Starting with the African worldview and laying a strong biblical foundation, he critiques the approach of the popular prosperity gospel that is so catching to many (African) Christians. His own proposed, contextual approach for poverty reduction in Africa stresses the importance of biblical work ethics, attitude to wealth, human development, women empowerment, cultural and social transformation, spiritual and moral transformation, solidarity, contentment, modesty, and simplicity. Last but not least, in his afterword, Boaheng points to some very practical steps.

For me this book stresses again the importance of biblical and holistic discipleship starting with the leaders of the church and Christian organizations as they model it and equip others. This is therefore a necessary resource for any good leader in this season of discipleship that has been called for by all the major Christian and mission movements in the world.

Rev. Jan C. Wessels
International Director, Faith2Share (UK)

This is an important book on the subject of poverty in Africa. The author approaches it from a theological perspective and offers a constructive critique aimed at correcting misplaced notions of wealth and poverty in the African context. It is highly recommended for the academy, church readership and national policy makers.

John D. K. Ekem, DTh
Kwesi Dickson-Gilbert Ansre Distinguished Professor
of Biblical Exegesis and Mother Tongue Hermeneutics,
Trinity Theological Seminary, Legon-Accra, Ghana

Poverty, the Bible, and Africa starts with a perceptive analysis of the African worldview and an overview of issues of poverty in Africa. From a foundation of in-depth biblical exegesis the author critiques current approaches to poverty alleviation in Africa, particularly prosperity theology, and develops an alternate biblically based and contextually sensitive response to the issues raised. Boaheng's combination of perceptive cultural insights and in-depth biblical analysis shines a prophetic light on the inadequacies of prosperity theologies in addressing issues of poverty. He challenges the church and society to a more biblical (and effective) response, highlighting the need for personal, cultural, and structural change both within the church and in wider society. An informed, perceptive and authentic voice, I highly recommend this book to anyone committed to deepening their understanding of the alleviation of poverty in Africa.

Mark Galpin, PhD
Postgraduate Programme Leader,
Tutor in Poverty and Justice Studies,
All Nations Christian College, Ware, UK

As the leader of a Christian relief and development organization and someone who lived and worked for fifteen years in Africa, I am deeply thankful for this unique and important book by Isaac Boaheng. For far too long the literature looking at the intersection of Scripture, poverty and Africa have been written with a predominantly external lens by authors from outside the continent. Boaheng brings solid exegesis as he reframes the challenges of poverty and injustice from an African perspective – with practical ideas for the church to be part of the solution. He does not hold back on challenging aberrant theology, colonial injustice, and issues such as corruption, which create barriers for people to experience "fullness of life." At the same time Boaheng helps unpack how the rich cultural heritage across African societies can be a strong foundation to build upon, rather than importing solutions which are culturally and contextually inappropriate from the global north. This should be on the required reading list for everyone involved with mission and development in Africa.

Matthew Maury, MBA
CEO, TEAR Australia
Vice Chair, Board of Directors, Micah Global

"The earth is the Lord's and all that is in it, the world and those who live in it . . ." (Ps 24:1). This verse seems to capture the sense of this book. In *Poverty, the Bible, and Africa*, Isaac Boaheng offers a fresh engagement of the thorny issue of poverty in Africa, not from a victim-blaming perspective as many do, but from the helpful premise that God owns everything. Human beings are God's stewards and all resources on earth are collectively held on behalf of God. The implication is the need for sharing, justice, and solidarity in addressing the problem of poverty, while dealing with contextual poverty-triggering factors. The strength of the book lies in its thorough engagement of Scripture and the African context. I wholeheartedly recommend this book.

Frederick Mawusi Amevenku, PhD
Senior Lecturer in New Testament Studies,
Trinity Theological Seminary, Legon-Accra, Ghana

This book is a necessary resource for global discipleship!

"Why a new book on poverty in Africa?" is the question the African author asks in the preface of his book. I want to applaud him for this very thorough and honest analysis of the challenges developing societies face and the approaches that the church in Africa has adopted or should adopt. Having worked for eighteen years in this beloved continent, I recognize so many things he writes.

Boaheng has only one goal in mind – to develop a theology of poverty that is both theologically sound and culturally appropriate for the context of Africa. However, it is not only a book for Africa and African Christians. I really hope and pray that the whole global body of Christ will read this book and learn from it. It is written in a very accessible language and format.

Poverty, the Bible, and Africa

Poverty, the Bible, and Africa

Poverty, the Bible, and Africa

Contextual Foundations for Helping the Poor

Isaac Boaheng

© 2020 Isaac Boaheng

Published 2020 by HippoBooks, an imprint of ACTS and Langham Publishing.

Africa Christian Textbooks (ACTS), TCNN, PMB 2020, Bukuru 930008, Plateau State, Nigeria.
www.actsnigeria.org

Langham Publishing, PO Box 296, Carlisle, Cumbria CA3 9WZ, UK
www.langhampublishing.org

ISBNs:
978-1-83973-033-7 Print
978-1-83973-034-4 ePub
978-1-83973-035-1 Mobi
978-1-83973-036-8 PDF

Isaac Boaheng has asserted his right under the Copyright, Designs and Patents Act, 1988 to be identified as the Author of this work.

All rights reserved. No part of this publication may be reproduced, stored in a retrieval system or transmitted, in any form or by any means, electronic, mechanical, photocopying, recording or otherwise, without the prior written permission of the publisher or the Copyright Licensing Agency.

Requests to reuse content from Langham Publishing are processed through PLSclear. Please visit www.plsclear.com to complete your request.

Unless otherwise stated, Scripture quotations are from the New Revised Standard Version Bible, copyright © 1989 National Council of the Churches of Christ in the United States of America. Used by permission. All rights reserved.

Scripture quotations marked (NIV) are taken from the Holy Bible, New International Version®, NIV®. Copyright © 1973, 1978, 1984, 2011 by Biblica, Inc.™ Used by permission of Zondervan.

Scripture quotations marked (NKJV) are from the New King James Version (NKJV). Copyright © 1982 by Thomas Nelson, Inc. Used by permission. All rights reserved.

Scripture quotations marked (ESV) are from The Holy Bible, English Standard Version® (ESV®), copyright © 2001 by Crossway, a publishing ministry of Good News Publishers. Used by permission. All rights reserved.

Scripture quotations marked (NJB) are from the New Jerusalem Bible, copyright © 1985 by Darton, Longmand & Todd LTD. Used by permission. All rights reserved.

British Library Cataloguing-in-Publication Data
A catalogue record for this book is available from the British Library

ISBN: 978-1-83973-033-7

Cover & Book Design: projectluz.com

The publishers of this book actively support theological dialogue and an author's right to publish but do not necessarily endorse the views and opinions set forth here or in works referenced within this publication, nor guarantee technical and grammatical correctness. The publishers do not accept any responsibility or liability to persons or property as a consequence of the reading, use or interpretation of its published content.

To
my wife, Adu-Agyeiwaa Gloria,
my mother, Mrs. Mary Ampomah,
my father, Mr. Noah Nti (posthumously),
and my three adorable children, Christian, Benedict and Julia.

To all people who have experienced or are experiencing poverty in their lives. I hope this small contribution to the public theological discourse on poverty will help reduce your plights.

Contents

Foreword xiii

Preface xv

Acknowledgments xvii

Introduction 1
    Why Another Book on Poverty for Africa? 1
    Overview of the Book 2

1   The African Worldview 5
    African Religious Worldview 5
    Sociopolitical Context 10
    Economic Context 12
    Conclusion 16

2   Poverty in the Context of Africa 19
    Perspectives on the Concept of Poverty 19
    Traditional African Perspectives on Wealth and Poverty 22
    Poverty as Absolute, Moderate and Relative 28
    Poverty and Economic Inequality in Africa 29
    Some Causes of Poverty in Africa 31
    Some Effects of Poverty in Africa 42
    Conclusion 46

3   Poverty in the Context of the Old Testament 47
    Key Biblical Terms for "Poor" 47
    Exegesis of Deuteronomy 15:1–11 51
    Exegesis of Isaiah 10:1–4 60
    Conclusion 68

4   Poverty in the Context of the New Testament 71
    Exegesis of Matthew 6:19–34 71
    Exegesis of 1 Timothy 6:6–10 89
    Theological Synthesis of Exegetical Analyses 95
    Conclusion 103

5	Prosperity Theology in Africa	105
	What Is Prosperity Theology?	105
	The Rise of the Prosperity Gospel	106
	The Planting of Prosperity Theology in Africa	107
	Major Teachings of Prosperity Theology	109
	Critique of Prosperity Theology	118
	Conclusion	140
6	A Contextual Approach for Poverty Reduction in Africa	141
	Contextual Theology in Africa	141
	Proposed Approach to Poverty Reduction in Africa	143
	Conclusion	168
	Afterword	169
	Bibliography	173
	Subject Index	185

Foreword

The vexed question of land-ownership and the all-engulfing spectre of dire poverty loom large in the landscape of Africa, with all her various histories. Such concerns, for over two millennia, have formed a core theme through the pages of the Hebrew Bible, as testified to in the central genres, from Law to History, from Prophecy to Wisdom. It is impossible to read Amos or Isaiah without realizing the enormity of God's passion for those whom society has swept into the fringes of social attention.

Yet African studies of such issues are few and far between. Therefore, it is with great joy that I welcome this published study from the pen of Isaac Boaheng, one of our emerging young scholars from Ghana.

The Bible is a rich source of information about land and poverty, given its large semantic range, especially in the Hebrew words for poverty and wealth, not forgetting the multiple terms for oppression and injustice. My prayer is that this work will encourage other young scholars from Africa and similar regions, where poverty looms large, to rise to the challenge of contextualizing the Bible and speaking prophetically into social issues like poverty and land-redistribution.

So often, as academics, we can lose focus from the safe surrounds of our comfortable universities and colleges, neglecting the need to train pastors and teachers who face first-hand the reality of the poor and marginalized. Such a study as this one makes it possible to place into the hands of such students a work that will challenge them and equip them to address these complex issues in clear biblical terms and with biblical authority. At the same time, we need biblically literate lay-people to speak into society and to encourage those with power and resources to use them wisely and justly for the good of all members of their society.

Rev. Prof. Bill Domeris, PhD
Senior Academic,
South African Theological Seminary,
Bryanston, South Africa

Foreword

Preface

Poverty is one of the greatest challenges facing Africa today. Poverty reduction strategies in many sub-Saharan African countries have not yielded much fruit. To try and tackle this major problem in the continent, many studies on poverty in Africa have been carried out and numerous books about it have been published and are available today. How do I then justify the publication of another book on poverty in Africa? A survey of the existing literature of poverty studies in Africa shows a lack of thorough engagement with Scripture and/or a lack of contextualization of biblical teachings on poverty in the African church. Consequently, the need to improve human life is a continuing theological concern in most African societies. *Poverty, the Bible, and Africa: Contextual Foundations for Helping the Poor* formulates a theology of poverty for Christians in Africa based on the teachings of Scripture and church tradition, as well as the socio-economic, religious and political needs of Africans. To this end, the book considers questions such as, what socioreligious contexts bind Africans together and inform the African understanding of wealth and poverty? What is the present poverty situation in Africa? What are the main biblical teachings on poverty and wealth? How effective and biblically grounded is the prosperity theology model towards poverty reduction in Africa? What contextual theology of poverty is relevant for Africa, and what implications does it have for Africans?

The book, which is organized in six chapters, devotes the first chapter to the African religious, political, economic and social worldview, while the second examines the poverty situation in Africa. Among others factors, this book identifies destruction of the environment, poor agricultural practices, bad leadership, corruption and mismanagement of public funds, negative cultural practices, expensive funeral celebrations, lack of education, large family size, inadequate access to employment opportunities, laziness, natural disasters, unfair distribution of national resources, and emigration of skilled human capital as the main factors perpetuating poverty in Africa.

Chapters 3 and 4 provide the biblical context through exegetical analyses of four biblical passages from the Law (Deut 15:1–11), the Prophets (Isa 10:1–4), the Gospels (Matt 6:19–34) and the Epistles (1 Tim 6:6–10). From the Scriptures it is clear that God frowns upon materialism, extravagance, love for riches, anxiety and worry that detract people from their loyalty to him. He encourages contentment, simplicity, modesty and sharing of resources with others. God does not command voluntary poverty, but he usually sides with the poor and helps them to improve their lives.

After the contextual frameworks in the first four chapters, the fifth chapter critiques the prosperity theology model of poverty reduction to ascertain whether or not this popular theological teaching is effective and appropriate for the African continent. Despite having some potential for fighting poverty, the theology has weak biblical support and is difficult to apply in the contexts of many Africans and their existential needs.

The main purpose of this study, which was the formulation of a contextual theology of poverty for Africa, is the focus of chapter 6. The chapter presents a contextual model for poverty alleviation which, unlike the prosperity theology model, passes both the contextual and the biblical-theological tests by incorporating biblical ideas such as God's ownership of all resources, humanity's role of stewarding God's resources, a communal view of resources or sharing of resources, the need to ensure justice in society, and working in solidarity with the poor, among other ideals, while at the same time addressing contextual issues such as lack of education and the cultural factors that impede economic progress (such as expensive funeral celebrations and traditions that deny women the right and access to economic resources). The book concludes with practical implications for the poor, the church and the state.

Written primarily for Africans, the book includes case studies from various countries in sub-Saharan Africa and reflects on their application for readers in the entire continent. Nonetheless, the book also offers valuable perspectives for people in other parts of the world where poverty is a major challenge. It is written in a way that makes it accessible to both scholars and ordinary readers and with the hope that it will be useful for Christians who are wrestling with poverty or are concerned with its reduction.

Isaac Boaheng
Sunyani, Ghana
2020

Acknowledgments

The dream of publishing this book was accomplished through the efforts of many individuals who are appreciated. It is, however, difficult to give credit to all involved, since so many people contributed in their special ways. My highest appreciation goes to the Triune God, in whom I live, move and have my being. I am indebted to the many authors and scholars whose work served as resources for the research that yielded this book. I am extremely grateful to Professor Bill Domeris of the South African Theological Seminary whose critical comments and review shaped the research which gave birth to this book. The leadership of the Most Reverends Robert K. Aboagye-Mensah and Professor Emmanuel K. Asante (past presiding bishops of the Methodist Church Ghana [MCG]), Titus Awotwe Pratt (the immediate past presiding bishop, MCG), and the Most Reverend Paul K. Boafo (presiding bishop, MCG) have contributed to my Christian, intellectual and leadership development in various ways. The Very Reverend Professor John David Kwamena Ekem and The Reverend Dr. Frederick Mawusi Amevenku have constantly encouraged me and supported my ministry and academic endeavors. I am very grateful to all of you.

I owe a profound gratitude to my parents, Mrs. Mary Ampomah and Mr. Noah Nti (posthumously), for their care, love and upbringing. May God richly bless my siblings, Mr. Yaw Boahen, Mr. Kofi Boachie, Mr. Samuel Boahen, Mr. Hayford Ampaabeng Kyeremeh, Mrs. Rachael Oforiwaa, Mr. Collins Frimpong, and Mr. Solomon Amoh for their encouragement and support. Many thanks to my wife, Mrs. Gloria Boaheng and children, Christian Adom-Boaheng, Benedict Adu-Boaheng and Julia Ampomah-Boaheng, for their sacrifice, encouragement and prayers.

I am also grateful to Reverends Daniel Asomah Gyabaah, Jonathan Amankwaa Oppong, Christian Meteku, Ebenezer Asibu Dadzie, Isaac Oduro-Boateng as well as Mr. Charles Adu-Ofori, Ms. Mary Twenewaa, Mr. Isaac Adu-Ofori, Mr. George Adu Prempeh, Mr. Seth Adu-Ofori, Mr. Samuel Adu Gyamfi, Miss Yaa Serwaa, Mr. Effah Korsa, Mrs. Afia Aframa, Mr. Asiedu Anthony and his family (Berekum) for their encouragement and support towards my ministry. Finally, I thank Professor Elizabeth Mburu and the reviewers, editors and designers of Hippo Books for shaping the manuscript to become what it is now.

Soli Deo Gloria! – To God alone be the glory!

Introduction

Why Another Book on Poverty for Africa?

Poverty is one of the greatest challenges facing the twenty-first century society. No country in the world is entirely unaffected by poverty. Global poverty keeps on rising, especially in developing countries. The issue of global poverty engaged the United Nations Millennium Summit, held in September 2000, which debated how to combat this global canker. The debates resulted in the formulation of the Millennium Development Goals (MDGs) with the number one goal being the reduction of extreme poverty by half by the year 2015. Although this target was worldwide, Africa was a prime focus because it is the continent with the greatest urgency for poverty reduction.

Africa consists of many developing countries that are currently experiencing multifaceted poverty, comprising economic, political, religious and social dimensions. In most African countries, poverty manifests itself in "bad roads, women and children walking barefooted and trekking long distances to get water and firewood, pupils studying under trees, dilapidated and ill-equipped health centers and scores of [other] poverty-driven problems."[1] African countries continue to experience economic challenges like poverty, high inflation, high budget deficits, increased cost of borrowing, increased fuel prices, frequent labor unrests, high unemployment rates and local currency depreciation in spite of the availability of natural resources, such as cocoa, diamond, bauxite, gold, oil and others.

Africa's poverty situation in the midst of her abundant natural resources has attracted scholarly attention from both secular scholars and theologians. Of particular interest to this book is the church's response to the issue. Out of the many responses from the church, the following four approaches are significant.[2] One approach considers poverty as a requirement for entering the kingdom of God. Another approach finds the solution to poverty in living a modest life. The third and the most influential response to poverty is prosperity theology. The fourth model finds a solution to poverty in proper stewardship of resources.

---

1. Aderonmu, "Local Government and Poverty Eradication," 201.

2. The approaches are found in Williams, *Christian Approaches to Poverty*, 81–146 and Asante, *Stewardship*, 50–67.

While previous writers must be commended for their contribution to the fight against poverty in Africa, there is a need for a more holistic approach to addressing poverty in Africa, an approach that engages Scripture more thoroughly and addresses the existential issues experienced by Africans. This book aims to provide such a holistic approach for tackling the problem of poverty in Africa.

Overview of the Book

This six-chapter book starts by providing a justification for a new approach to addressing poverty in Africa in the Introduction. Chapter 1 examines the African context in terms of religious, political, economic and social developments from the precolonial era, through to the post-independence period. Chapter 2 deals with the poverty situation in Africa with examples from various parts of the continent.

Chapters 3 and 4 provide the biblical context for the book through exegetical analyses of four biblical passages in both the Old and New Testaments (Deut 15:1–11; Isa 10:1–4; Matt 6:19–34; 1 Tim 6:6–10). Other biblical passages are also discussed to provide a broader biblical perspective on the subject while at the same time presenting a focused examination of these key passages. Key conclusions from the analyses are that God frowns on materialism, extravagance, love for riches, and anxiety and worry that detract one from loyalty to him. He encourages contentment, simplicity, modesty and sharing of resources with others. Furthermore, though God does not command voluntary poverty, he sides with the poor and helps them to improve their lives.

Chapter 5 assesses prosperity theology in the light of Scripture and the African cultural setting to ascertain whether or not this popular theological teaching is effective and appropriate for the African continent. Though prosperity theology has some merits, it lacks contextual application to the African situation and has weak biblical support.

The book reaches its climax in the sixth chapter where a contextual approach to poverty in Africa is formulated based on Scripture, tradition and the sociopolitical and socioeconomic situation of Africans. The proposed contextual model, unlike the prosperity theology model, passes both the contextual and the biblical-theological tests by incorporating biblical truths such as God's ownership of all resources, human duty in stewarding God's resources, a communal view of resources or sharing of resources, the need to ensure justice in society, and living in solidarity with the poor. At the same time, this model addresses how to deal with issues such as lack of education and the cultural factors that fight against economic progress (for example, expensive funeral celebrations, and norms that deny women an equal right to economic resources as men). The book concludes with an afterword that recaps the major points discussed and gives implications of a biblical approach to penury for the fight against poverty in Africa.

Having outlined the purpose, the justification and the outline of the book, I now proceed to consider what socio-economic, religious and cultural settings bind Africans together.

1

The African Worldview

Every theology is contextually informed. That is to say, all theological formulations are for particular contexts. Aware of this fact, my goal in this chapter is to discuss the African context in terms of religious, political, economic and social developments from the precolonial era, through to the post-independence period. This will not only help us to appreciate the traditional African worldview that informs African perspectives on poverty and wealth but will also give a clear view of the contextual issues that should be given attention when formulating a theology of poverty for the African continent.

African Religious Worldview

The African worldview is intensively and pervasively religious. Emmanuel K. Asante rightly observes that from an African perspective, there is no "sharp distinction between the sacred and the secular, the religious and the non-religious and between the spiritual and the material."[1] Asante's point is that in all that the African does, there is religion at work. Therefore, the religious worldview of Africans is crucial to understanding their way of life. This section examines the four distinctive markers of African Traditional Religion, namely, belief in God (or the Supreme Being), lesser divinities, ancestral spirits, and the lower spirit powers (amulets and talismans), in order to help us appreciate the religious context of Africa into which Christianity was introduced. The emphasis on each of these components of the belief system, however, varies from one society to another. I now turn to outlining each of these key aspects of African Traditional Religion.

---

1. Asante, *Issues in African Traditional Religion*, 2.

Belief in God

John S. Mbiti once stated that the European missionaries who introduced the Christian gospel to Africa did not bring God to Africa; instead, God who was already present in Africa brought them.[2] The African traditional belief system totally agrees with Mbiti's position in that long before their contact with Christian missionaries, Africans expressed their belief in God in various aspects of their traditional life.[3] For example, Africans express their belief in God through proverbs. The proverb "No one points out God to the child" underlines the belief that God's existence is self-evident. The proverb "If you want to say something to God, say it to the wind" underscores the belief that God is spirit and omnipresent. The Langi of Uganda say, "He is like air," the Ngombe of the Democratic Republic of Congo say, he is "the One who fills everything" and the Burundi say, "He who is met everywhere."[4] God's love and care for humanity is evident in the proverb "It is God who drives flies from the tailless animal." That God is the Creator and Father of humanity is expressed in the proverb "All people are God's children, none is the earth's child." God is also known to be Omnipotent; the All-Powerful One, for which reason the Zulu of South Africa assert that He is the One "who roars so that the nations be struck with terror."[5]

Africans also express belief in God during traditional rites and ceremonies like outdooring ceremonies for newly born babies,[6] funerals, marriage, festivals and puberty. For instance, people use the expression "God hates sin, that is why he gave each person a name" during naming ceremonies to express their idea of the holiness of God. Libation prayers in most African societies recognize God as the one who is the controller of destiny and determiner of the outcome of prayer (or libation). More so, cultural (*Adinkra*) symbols are used to express beliefs about God. For example, the Akan cultural symbol labelled "God's eye," which is the shortened version of the expression "God's eye sees all hidden things," emphasizes God's omnipresence and omniscience.[7]

---

2. Mbiti, "Encounter of Christian Faith," 817.
3. Boaheng, "Early Christian Missions," 228–229.
4. O'Donovan, *Biblical Christianity*, 47.
5. O'Donovan, 53.
6. The outdooring ceremony is the official naming ceremony for babies born into African homes. In the process the child is told that he or she was created by God and that God has given him or her the responsibility to choose right and reject wrong.
7. Arthur, *Cloth as Metaphor*, 129.

The presence of theophorous names[8] in almost all indigenous African societies signifies that indigenous Africans believed in God. The Ga name *Nyonmo Baatsoo*, (God will provide); Igbo names such as *Chibuzor* (God first), *Chukwuka* (God is greater) and *Chukwudi* (God exists); Yoruba names such as *Oluruntobi* (God is great) and *Olorunkoya* (God decries oppression); the Akan name *Nyamekyε* (God's gift) and Ewe names such as *Mawunyo* (God is kind), *Mawusi* (in God's hands, an affirmation of God's supreme protection), *Mawunyega* (God is the greatest), *Mawuto* (God's gift) and *Mawuli* (God exists continually) are examples of theophorous names pointing to the belief in the existence of God. These names were given to people long before the advent of Christianity in Africa. In addition, African societies have different names or appellations given to God based on their conception of the Supreme Being and the attributes they ascribe to him such as his self-existence, transcendence, immanence and providence; and his role as creator and provider. He is viewed as the most powerful being from whom others derive their powers and other attributes.[9]

Belief in Lesser Divinities

According to Mbiti, "the spiritual world of African people is very densely populated with spiritual beings, spirits and the living-dead."[10] The traditional African worldview recognizes a group of beings known as lesser deities comprising idols, magical powers, totems and so on.[11] The lesser deities are differentiated from the Supreme Being on the ground that unlike the lesser divinities, God does not have a shrine and a priest in the religious life and thought of Africans. In other words, God is not restricted to a specific shrine or priest, neither is he worshipped through specific shrines nor served by specific priests. Lesser deities are worshipped through objects such as stones, wood, and carvings. These objects are believed to be intermediaries between God and humanity. The combined power of these divinities is nowhere near that of the Supreme God. The Supreme God has no coequal.

Lesser divinities did not come into existence by their own volition but by God's divine ordering.[12] They serve God to fulfill certain functions and just

---

8. These are names derived from the nature of God.
9. Mbiti, *Introduction to African Religion*, 47; Boaheng, "Exploring Relationship," 58.
10. Mbiti, *African Religions and Philosophy*, 74.
11. Edu-Bekoe and Wan, *Scattered Africans Keep Coming*, 24, 27.
12. Mbiti, *African Religions and Philosophy*, 74–75.

below him in the hierarchy of powers, each lesser divinity having its own area of competence.[13] Two groups may be identified; the first comprising mythological figures, or tribal heroes or heroines, who take the forms of mountains, rivers, forests, the sun, the moon, the stars, and the mother earth. The second category comprises divinities relating to different aspects of life, society and community, including divinities of the sea or the waters, rain, thunder, fertility, health or sickness, planting or harvest, tribal, clan or family life.[14] The lesser divinities have power, which they may use to bring fortune or misfortune to people.

Belief in Lower Spirit Powers

Africans believe that anything that happens in the physical world has a spiritual antecedent, hence they try to find the spiritual cause(s) of whatever happens in their lives. Most African societies believe that the world is full of spirits residing in various places such as stones, tombs, haunted homes, trees and so on.[15] These lower spirits (and lesser divinities in terms of power) may be benevolent, those that wish people well and help people to live good life, or malevolent, those which bring misfortune to people. Great care is taken in dealing with these spirits. For example, libation must be poured before cutting down a tree perceived to have a vindictive spirit. Hunters who hunt animals perceived to have vindictive spirits are expected to have spiritual protection, or else their life might be lost before, during, or after the hunt. The spirit world is divided into two categories: the world of non-human spirits, and the world of the spirits of the dead.[16] Lower spirit powers in African worldview include such objects as amulets, charms, talismans or beads, which people wear around the waist, neck or wrist; evil spirits (associated with witches), which are believed to be extremely hostile to humans and live on tall trees; and dwarfs, powerful ethereal beings with feet facing backwards, which are believed to live in forests and sometimes help herbalists find herbs.[17] All these entities are believed to be less powerful spirits that operate in objects. There are various other lower spirits, each having control over a certain aspect of life. Some lower spirits are responsible for marriage, fighting, protecting against witchcraft, trading, farming, fertility, sports, learning and hunting. Because these spirits

---

13. Asante, *Culture, Politics and Development*, 35.
14. Asante, 35.
15. See Asante, 35.
16. Edu-Bekoe and Wan, *Scattered Africans Keep Coming*, 27–28.
17. Kyeremanteng, *Akan of Ghana*, 94.

can affect people's lives either positively or negatively, it is important for people to maintain a good relationship between the human world and the spirit world.

Belief in Ancestors

Another key feature of the African religious worldview is the belief in ancestors and their veneration. Most African societies believe that death is a transition of the soul of the departed to the world of the ancestral spirits where it continues to live. Thus, death is a journey to the underworld rather than a break with earthly beings.[18] The world of spirits or ghosts is believed to be located somewhere in the deep of the earth (the underworld, underground or netherworld).[19] Ancestors are spirits of heroes and heroines who, after death, have acquired superhuman powers and are able to affect the lives of the living.[20] Africans describe ancestors "as that part of the clan who have completed their course here on earth and gone ahead to the other world to be elder brothers of the living at the house of God."[21]

The qualifications for becoming an ancestor include the following: dying a natural death at an old age after leading a decent life; leading a life worthy of emulation; having children; and a proper burial with elaborate funeral rites.[22] Peter Sarpong captures this point as follows: "No one wants to remember a good-for-nothing person, a thief, a murderer, a rapist, or people who, in general, have no respect for themselves. It is those whose lives are worth emulating that are venerated as ancestors."[23] The roles of the ancestor include: presiding at family meetings and, like the police, ensuring that law and order is maintained in the society. Ancestors constantly watch over their families like a "cloud of witnesses," punishing evil doers and rewarding good deeds.[24] More so, ancestors are the custodians of customs and traditions of the people and serve as mediators between the world of the living and the world of the dead. Their mediatory role is the reason they receive libation and sacrifices (during festivals and other occasions) from the living. In all, ancestors are venerated, not worshipped or deified.

---

18. Asante, *Culture, Politics and Development*, 36.
19. Asante, *Theology in Society*.
20. Asante, *Culture, Politics and Development*, 35–37.
21. Pobee, *Towards an African Theology*, 46.
22. See Seale and van der Geest, "Good and Bad Death," 883–886.
23. Sarpong, *People Differ*, 98.
24. Asante, *Culture, Politics and Development*, 36.

Sociopolitical Context

African social structure gives priority to the community over the individual. Each person belongs to a family comprising the living, the dead, and the yet-to-be-born. Jomo Kenyatta rightly avows that, "The land not only unites the living members of the tribe but also the dead ancestors and the unborn posterity."[25] Two types of family exist, namely the nuclear and extended families. The nuclear family comprises the spouses and their children while the extended family is made up of parents, children, grandparents, and others. Families come together to form a clan which also bonds people together. Asante has observed that, in Africa "the value of humanity is, intrinsically, linked with that of the unity of all people, whether biologically related or not."[26] John Pobee describes this interdependence in the Akan ontology as *Cognatus ergo sum* meaning "I am related by blood, therefore, I exist or I exist because I belong to a family."[27] This corresponds to the Ubuntu philosophy of "I am because you are, you are because I am." This is what O'Donovan rightly refers to when he writes, "Africans tend to find their identity and meaning in life through being part of their extended family, clan and tribe. There is a strong feeling of common participation in life, a common history, and a common destiny. The reality in Africa may be described with the statement: 'I am because the community is.'"[28] These affirmations underscore the importance of interdependence, unity and peaceful coexistence among Africans.

Therefore, the African society is expected to give its members the sense of belonging through acceptance, common ownership of resources (such as land), and sharing of individual problems.[29] The saying "The stranger does not sleep on the street"[30] teaches people the need to open their doors to strangers and to be generous and hospitable to them. J. V. Taylor has rightly observed that in Africa, "an individual who is cut off from the community organisation is a nothing."[31] For the above reasons, each African tries to maintain the societal norms so as to avoid being cut off from the community. Unlike Westerners, Africans freely visit each other without the need for prior notice. Such visits are basically meant for socializing rather than some kind of measured outcome.

---

25. As cited in Barrett, *Schism and Renewal*, 123.
26. Asante, *Issues in African Traditional Religion*, 35
27. Pobee, *Towards an African Theology*, 49.
28. O'Donovan, *Biblical Christianity*, 4.
29. Edu-Bekoe and Wan, *Scattered Africans Keep Coming*, 29.
30. Asante, *Issues in African Traditional Religion*, 35.
31. Taylor, *Primal Vision*, 100.

In the street, people meet and exchange elaborate greetings and find out about the well-being of one another's family. Clearly, traditional African community is built on "mutual trust, listening, helping, sacrifice, self-denial, equality and personal freedom . . . respect for elders, unity, cooperation, hospitality, inclusiveness, celebration, accompaniment and greeting."[32]

The African precolonial political system was characterized by decentralized forms of governance, whereby the leadership of the community or tribe was entrusted to local traditional leaders (chiefs or kings).[33] The traditional African structure of leadership is hierarchical. Traditional African political structure and government is practiced at different levels within the hierarchy of chieftaincy. At the family level, the family head has the highest authority. There are chiefs who are responsible for the administration of small villages and others who are responsible for the administration of towns. The state chief or paramount chief is the head and highest authority in every traditional area. Chiefs were the custodians of land in precolonial Africa. They were responsible for ensuring the preservation of land, rivers, trees, and other natural resources.

The introduction of colonial rule with its indirect system of administration, comprising new political structures such as the civil service, local government ordinances, and taxation, led to the reduction of the duties of the chief to cultural matters.[34] The colonialists formulated by-laws to regulate the rights and responsibilities of chiefs and their traditional councils. Chiefs were reduced to collectors of royalties charged on certain farming and mining operations. The colonial system of administration eventually weakened the authority and influence of many chiefs.[35]

At one point in the history of Africa, people began to fight for independence from colonial rule. Ghana (formerly the Gold Coast), in 1957, became the first sub-Saharan African country to gain independence and by 1970, most African nations were free of colonial rule. Today no African country is under colonial rule. However, the post-independence history of most African countries has been characterized by social and political violence and bloodshed through coups d'état and military rule.[36] Still, most of these countries have gone back to constitutional rule and are currently enjoying a relatively stable political atmosphere. What impact has colonialism, Africa's independence, and its

---

32. Nihinlola, *Theology Under the Mango Tree*, 82–83.
33. Kyeremanteng, *Akan of Ghana*, 55.
34. Kyeremanteng, 55.
35. Kyeremanteng, 55.
36. Owusu, "Military Coups in Ghana," 6–10.

political situation had on its economic growth? I will attempt a response to this question when I discuss the economic context of precolonial Africa in the next section.

Economic Context

Economic activities in precolonial African mostly involved the management of the natural resources available to the people. For example, most Africans who lived in forests cultivated crops such as yam, plantain, cocoyam, cassava, and orange for consumption. Others engaged in hunting activities and the rearing of livestock like goats, cattle, and sheep. Blacksmithing was common among African farming communities (such as the Yoruba and Akan) who made cutlasses, hoes, fishing hooks, and other iron tools by smelting iron from a special stone. Those living along the coast were mainly fishermen.[37] In fishing communities men fished and women processed the highly perishable fish by smoking, salting, or drying. Women also engaged in salt production.

Even though trading took place between communities in precolonial times, the continent was isolated from other parts of the world in terms of international economic activities. The Ghana, Mali, and Songhai empires witnessed some international trade (for example in gold) and the raising of revenue through taxation on foreign trade to support the budget of the empire.[38] Initially, the barter system of trade was used before various cultures started using means of purchase such as cowrie shells around the fifteenth century. The poor road network, however, limited the growth of trade in most societies.

The economic merits and demerits of colonialism in Africa has been a subject of debate among scholars. According to Joshua Dwayne Settles, the goal of colonialism was "to exploit the physical, human, and economic resources of an area to benefit the colonizing nation."[39] The little developments experienced in Africa were geared towards achieving this agendum.[40] Ultimately, the natural development of African economic life was halted. Settles contends that "African economies were advancing in every area, particularly in the area of trade" prior to colonialization.[41] Toyin observes that colonialism led to the introduction of

---

37. Odotei, "Pre-Colonial Economic Activities of Ga," 60.
38. Settles, "Impact of Colonialism," 3.
39. Settles, 3.
40. Settles, 3.
41. Settles, 3.

Western education, which elevated the level of education in Africa.[42] Boaheng, on the other hand, argues that the educational policies of the colonial masters ended up breaking the tie between educated Africans and their families, to the extent that the elite felt ashamed of their roots.[43]

The imposition of colonial rule on Africans brought about permanent changes in African ways of thought, economic trends, and political structure. For example, the concession company colonies of Ruanda and Urundi were transformed into the post-independence Rwanda and Burundi crop-based economies.[44] European settlers controlled economic resources in most African countries, engaging in mining and cash crop farming activities in South Africa, Zimbabwe, and parts of Angola, Mozambique, Democratic Republic of Congo, Kenya, Zambia, and other countries.[45] However, the agricultural economies of countries such as Senegal, Ghana, Sierra Leone, Nigeria, Uganda, and Tanzania had Africans participating in crop production (though in some cases Africans were not allowed to own land), while the marketing aspects were controlled by the foreign Europeans.[46] In all, economic activities in the African colonies were geared towards meeting the food demands of the colonial masters. Colonialism and the division of Africa by colonial masters eventually halted the natural economic development of the continent.[47]

Colonialism brought about some infrastructural developments such as roads, harbors, schools, hospitals, and so on; yet, these infrastructures were put in place to serve the interest of the colonialists.[48] For example, the road and railway networks ended up enhancing the transportation of raw materials to the harbors for export. In addition, colonialist influence on the demarcation of borders ended up generating partisan politics, ethnic conflicts, and civil unrest, which eventually retarded economic growth.

According to both Amoah and Settles, the introduction of the transatlantic slave trade and the negative impact of colonialism was generally a contributing factor to the poverty situation in Africa.[49] For Settles, the slave trade led to the high demand for slaves, which eventually subordinated the indigenous African

---

42. As cited in Sangmor, "Impact of Colonialism," 17.
43. Boaheng, "Early Christian Missions," 219.
44. Mkandawire, "Tax Efforts," 164–169.
45. Khan, Morrissey, and Mosley, "Colonial Legacy," 2.
46. Khan, Morrissey, and Mosley, 2.
47. Settles, "Impact of Colonialism," 3.
48. Odotei, "Pre-colonial Economic Activities," 59–74.
49. Amoah, "African Traditional Religion," 3–7; Settles, "Impact of Colonialism," 56.

economy to the interests of Europe in that the trade substituted "European manufactured products for those products which normally would have been made locally."[50] Peter Wicins rightly contends that as a result of the uneven trade associated with the colonial economy, "[e]ven innocuous imports such as textiles, competed damagingly with local products, with the result that the technological gap between Africa and Europe . . . widened to such an extent that African technology failed to progress."[51]

Eventually, Africa became a source of human resources and a consumer of finished goods, not a manufacturer of goods. Rather than the colonial masters helping Africa turn its raw materials into finished goods so that the continent could export products and increase its wealth, they took the natural resources away at virtually no cost.[52] In terms of human resources, the slave trade deprived the continent of its best people, people who would have contributed immensely to Africa's development. Not only did local leaders fail to protect their subjects, some involved themselves in the trade.[53] K. G. Cannon has observed that local African leaders took advantage of their trade relations with the Europeans to enrich themselves at the expense of the masses, a situation which has led in part to the negative perception people have about African leaders and their wealth.[54]

The independence of African states from the late 1950s onwards became a turning point in Africa's economic history. For instance, the first president of Ghana, Dr. Kwame Nkrumah, who was hailed as the *Osagefo* or redeemer, laid economic foundations based on the production and export of cocoa (of which the country was the world's leading producer), gold, and timber.[55] At the time, many African countries had positive indications of a brighter future in terms of having relatively good transportation networks, high per capita income, low national debt, advanced educational systems, and sizable foreign currency reserves.[56]

After taking over from the colonial masters, most African leaders realized that the colonial socioeconomic and political systems were motivated by an individualistic worldview that opposed the African communal heritage. The

---

50. Settles, "Impact of Colonialism," 56. See also Yeboa-Mensa, "Reducing Poverty," 92.
51. As cited in Settles, "Impact of Colonialism," 4.
52. Settles, 4.
53. Ogundele, "Understanding Nigeria," 8.
54. Cannon, "An Ethical Mapping."
55. Owusu, "Military Coups in Ghana," 6.
56. Owusu, 6.

promotion of economic policies based on African cultural settings became necessary. In Tanzania, for example, Julius Nyerere (the first president), having realized that "the inherited colonial, social and economic system was a poor tool to mobilise and empower people to work for the improvement of their living conditions"[57] developed and popularized the concept of *Ujamaa* as the basis of his policies for social and economic development. The *Ujamaa* (familyhood) ideology is essentially an African socialist approach to poverty reduction which emphasizes personal resource development (self-reliance); joint effort in national development; communal labor among rural settlers; social justice; equal opportunity for all; just distribution of wealth; nationalization of commerce, industry, and natural resources as means of achieving "social cohesion, stability and peace, which are the essential elements of meaningful political freedom, social and economic change."[58]

The *Ujamaa* concept promoted the nationalization of land which eventually solved the problem of landlessness among the poor; the communal labor system also led to national solidarity and patriotism. The "familyhood" foundation solidified self-reliant village societies and made it easier to have social services distributed to the majority of Tanzanians.[59] Through education, people gave up negative cultural practices which hindered their progress in life. Free compulsory education was given to develop the human resources of the country. More so, the *Ujamaa* ideology inculcated African values in the educational system so as to raise socialist leaders who place the interest of their people first in all decision-making processes, thereby addressing political and socioeconomic inequalities.[60] The effect was the improvement in people's living standards and the closing of the socioeconomic gap between the poor rural settlers and rich urban dwellers. *Ujamaa* also influenced African socialist ideas in other parts of Africa in the 1970s. However, with time *Ujamaa* failed to lift Tanzanians out of poverty, leading to president Nyerere's retirement in 1985.

In spite of attempts by various governments to eradicate poverty, Africa's political independence has not had much impact on its economy (as I demonstrate below). In Nigeria, for instance, various attempts by successive governments to grow the country's economy after independence could not sustain the country's economic growth. In the early 1980s, the country declined

---

57. What I have quoted is Nyerere's idea which Kimilike, paraphrased in Kimilike, "African Perspective," 90.

58. Kimilike, "African Perspective," 90–91.

59. Kimilike, 92.

60. Kimilike, 92.

from a middle-income state status to become one of the world's poorest countries.[61] Since then the country continues to have economic decline. According to Otu et al., "The incidence of poverty in Nigeria had worsened between 1980 and 2010 with the number of Nigerians living below the poverty line increasing from 17.1 million in 1980 to 112.5 million in 2010."[62]

The Heavily-Indebted Poor Country (HIPC) initiative which was launched in 1996 by the International Monetary Fund (IMF) and World Bank became a blessing to many African countries who owed so much external debt that the repayment of the interest on their loans alone could bring their economies to a standstill. This initiative was meant to provide "debt cancellation (rather than palliatives such as debt rescheduling, and interest rate reduction) as the main means to ease the debt burden of the poorest and most indebted countries. It also radically included debt cancellation owed to multilateral institutions such as the World Bank, the International Monetary Fund, the African Development Bank and the Inter-American Development Bank."[63] According to Edoun and Motsepe, the economies of many African countries had become so poor that the twenty-second meeting of the Committee of Experts of the Conference of African Ministers of Finance in May 2003 noted, "that in many African countries, domestic debt burden is causing severe problems in terms of fiscal sustainability, high interest rates and crowding-out of private sector investment."[64] It was further noted that in many African countries, "The domestic debt burden further hampers the development of the private sector, as firms do not receive prompt payment for providing goods and services."[65] African countries which have benefited from HIPC include Mali, Niger, Sierra Leone, Ghana, Zambia, Ethiopia, Guinea-Bissau, Uganda, and Senegal. Most of the countries that have benefited from HIPC are in sub-Saharan Africa. Yes, even today, many of these African countries still face many social problems including poverty.

Conclusion

This chapter has outlined the African context that is referred to in this book. Among others, the following facts were noted. First, atheism or agnosticism are

---

61. See Chukwuma, "Reducing Poverty in Nigeria," xxx.
62. Otu et al., "Analysis of Poverty," 175.
63. UNDP as cited in Edoun and Motsepe, "Critical Assessment," 380.
64. Edoun and Motsepe, 380.
65. Edoun and Motsepe, 380.

foreign to the traditional African worldview. Traditional Africans believe in the existence of the Supreme Being who has no coequal and hence is completely distinct from any lesser deity. This kind of belief system is different from that of ancient Greece where people believed in a pantheon of gods. African traditional religious thought was noted to be monotheistic, not polytheistic. Second, African social life was based on a communal rather than the individualistic worldview that characterizes the Western world. Africans do all they can to be accepted as part of the community, because to be cut off from the community is equivalent to losing one's human value. Third, the chapter notes that poverty has been a characteristic of African societies from precolonial times to date and that colonial policies worsened the poverty situation in many African countries. With this foundation the question that must be addressed is: What is the current poverty situation in Africa? The next chapter seeks to answer this question.

2

Poverty in the Context of Africa

The previous chapter discussed the traditional African worldview as a way of outlining the African context. This chapter continues the discussion by looking at the prevailing situation of poverty in the context of Africa. I begin with the concept of poverty from the perspectives of economists, and then consider the traditional African view of wealth and poverty. Finally, I will discuss the causes and challenges of poverty in contemporary Africa. The limited scope of this book does not allow discussing cases from every African country, but I have cited selected cases from countries in every region of sub-Saharan Africa. The discoveries in this chapter will inform the formulation of a theology of poverty that addresses the needs of Africans (later in chapter 6).

Perspectives on the Concept of Poverty

In this section, I discuss the concept of poverty as seen from the perspective of the field of Economics. Understanding the economic dimension of poverty is crucial because most of the approaches to poverty reduction by governments in Africa focus on the economic aspects of the problem. Defining "poverty" is extremely difficult due to the dynamic and multifaceted nature of this term. A survey of literature on poverty shows that scholarly perspectives on poverty fall under three categories.

The Economic Deprivation Approach

The first perspective on poverty considers it as an economic concept. From this perspective, poverty is defined as a state of economic deprivation.[1] Opinions

---

1. Khan and Hassan, "Incidence of Poverty," 21.

about what constitutes "economic deprivation" vary. Scholars[2] define poverty as the lack of essential necessities for human life or lack of the capacity to acquire these things. According to this view, temporal economic deprivation does not constitute poverty but permanent deprivation does. Therefore, a person who becomes homeless due to a natural disaster (such as a fire outbreak or flood) but gathers enough resources to put up another house in the next few weeks is not to be considered poor within the short duration of their homelessness.[3]

Wagle's perspective on poverty centers on income or the standard of living. He explains poverty as a state in which one lacks income or other economic resources required for maintaining a minimum living standard.[4] Wagle, however, considers it inappropriate to set a universal minimum income in defining who the poor is.[5] He does not agree with such thresholds because, in his opinion, it is not just how much one earns but the capacity to consume that determines who is poor and who is not.[6] Pantazis, Gordon and Levitas agree with Wagle and argue that someone may earn a relatively small amount but save more than one who earns relatively high income.[7] Therefore, what matters is how much one saves, not just how much they earn.

The Capabilities Deprivation Approach

A. K. Sen is responsible for the second perspective on poverty. Sen's approach employs two key terms, namely functionings and capabilities.[8] Functionings means the things one succeeds in doing or being, such as being healthy, while capabilities are the freedom to achieve valuable functionings, such as the ability to enjoy social life and self-esteem.[9] Sen pointed out at least two pitfalls of the resource-centric approach to the understanding of poverty.[10] First, he argued, human needs vary between communities, families, and even individuals in such a way that different communities, families, and individuals need different amounts of resources to achieve the same capabilities. Second, income alone

---

2. They include Citro and Michael, *Measuring Poverty*; Khan and Hassan, "Incidence of Poverty," 21.
3. Smeeding, "Public Policy."
4. Wagle, "Multidimensional Poverty Measurement," 58, 67.
5. Wagle, 58–67.
6. Wagle, 59–61.
7. Pantazis, Gordon and Levitas, *Poverty and Social Exclusion*, 39–40.
8. Sen, *Development as Freedom*.
9. Sen, 75.
10. Sen, "Capabilities, Lists," 79–80.

cannot be used to measure poverty because it is only one of the factors that determine what people can do and be.[11]

According to Sen's approach, human well-being relates directly to how capably one can freely do the things they value doing or being. It could be deduced that this approach puts a premium on what the individual values rather than what policymakers wish for them. Sen embraces diversity, substantive freedom, agency, and participation such that what one can do or be (rather than what one has or feels) determines whether they are poor or not.[12] People with low levels of capabilities are considered poor and those with high levels of capabilities are considered rich. Poverty therefore refers to low-level human capabilities and poor access to the means to achieving these capabilities.[13]

The Social Exclusion Approach

The social exclusion approach is the third perspective on understanding poverty. The social exclusion that poverty brings may be in the form of "either economic dimension (exclusion from the labor market opportunities to earn income) or a purely social dimension (exclusion from decision-making, social services, and access to community and family support)."[14] This approach to poverty emerged in France in the 1970s and 1980s as a means of explaining the precarious situation of the disadvantaged and marginalized due to their inability to take part in the major economic, political, and social enterprises.[15] The meaning of the expression "social exclusion" has metamorphosed over the years.[16] In the 1970s many people became unemployed due to decline in business activities. In such a context, the term exclusion was used to denote the process that led to the expulsion of people from the job market. In the 1990s, prevalent human rights issues led to defining "excludees" as those who are "partly or completely outside the effective scope of human rights."[17]

The social exclusion approach differs from the economic and capability deprivation approaches in that the latter focus on individual characteristics and circumstances while the former shifts attention to the relational quality

---

11. Sen, 79–80.
12. Sen, 77–79; Hick, "Poverty as Capability Deprivation," 304.
13. Sen, 77–79; Hick, "Poverty as Capability Deprivation," 304.
14. As cited by Mathole, "Christian Witness," 46.
15. Wagle, "Multidimensional Poverty Measurement," 42–45.
16. Wagle, 58, 60.
17. Strobel cited in Wagle, 42.

of life (its social dimension). According to the exclusion approach, one may have high income and still be poor if there is lack of social order and hence, insecurity in the community. Moreover, the analysis of exclusion involves the study of societal structure and the conditions of the marginalized groups, such as minority groups and the landless. Social exclusion therefore involves cultural, institutional and social dimensions, which are absent in the first two approaches. It advocates for the need to redistribute opportunities and resources in order to improve the lives of the marginalized.

I must state at this point that while the economic dimension of poverty is very crucial in defining poverty, the concept of wealth and poverty in Africa and in Scripture goes beyond the economic dimension. There are social, religious, and spiritual dimensions to the problem (as I will discuss later).

Traditional African Perspectives on Wealth and Poverty

Imagery of poverty abounds in many African languages, showing that poverty has been a human challenge in the continent since time immemorial.[18] In search of an indigenous African understanding of poverty, I reflect on, and establish, the thinking pattern of Africans on poverty, especially as evident in proverbial materials.[19] Different terminologies are used in Africa for "poverty," "the poor," and "wealth." The term for poverty among the Bena of Tanzania is *muhangala* (deprivation); among the Akan of Ghana it is *ohia* (the lack of, being in need); among Igbo of Nigeria it is *ogbenye* (community to give[20]) and among the Yoruba of Nigeria it is *aku-ise* (carrying misery).[21] According to Kimilike the semantic content and function of poverty in the African perspective comprises lack of basic necessities of life including food, shelter, education and clothing; social exclusion, and deprivation of economic resources, especially land; childlessness, failure to meet membership requirements for "some sacred socio-cultural institutions or cults" and "[b]eing bodily weak, lazy, a loiterer, an idler, incapable of planning for one's future, incurring high indebtedness

---

18. Kimilike, "African Perspective," 84.

19. Proverbs are didactic materials for child-rearing, and linguistic and religious instruction for the society, and constitute a source of cultural values and wisdom applicable to the societies from which they emerge. Kimilike, "African Perspective," 101. They emerge from people's experience of reality and circulate freely in their community.

20. It refers to one whose survival depend on the collective effort of the society.

21. Kimilike, "African Perspective," 83–84.

without the ability to repay debts."[22] It follows therefore that the African concept of poverty has both personal and communal dimensions.

The African concept of wealth or prosperity includes not only material success but also fullness of life, fertility, peace, and other things.[23] Pobee gives useful insights into the Akan concept of prosperity (or well-being) which also applies to most African societies: Prosperity includes ideas such as "*nkwa*, which embraces life, vitality, good health, longevity; *adom*, God's gifts of food, life, any favour that the spirit world may shower on the living; *asomdwee*, peace of self (body and spirit), the family, the clan and human kind," as well as "*abawotum*, procreativity, potency, fertility of individuals as of clan . . .; *anihutum*, good and powerful eyesight and perception; *asotatum*, good hearing power; and *amandoree*, rainfall on the tribe as well as the increase and general prosperity of the family, clan and tribe."[24] With this background, I proceed to consider some of the traditional African wise sayings related to wealth and poverty.

Poverty as Social Exclusion

As mentioned earlier, Africans hold a communal worldview of life. For this reason, an African needs to feel part of, and be accepted by, the community because his or her existence depends more on community support than individualism. The Akan saying "The sibling of a rich person is money" underscores the fact that a wealthy person's need for companionship is satisfied by their wealth.[25] It does not mean that wealth is the literal sibling of the wealthy but that wealth creates opportunity for the wealthy to have many companions. People tend to visit the rich more frequently than the poor for the obvious reason that they might get something from the rich. The Yoruba version of the saying is "Lack of money is lack of friends; if you have money at your disposal, every dog and goat will claim to be related to you," which also underscores the fact that no one wants to visit or be associated with the poor because the poor have nothing to offer them; therefore, to be poor is to have a lonely life.

The Akan saying "The poor man and the rich man do not play together" also indicates that poverty is a form of social exclusion. We mentioned earlier that some African communities (such as the Akan and Yoruba) are highly

---

22. Kimilike, "African Perspective," 85–86.
23. See Anim, "Prosperity Gospel," 70.
24. See Anim, 70.
25. Anim, 70.

hierarchical. Only those at the same social level move together, for which reason people say, "Birds of equal status play together." Therefore, in these traditional African communities, the poor befriend the poor and the rich befriend the rich. Some rich families do not allow their members to marry into a poor family. A Nigerian movie entitled *Worlds Apart* depicts this culture very well. In this movie, the parents of a rich man discourage him from marrying a poor woman he loves due to the economic gap between their families. With this kind of attitude, the poor continue to be poor and the rich protect their riches.

Poverty Is Dehumanizing

Traditional African societies consider poverty dehumanizing and undesirable, hence the sayings "Poverty is a disgrace and dehumanizing" (Ghana) and "Poverty is slavery" (Somalia). Poverty causes one to become destitute, humiliated, and eventually to deviate from societal norms. Poverty exhibited in lack of food, shelter, and clothing usually makes one lose respect and dignity in society. The poor in most African societies are not respected; they are insulted and not taken seriously. They are vulnerable and objects of exploitation and injustice. The saying "The poor is not able to convince a child of his love" underscores the point that poverty may prevent a parent from showing affection to their child. Another proverb, "It is poverty that turned an Akan person into an animal," also points to the dehumanizing nature of poverty. A Bena proverb "Being poor is being a dog" sums up the discussion. The poor are powerless and unable to use their rights to improve their lives.

Wealth as Something Desirable

That indigenous Africans consider wealth as something desirable is expressed in many sayings. The Bono saying "The rich eats what is sweet" points to the fact that all the desirable things in the community eventually get to the rich. There is also an Akan saying that "the corpse of a rich person is more respected and glorious than a living poor person." In other words, it is worse to be poor and alive than to be rich and to die (even while) young. This saying assumes that the poor have no hope in life and their lives are almost aimless. The rich, on the other hand, no matter how short their lives, are perceived as having the opportunity to taste the sweet things in the world and so they die happily. The respect the rich person gains after death in terms of the kind of tomb for the burial, the number of people who wail at the funeral, and the manner the corpse is handled is far better than that accorded a poor person, sometimes even when they are alive.

A similar saying is, "It is poverty that will make one say medicine is not good." The poor person says, "medicine is not good" because they lack the money to buy the medicine required to cure their diseases. Eventually, the poor person is likely to die young. The rich person, on the other hand, is able to use their wealth to postpone death through medication and treatment, the cost of which the poor cannot afford. Therefore, even though Africans believe that death is inevitable, it is also a common view that wealth can prevent certain deaths. A related saying, "Wealth is blood but poverty is a misfortune," uses blood metaphorically to signify life and good fortune. Therefore, in that sense, to have wealth is to live a long life but being poor is a misfortune that may shorten life.

Wealth Offers Opportunities and Authority

A common saying among poor Akan people is "By the time that the poor gets money, their chances of traveling would have been blocked." Most Akan people travel in pursuit of greener pastures. Such travels are, however, mostly expensive and only the rich end up participating. The poor are saying that by the time that the chances for such travels are available, they do not have the means (funds) to pay for them and by the time that they have the means, their way is blocked. The point is that the poor are unable to travel for greener pastures and remain stuck in poverty.

The saying "The rich man is an elder" reminds us of the story of Jacob and Esau in the Bible, in which Esau's hunger makes him sell his birthright to his younger brother Jacob in return for food (Gen 25:29–34). In various African communities, many people indirectly or unconsciously sell their birthrights to their wealthy siblings. Usually, it is the eldest child who must take responsibility for the family needs. If it happens that they are unable to meet these needs, a younger sibling who is more financially endowed may take this responsibility, and eventually be regarded as the elder one (not based on time of birth but based on the role they play in the family).

The saying "If a woman becomes wealthy, she changes into a man" is rooted in the social status of African women. I have already stated that the patriarchal nature of most traditional African societies makes women have virtually no authority. In some societies, women are regarded as properties of their husbands and are not allowed to challenge their husbands or other elderly men on any issue. The social status of African women is, however, changed when a woman becomes rich. Wealth brings authority to women who are then allowed to contribute their quota in decision-making and community development.

Poverty Brings Out Creativity

In some parts of Africa, sayings are used to show poverty may make people want to improve their lives. That necessity is the mother of invention is depicted by the Ghanaian saying "Poverty makes one think (creatively), or causes one to be creative." This is also depicted by the Akan proverb "If a poor person has nothing else, they have at least a [sweet] tongue with which to defer the payment of his/her debts." The Bena saying "The mouth is a release" also underscores the proper use of the tongue to defer a debt or tone down a difficult situation. Certainly, poverty does not take away a person's ability to plan or think.

This point is expressed by Ghanaian highlife musician Moses Kwaku Oppong, the founder of the Kakaaku Band, in a song entitled "*Ohia ma adwendwene.*" The song depicts two animal characters, a tortoise and a mona monkey, as two close friends. The monkey's mother died and it asked the vulture to inform the tortoise about the bereavement. Upon hearing the news, the tortoise told the vulture to express the tortoise's condolences to the monkey and tell the monkey that tortoise will be there to mourn with the monkey on the day of the funeral. The vulture mocked the tortoise since the tortoise had no wings to fly to the top of the tree where the funeral was to take place. After a while, the tortoise told the vulture that on the day of the funeral the vulture should come to the house and pick up a sack at a given location and take it to the monkey, informing the monkey that the tortoise was on the way.

On the day of the funeral celebration the vulture came and picked up the sack, carried it to the monkey and told the monkey what the tortoise had said. The monkey wondered how the tortoise could attend the funeral. After opening the sack, the monkey found the tortoise in it. Clearly the tortoise's lack of wings to fly made it invent a way to get to the destination. This story perfectly illustrates the Cameroonian proverb "Knowledge is better than riches."

One Should Not Give Up Hope Because of Poverty

Traditional African societies deal with poverty by encouraging the poor to help themselves to improve their lives rather than give up hope. This is a form of social creativity. Social creativity refers to "a social mechanism employed by groups to resist pressure."[26] For example, by applying social creativity, someone who has been defeated in a competition may decide to avoid any comparison with the one who defeated them. The defeated person then chooses to compare themselves with those they can defeat. In so doing, people are able to comfort themselves even in times of crises. Traditional African people use social creativity to manage their poverty situation with the hope of improving their lives.

The African proverb "Do not commit suicide because of poverty, because you do not know what good thing may come your way" and the saying "The dead person is the poor person, if a person is alive they are not too poor" advise the poor to live with the hope of overcoming their situation in future. The proverb "If you have life you have everything" underlines the fact that longevity is a source of hope. Until death, one's life situation may change at any time. The poor must not give up hope, but work hard to improve their situation rather than resorting to idleness, which causes and increases poverty.

Benefits of African Communal Worldview of Wealth

Earlier, it was noted that poverty leads to social exclusion. Social exclusion contradicts the African communal lifestyle. Traditional society opposes social exclusion with the Akan, for example, saying that "If your mother is poor, you do not forsake her and adopt another." This saying underscores the fact that poverty should not lead to the breakdown of African communal (familial) relationships. The communal worldview of African societies is reflected in the ownership of wealth. In African, wealth is community-centered in that no matter who it belongs to, it is intended to be used for the well-being of the entire society. This fact is expressed among the Akan with the saying "If there is a *sika peredwan*[27] in a town, it belongs to the whole community." That is to say, the value of wealth is found in the generosity of the owner and wealth does not belong to the owner alone.

Therefore, in African communities it is wrong for one to accumulate wealth while others are suffering. Wealth is a common good that is intended to be shared with the needy to ease their plight. This is one of the ways of dealing with poverty in African traditional society. The common ownership of land, which is a major means of human survival, also promotes poverty reduction

---

26. Kissi, "Reading Hebrews," 31.
27. *Peredwan* was a unit of British colonial currency that was used in Ghana until 1957 (gold valued at £8.2s).

in the society. Therefore hospitality, a sense of belonging, sharing of resources, and showing compassion, respect and reciprocal responsibility that exist in African societies can be means of reducing the plight of the poor. Traditional African societies also fight against poverty through a collective responsibility to the family and society. Family members will do all they can to help their poor members maintain their human dignity. We said earlier that the human being, family and community are defined in terms of the values of solidarity and participation. It is believed that generosity to the poor will bring good fortune on the benefactor from the gods and ancestors while lack of generosity incurs the wrath of these entities. Everyone is therefore ready to share the little they have with others. This way the well-being of orphans, widows and the weak is sustained in traditional African societies. Therefore, African traditional values require that the needy are not abandoned.

It is also held that if one does not distribute their wealth for the benefit of others, they may lose it. This thought is depicted in the Ghanaian saying "Money has wings." It can fly from the selfish person to one who is generous. In support of this view is the Somali proverb, "One cannot count on riches." Therefore, the rich must help others with their wealth and at the same time avoid living extravagant lives.

The idea that wealth is intended to serve the whole community also makes people hate tightfisted rich people. Thus, the rich may have enemies if they do not show concern for the welfare of others. Yet, at the same time people become envious of rich people and become enemies with them simply because God has blessed the rich with wealth. This happens when the poor feel that the rich have had advantages that the poor did not have. The Swahili proverb "Much wealth brings many enemies" is a lesson to the rich to ensure that they avoid situations that can make them enemies of others. The saying also serves as comfort to the rich who by no fault of theirs have enemies simply because they have riches.

Poverty as Absolute, Moderate and Relative

Poverty in Africa comes in three different levels, namely absolute or extreme poverty, moderate poverty, and relative poverty. Absolute poverty refers to the lack that makes it impossible to meet basic physical human needs for survival including food, healthcare, drinking water, education for children, shelter, clothing, and sanitation. This level of poverty is the worst because without these basic needs human health and life are threatened. In Nigeria and other parts of Africa, some of the people affected by absolute poverty are the beggars found in "streets, railway line tarmac, carparks, vehicles terminus, market squares, hospitals, and schools."[28]

Moderate poverty refers to a situation where people barely meet their basic needs. In this case there is the need to forfeit other needs in order to acquire basic necessities of life. Those in this category are not in danger of dying, but they only survive physically, and do not have the means to enjoy life, though they are better off than those in the first category.

Relative poverty refers to a situation whereby one finds themselves poor because his income is far less than the average income of the society in which they live. In this case one is considered poor relative to others. The idea of relative poverty is based on an assumed, generally accepted, living standard in a community at a particular time. This poverty is common among urban dwellers such as people in cities like Abuja, Accra, Bamako, Monrovia, Nairobi, Lagos, Pretoria, Sunyani, and others. Someone considered rich in their village may be considered poor when they move to the city, where richer people reside. This leads to the concepts of rural poverty and urban poverty. The former focuses on issues such as food insecurity, childlessness, disability, and lack of property (such as farmland), while the latter comprises lack of employment, the unavailability and inadequacy of social services, absence of skills training, and lack of capital and education.

Poverty and Economic Inequality in Africa

Economic inequality in Africa is high and complex. Seven out of the ten most unequal countries in the world are found in Africa.[29] Inequality may be considered in terms of outcomes like income, consumption, and wealth, or in terms of opportunity. Inequality in outcome has to do with the economic gap between the richest and the poorest. The major factors that bring about this gap include inequality of opportunities and individual efforts as well as one's ability or inability to take risks. Inequality of opportunity has to do with situations over which one has little or no control (including parents' education level, place of birth, whether rural or urban), and yet have the tendency to determine what the future will be. In this sense, one may be considered "born poor" if they are a "beneficiary of less investment in human development, which determines future living standards."[30] The reality of inequality underlines

---

28. Chukwuma, "Reducing Poverty in Nigeria," xxviii.
29. Beegle et al., *Poverty in a Rising Africa*, 117.
30. Beegle et al., 117.

"the lack of a level playing field" for all people.[31] The idea that being born poor has a direct influence on one's aspirations and success (or that the environment into which one is born impacts their success in life) is underlined in the Bono saying "The one who is born on a mountain easily becomes tall while the one born in a valley struggles before becoming tall." One born into a poor family may think that it is not possible to become rich and such a feeling and thought may keep them poor throughout life.

I now proceed to cite cases from some African countries to further explain the issue of economic inequality. In Zambia, the majority of people live in rural areas and the rural residents have a higher incidence of poverty compared to urban residents.[32] Rural areas lack social amenities such as electricity, schools, health facilities, and motorable roads. The reason is that most industries and investments are found in the urban areas; the government has paid more attention to copper mining at the expense of rural development, the result of which is the mass exodus of people from rural areas to urban areas.[33] This movement of people results in congestion and a high crime rate in urban areas.

In South Africa, the economic situation shows a similar trend. Maluleke observes that in South Africa, development (in terms of "communication, health services, electricity, good road networks and water supply") is concentrated in urban areas.[34] There is also a wide gap between Blacks and Whites in South Africa, and Giliomee has lamented that, "The vast discrepancies in wealth between Blacks and Whites are simply not compatible with nation building. At the very least, a progressive equalizing of life chances is essential."[35] Apartheid legislations and policies entrenched skewed distribution of the national cake in such a way that to be born Black makes one a likely candidate for poverty.[36] This situation in a post-apartheid South Africa is disturbing. The obvious conclusion from the findings of this section is that, unless wealth is redistributed and incomes made to be more equal, poverty will always remain a burden to Africans.

The *2016 Poverty Profile for Somalia* shows a high level of economic inequality between the poor and the rich in Somalia which is more noticeable

---

31. Beegle et al., 117.
32. Chimfwembe, "Pastoral Care," 68.
33. Chimfwembe, 69.
34. As cited in Chimfwembe, 69.
35. As cited by Mathole, "Christian Witness," 21.
36. As cited by Mathole, 23.

in urban areas than in rural ones.[37] In the rural areas, the low economic level is nearly the same for everyone, and at a level where each one can survive, unlike in the urban areas where the wealthy have more than they need while the poor have too little to survive. But the poverty level in the rural areas causes a lot of rural dwellers to lag behind in terms of education as compared to their urban counterparts. The report further noted that there has not been much achievement in bridging the gap between the poor and the rich in the past few years, though there are positive indicators that success could be achieved soon.[38] Two of the main reasons that perpetuate the economic gap between the poor and rich include disparities in education level between the poor and non-poor households and the high rate of rural unemployment. Any attempt to bridge the existing economic gap should aim at creating sustainable employment for the rural areas and increasing the literacy rate among rural settlers.

In their study on Ghana's poverty situation from the 1990s to 2006, Coulombe and Wodon commended the country's commitment towards the achievement of the Millennium Development Goals (MDG), particularly its ability to reduce poverty by half in 2006 (nine years earlier than the MDGs target).[39] Nonetheless, they observed economic inequality in the country and argued that Ghana could have achieved this feat earlier (before 2006) if the gap between the poor and the rich had been checked. Their research brought to the fore the fact that Ghana's poverty reduction strategies did not benefit the northern Savanna Region as much as they did the middle and southern parts of the country.[40] Therefore, being born in the northern savanna part of the country makes one a likely victim of poverty.

This brief survey points to similar trends in socioeconomic inequality in African countries. This means that in most African countries one's chances of succeeding in life depends on where they were born, or where they live. With this background, I now proceed to consider why poverty continues to be a challenge to Africans.

Some Causes of Poverty in Africa

Africa is endowed with the natural resources required for sustainable development. Yet at the same time the continent is filled with people living in

---

37. World Bank, *Somali Poverty Profile 2016*, 8.
38. World Bank, 10.
39. Coulombe and Wodon, "Poverty, Livelihoods, and Access," 21.
40. Coulombe and Wodon, 21 and 25.

abject poverty. The obvious question to ask is "Why is Africa a poor continent in spite of its abundant resources?" Assessing the causes of poverty in Africa is helpful in understanding why Africans remain poor in the midst of abundant resources. To this issue I now turn.

Environmental Destruction

Environmental destruction is one of the major causes of poverty in many African nations and, at the same time, poverty can also lead to environmental destruction.[41] Environmental degradation in Africa manifests itself in rapid rates of depletion of natural capital. God has blessed the continent with different natural resources for socioeconomic development. Africa is blessed with resources like diamonds, coffee, timber, oil, sugar, salt, gold, iron, cobalt, uranium, copper, silver, bauxite, petroleum, cocoa beans, and tropical fruits. In the process of harnessing these resources, some societies sometimes experience serious environmental problems. For example, overexploitation of a country's natural resources and unsafe practices including excessive cutting down of trees, illegal mining activities, chemical means of harvesting fish, and so on, has led to diverse environmental problems like land degradation, soil erosion, pollution of rivers, streams and lagoons, air pollution, and desertification. In the forest zones, people often resort to cutting down trees for firewood or charcoal, a practice that may lead to desertification and render the land incapable of supporting plant life. Such a situation not only costs the country and individuals huge sums of money but also makes people poorer by destroying their means for production.

Poor Agricultural Practices and Road Networks

Poor agricultural practices contribute to (rural) poverty in many African societies[42] where the agricultural sector is a major contributor to national development in most countries.[43] In Ethiopia, for instance, about 80 percent of the populace engage in agricultural activities. Most of these are rural settlers who lack basic amenities like electricity, health care and educational facilities.[44] Technological advancement in the agricultural sector is very slow and so

---

41. Asante, *Stewardship*, 185.
42. Adjei, "Poverty in Ghana," 48.
43. Cunguara, "Assessing Strategies," ii.
44. Gomez, "Main Causes of Poverty."

farmers continue to rely on rainfall for cultivation (due to lack of irrigation facilities), and on human labor for cultivating their crops (due to lack of technologically-advanced farming equipment).[45] The capital-intensive nature of labor-intensive farming practice restricts many farmers from setting up large farms. There is also the subdivision of land resulting from population pressure, meaning that farmers have very small farms that may not meet household food needs. Many farmers are only able to cultivate a little more than what they can consume. Also, pest control methods are ineffective and so pests and diseases sometimes reduce yield drastically. The end result is the inability of many African countries to achieve self-sufficiency in food production.

Most roads leading to many African farming communities are unmotorable[46], making it impossible for some farmers to transport their produce to urban areas for marketing. Consequently, an appreciable quantity of farm yields in farming communities rots in farms, causing financial loss to those already farming and discouraging potential farmers.[47]

Underdeveloped markets, poor post-harvest storage practices, and lack of markets forces many farmers to compete for buyers, a situation which eventually gives buyers the power to determine the prices of foodstuffs, without considering the farmers' cost of production and denying them much needed profit. Africa's inability to add value to farm produce through processing also makes farmers sell their produce such as cocoa, coffee, and cashew as raw materials at cheap prices. I believe that this observation is true in many African countries. The results of all these challenges is that, at the end of the year, many farmers in Africa are unable to pay their creditors (let alone make a profit), in spite of their hard work. This situation makes many farmers enter every farming season with debt incurred in the previous season and often contributes to a cycle of poverty.

Bad Government Policies

In Africa, poverty is often politically driven. Government policies are expected to benefit the citizens. Unfortunately, in our part of the world, politicians mostly formulate policies that turn out to establish and legitimize some form of exploitative means of distribution of opportunities, income and wealth, relying on the use of state power. The available resources are used to satisfy the wants

---

45. Cunguara, "Assessing Strategies," ii.
46. Adjei, "Poverty in Ghana," 49.
47. Adjei, 50.

of a few while many lack the basic life necessities. More so, legislatures enact laws that endorse a huge gap between the salaries of politicians and other civil workers, the result of which is economic disparity.

Many African countries do not have strong governance systems. "Weak governance in Africa is characterized, in many of the countries, by a combination of such elements as poor institutional performance, inadequate parliamentary oversight, lack of judicial independence, political instability, nonexistent or insufficient budgetary accountability, no respect for the rule of law or human rights, and rampant bureaucratic and political corruption."[48] Many African countries have experienced political instability. Those with stable political structures also lack proper government machinery and oversight. The judicial services in most countries do not enjoy autonomy, the result of which is the lack of rule of law. In such a situation, Africa's socioeconomic development cannot be realized.

Corruption

The high level of corruption and mismanagement of public resources is another contributor to poverty in Africa.[49] By corruption, I mean the misappropriation of public funds or property by a person who has the mandate to safeguard and protect them. The seriousness of corruption in Africa is evident from the 2018 Corruption Perceptions Index. The report found that sub-Saharan African was the most corrupt region in the world. An Africa country, Somalia, was found to be the world's most corrupt nation.[50] Other African countries that fall within the first ten most corrupt countries include South Sudan (third in the world), Sudan (sixth), Guinea Bissau (seventh), Equatorial Guinea (eighth), and Libya (tenth).[51] The high rate of corruption in most of these African countries is coupled with ineffective institutions and weak democratic values, which hinder anti-corruption progress. This observation buttresses the assertion by Delia Rubio (chair of Transparency International) that "Corruption is much more likely to flourish where democratic foundations are weak and, as we have seen in many countries, where undemocratic and populist politicians capture democratic institutions and use them to their advantage."[52]

---

48. Hope, *Poverty, Livelihoods, and Governance*, 155–156.
49. Hope, 156.
50. Transparency International, *Corruption Perceptions Index 2018*, 1.
51. Transparency International, 1. Somalia has been at the bottom of the chart since 2006.
52. Transparency International, *Corruption Perceptions Index 2018*, 1.

Corruption is increasingly viewed as a key hindrance to sustained socioeconomic development in sub-Saharan Africa. Corruption is common in many parts of Africa, though its extent varies from rare to widespread and systemic. The media are constantly filled with stories of misappropriation of government funds, an act which eats deeply into a nation's economy. In Africa, corruption ranges from the petty bribe received by a secretary in the office or the police at a checkpoint to the huge bribe taken by a high ranking government official to award contracts, and so on. In Africa, corruption is not only evident in the public sector but is also found in the private sector. To substantiate his position that corruption is deeply entrenched in the public sector of Kenya, Boniface Nikamiti cites the case of Goldenberg International "where the company through authorization by senior government officials received compensation for minerals not exported."[53] He also refers to evidence from a report by the Controller and Auditor General which reveals that the Kenyan government's system of financial management was characterized by laxity and weak financial controls.[54] Apparently, the continual presence of corruption in Africa points to loopholes in governance across much of the continent.

Corruption fights against efficiency in service delivery because often people are able to bribe supervisors and accept mediocre services. Many public officers use their position to illegitimately amass wealth for themselves instead of promoting the welfare of the citizenry. Some politicians steal the nation's money and deposit it in foreign bank accounts. Members of the police force, which are expected to ensure justice, involve themselves in corruption (especially the traffic police). Christians, who by nature are expected to be corruption-free and to fight corruption, also get caught up in high-level corruption because, in many cases, the vice is almost "normalized" in African nations. The unreasonably high cost of projects executed by governments in Africa as compared to the cost of similar projects when undertaken by the private sector points to the pervasive nature of corruption.[55] Ultimately, corruption undermines national development, weakens the economy, leads to economic inequality among citizens and makes a country poorer.[56]

---

53. Nlkamiti, "Does Corruption Affect Poverty?," 8.
54. Nlkamiti, 8.
55. Adjei, "Poverty in Ghana," 51–55.
56. Adjei, 52.

Cultural Practices

Certain cultural practices contribute to poverty among Africans. For example, poverty among African women may have cultural underpinnings. Most African societies are patriarchal in nature, with socioeconomic structures that contribute to poverty among women. Poverty is often distributed along gender lines. The 2002 World Bank Conference in Nairobi noted that "[w]ithin Africa poverty affects women and children disproportionately. The voiceless and the powerless are most often women."[57] This happens because of unfair patriarchal structures in most indigenous African societies that tend to sideline women, treat them as slaves, and prevent them from owning economic resources, thereby making them more prone to poverty than men. In some traditional African communities, women are denied the right to access resources such as land, buildings, livestock, poultry, water bodies, farm produce, bullocks, radio, bicycle, motor vehicles, and labor. Many widows who could have improved their lives with the resources left behind by their late husbands end up living in poverty because traditional customs do not allow them to inherit these resources. As an African, I believe that in most communities, this custom is rooted in the fact that the dowry (in the form of cows, dogs, cowries and cash) paid during marriage is regarded as giving the man and his family ownership of the woman. The patriarchal nature of traditional African society is a hindrance to the fight against poverty among women who continue to remain powerless to change the structures that contribute to the plight.

Another cultural practice that contributes to poverty among women is widowhood rites.[58] In most African societies widowed women are exploited financially, emotionally, sexually, and socially in the process of fulfilling cultural rites of widowhood. In Nigeria and other parts of Africa, widowhood rites comprise "socialization processes that condition women to passivity and dependence."[59] Traditional customs often do not permit the widow to undertake any social or economic activity throughout the period of the widowhood.[60] Widows undergo rituals such as living in seclusion, following a prescribed dress code, walking barefooted, shaving their hair, and fasting for extended periods of time, among other requirements.[61] Such requirements are not compatible with undertaking any business venture during the entire period of widowhood.

---

57. As cited in Mathole, "Christian Witness," 29.
58. Adjei, "Poverty in Ghana," 57.
59. Genyi, "Widowhood and Nigerian Womanhood," 68.
60. Genyi, 68.
61. Genyi, 69.

Some societies may require widows to observe widowhood rites for about a year, and one can only imagine how a poor widow would cater for her needs and those of her children in such circumstances. Often, as a result of observing widowhood rites, the widow and her family end up in poverty.

Moreover, the cultural requirement for fulfilling funeral rites before and during burials also exposes many African families to poverty, especially in the rural areas of the continent. Funeral rites are often expensive in Africa because of the belief that an elaborate funeral will enhance the entrance of the spirit of the deceased into the afterlife. In Africa, funerals offer people the opportunity to celebrate the life of the dearly departed and people "may spend as much money on funerals as on weddings, sometimes even more."[62] Some people take out loans in order to celebrate funerals of loved ones.[63] It is also a common practice to share funeral costs among family members who may become indebted because of frequent funerals in their family. The time spent planning and attending funerals also keeps people from engaging in economic activities to improve their lives. In South Africa, it has been observed that a family "may become permanently poorer following the death of a household member in part because of the obligation it faces to bury members in a manner that reflects both the household's status and the member's status within the community."[64] The size of the funeral gathering, its expenses and extent of feasting are informed by the age of the deceased, their social status and the wealth of the deceased person's family. In KwaZulu-Natal "the feast following a man's funeral will involve slaughtering a cow (an expensive proposition),while that following a woman's will involve slaughtering a goat (at lesser expense)."[65]

High Rate of Illiteracy

The lack of education is another key contributor to income poverty;[66] it both causes and perpetuates poverty. There is a high illiteracy rate in many parts of Africa. The United Nations Educational, Scientific and Cultural Organization (UNESCO) Institute for Statistics (in 2017) observed that the world's lowest

---

62. Newton, "Long Goodbye," http://edition.cnn.com/2014/03/11/world/africa/on-the-road-ghana-funerals/.
63. Bax, "In Ghana."
64. Ardington, Bärnighausen, Case, and Menendez, "Economic Consequences," 17.
65. Ardington, Bärnighausen, Case, and Menendez, 17.
66. Ghana Statistical Service, *Ghana Poverty Mapping Report*.

literacy rates are in sub-Saharan Africa and in Southern Asia.[67] The report listed the following countries among those whose adult literacy rates fell below 50 percent: Benin, Burkina Faso, Central African Republic, Chad, Côte d'Ivoire, Ethiopia, The Gambia, Guinea, Guinea-Bissau, Liberia, Mali, Mauritania, Niger, Senegal, Sierra Leone, and South Sudan.[68] The report was explicit that access to education was a major problem in most African countries.

Education is one of the forces that fosters sustainable development. The skills needed to acquire a job, establish a business, manufacture, and to manage available resources, among others tasks, are all acquired through education. Imagine how difficult it is for an illiterate person to keep basic records of their daily business activities or prepare a financial account of their yearly activities. There are instances whereby people, for lack of knowledge, unintentionally sell their goods at prices lower than the cost price. Illiteracy can also lead to poor health or nutrition deficiency, gender inequality, and poor productivity, all of which hinder economic progress. Another aspect of education is the fact that the education systems of some countries do not equip graduates with the skills required to meet the development needs of the society.[69] The education systems of most African countries lay more emphasis on theoretical education rather than practical learning. Consequently, by the time many students graduate from university they have little experience for the job market.

Large Family Size

In Africa, a large family size has the potential of making people poor.[70] Generally speaking, many Africans have the desire to have large families. Childlessness is a serious problem for an African couple because to not have children after marriage is viewed as a misfortune. A woman proves her worth by her ability to conceive and give birth. An Akan woman who gives birth to the tenth child is rewarded with a sheep, referred to as *Badudwane* (tenth-born sheep). But as it often turns out, it is the poor who usually desire to have more children, not the rich. Most of these people are farmers and having a large family ensures that more farmhands are available. At the end, having many children increases expenditure and reduces a family's chances of saving. Most children from such

---

67. United Nations Educational, Scientific and Cultural Organization (UNESCO) Institute for Statistics, "Literacy Rates Continue to Rise," FS/2017/LIT/45.

68. UNESCO Institute for Statistics, "Literacy Rates Continue to Rise," FS/2017/LIT/45.

69. Hope, *Poverty, Livelihoods, and Governance*, 155.

70. Anyanwu, "Marital Status," 7.

families do not get an opportunity to attend or finish school. The scarce resources available to the family are shared among a large number of people, making it easy to fall into poverty and difficult to break out of the cycle of poverty.

Lack of Employment

Inadequate access to employment opportunities is another reason why many Africans are poor. There is a strong correlation between unemployment and poverty. People can save if they are gainfully employed. However, most African countries are currently experiencing high unemployment rates.[71] For example, the high unemployment rate in South Africa is the main reason for the xenophobic attack on foreigners in some South African communities.[72] In Ethiopia, there is mounting unemployment in urban areas, which calls for immediate measures to create more employment.[73] Today, there are many graduates in Africa who wander the streets without anything gainful to do for a living and hence are unable to afford the basic necessities of life, including food, clothing and shelter.[74] The obvious results of this state of affairs are the high crime rate, illegal mining, and so on, that are seen in most African countries today.[75] The unemployment and under-employment situation in Africa, particularly among the youth, also results in the mass exodus of Africans to Europe and (especially) North America to seek for greener pastures which most do not really find. Many of these people eventually get stranded abroad.

Laziness

People may also become poor due to laziness. Laziness may comprise an unwillingness to engage in productive activity. As Kimilike observes, "a lazy type of person works under the stress of necessity and tries to make his or her living from hard-working people by continual begging, stealing and other fraudulent means."[76] Eze argues that "lack of participation can be considered one of the major factors that contribute to the constant existence of poverty and refers to one's inability to take part in some activities that could help

---

71. See Poku-Boansi and Afrane, "Magnitude and Impact of Youth," 74–80.
72. Dahir, "These Charts Show Migrants," September 13, 2019.
73. Enquobahrie, *Understanding Poverty*, 12.
74. Adjei, "Poverty in Ghana."
75. Poku-Boansi and Afrane, "Magnitude and Impact of Youth," 74–78.
76. Kimilike, "African Perspective," 87.

him or her to make a living."[77] Though traditional African values frown upon laziness, it has become common these days especially among people from wealthy homes. Many people from rich families want to enjoy life but are not ready to work hard. They normally depend on the breadwinner in their family for survival and spend their time on detrimental social activities such as gambling, alcoholism, womanizing and the like.

If the bread winner dies, these people are left on their own to struggle for a living. They consume whatever was left by the deceased without working hard to add to it. After consuming what they have, they are left poor throughout the rest of their life due to their lazy attitude. Other people may develop laziness after trying to work hard for success but failing. This attitude of despair towards work may be the result of "unjust socio-economic structures of the community, that is, the existence of an inequitable distribution of resources."[78]

Natural Disasters

Natural disasters such as drought, fires, earthquakes, floods and war also bring many Africans to poverty. Many African countries have experienced wars in their history, which have contributed to loss of lives and livelihoods, and forced many to flee live as refugees in neighboring countries. Those who remain behind find it difficult to survive as a result of losing their sources of incomes or breadwinners. Many people have also become poor due to fire outbreaks. Many rural settlements and some business establishments in Africa are made of mud and roofed with grass or thatch, making them prone to fire. Drought, the frequency of which has increased in the continent, is also a major threat to incomes and livelihoods. In 1973–1974, Tanzania suffered a severe drought that adversely affected maize production (the major subsistence food crop), leading to a higher cost of living and poverty.[79] In 1983, Ghana experienced a nationwide fire outbreak which led to famine and poverty at record levels and Uganda's war against Tanzania from 1978 to 1979 brought economic hardship to the two countries.

---

77. Eze, *Understanding Poverty*, 170.
78. Kimilike, "African Perspective," 8.
79. Kimilike, "African Perspective," 93.

Poor Health

Poor health may also render people incapable of working towards their economic development. The issue of HIV/AIDS in this regards needs special consideration due to its devastating effect on the progress of the continent. Pobee says that the HIV/AIDs pandemic "signals a crisis facing the society, the family, the nation and the world. Pandemic is a reminder that HIV/AIDs is a human tragedy and issue." Of the 42 million people living with HIV/AIDs in the world, 29.4 million (70 percent) are in the sub-Saharan Africa where only 10 percent of the world's population live.[80] South Africa, Nigeria and Ethiopia are the top three countries in terms of HIV/AIDs infection in Africa. The number of people infected are respectively 5, 4 and 3 million.[81] This disease and others may lead to joblessness, a situation that is likely to make one depend on others for survival. African societies with many sick people who no longer have the capacity to work, end up with high economic dependency, which leads to poverty.

Emigration of Skilled People

The emigration of skilled people from various parts of Africa to other parts of the world (particularly Europe and North America) to seek greener pastures is another major contributor to Africa's poverty.[82] This emigration, also referred to as brain drain, reduces Africa's capacity "to effectively and efficiently deliver public services and contribute to the skill pool requirements of the private sector."[83] In the colonial era, Africans were forced to go and serve abroad. However, today Africans are eager to leave the continent for countries, mostly in West, that they consider as having stronger economies, and better education and employment opportunities. It is difficult to control these departures because people choose where they want to live or work. Some of these Africans have attended schools abroad and chosen to not return home to their countries; others have acquired education in their home countries and decided to live and work outside the Africa.

It is estimated that about twenty thousand skilled Africans leave for developed countries every year.[84] Whether through slavery or emigration,

---

80. Nihinlola, *Theology Under the Mango Tree*, 173.
81. From Nihinlola, 173.
82. Hope, *Poverty, Livelihoods, and Governance*, 153.
83. Hope, 153.
84. Hope, 154.

Africa has lost the services of many well-trained individuals who have the expertise to help develop African countries. A study in the year 2000 found that 10.4 percent of African tertiary graduates travel to other parts of the world to seek for job opportunities.[85] For countries such as The Gambia, Cape Verde, Sierra Leone, and Mozambique, the emigration rate is more than 45 percent. The effect of this brain drain is that many African societies and countries have lost the human resources they require for sustainable development.

Some Effects of Poverty in Africa

The effects of poverty in Africa are many and varied and include low human productivity which limits the resources available to meet human basic needs such as food and adequate shelter. Poverty also prevents many people in Africa from accessing adequate health care and education. It also causes long-term social problems in the continent.

Inadequate Food and Housing

The United Nations Sustainable Development Goal 2 is stated as follows: "By 2030, end hunger and ensure access by all people, in particular, the poor and people in vulnerable situations, including infants, to safe, nutritious and sufficient food all year round."[86] Africa is making progress in the fight against food insecurity. In 2015 it was observed that the prevalence of undernourishment in Africa had fallen from about 34 percent in 1991 to 20 percent. Yet, lack of food is still a problem in Africa today despite the continent's large landmass.[87] The majority of Africans are farmers and yet the continent is not self-sufficient in food. Some African countries, including Nigeria, continue to import food such as rice, millet, and maize, which could be produced locally in abundance if the agricultural sector was strengthened. Food insecurity in the continent is rising and some of the areas that suffer most from lack of food include the Lake Chad Basin, Central African Republic, Democratic Republic of the Congo, Somalia, and South Sudan. As noted earlier, farmers in Africa are unable to produce enough food to feed themselves and for selling because of the overreliance on traditional methods of farming. Potential farmers are

---

85. Hope, 154.

86. Morton, Pencheon, and Squires, "Sustainable Development Goals," 84.

87. Donkor, "Role of MMDAS," 31; Ghana Statistical Service, *Ghana Poverty Mapping Report*.

discouraged because farming is not a lucrative enterprise. The results of the lack of food include malnutrition, hunger, and poor health. In places where food is available, poor people are unable to afford it. It is therefore not surprising that sub-Saharan Africa has the highest prevalence of undernourishment in the world.[88]

In addition to having sufficient food, access to shelter is one of the basic necessities of life. A rapid increase in housing facilities is required to match the needs of an ever increasing population and urbanization in many African countries and urban centers. However, years of government underinvestment in building new houses means many cities and towns in Africa have inadequate housing. Consequently, in urban areas it is common to find people dwelling in unsuitable conditions in kiosks, streets, tents, cargo containers, and other forms of informal housing. Exposed to the elements and diseases, some (of the mostly poor people) end up losing their lives due to the adverse living conditions. Others move from place to place when natural disasters like floods strike. To sum up, the accommodation problem facing many Africans today is a clear manifestation of the high poverty levels of African societies.

Poor Health Facilities

Africa's poverty situation is attested to in its deficient health care system.[89] Hospitals are the main health care facilities available to people in Africa, but the lack of funds for training health personnel has resulted in a very high patient-to-doctor ratio in many African countries, including Ghana.[90] In many countries across sub-Saharan Africa patients queue from morning till evening without getting seen by qualified health professionals. Many also have to travel long distances to access health services.

Health facilities in many African countries are in deplorable situations. People die because of lack of medicine, lack of beds, and so on. In Africa, a patient may die before reaching a health facility because of poor transport networks and long distances to hospitals. Transfer of patients between hospitals is also usually not done with much care for the sick. Quite recently, a Ghanaian man died in the process of being transferred to a different hospital because the new hospital had no available beds.[91] In many hospitals, patients have to

---

88. Lausund, "Social Protection for Enhanced Food."
89. Donkor, "Role of MMDAS," 66.
90. Adjei, "Poverty in Ghana," 66.
91. Adogla-Bessa, "Man, 70, Dies."

sleep on the floor, benches, or trolleys while receiving treatment or undergoing medical procedures such as blood transfusion. There are hospitals in Africa where mothers deliver children on the floor because of lack of beds![92]

Infant mortality is also high in many African countries.[93] Ambulance services are often unavailable in many parts of the continent, meaning that many patients die because they cannot access hospitals during emergencies. Most African governments are unable to foot the cost of healthcare delivery to their citizenry and they resort to foreign-sourced loans and grants to provide this critical service. Aside from this, the poor terms of service for health workers lead to regular strike actions by doctors and nurses, which leads to further patient deaths. Though national immunization campaigns are on the increase in many countries, many African children below three years of age have not been vaccinated against the main childhood killer diseases, namely tuberculosis, polio, diphtheria, whooping cough, tetanus, and measles.

Poor Education Systems

There is a close link between education and poverty reduction. This is so not only because education increases one's skills and productivity, but also because it emancipates one's mind from sociocultural practices that have the potential of keeping one in poverty. Yet, in Africa, poverty has led to poor education systems and a high illiteracy rate. Hope has observed that "the state of education in Africa, from primary to tertiary, has been plagued by the lack of funds . . . teachers, and textbooks, as well as inadequate school buildings."[94] Many African countries have rolled out policies to increase the Net Attendance Rate (NAR)[95] with countries such as Burundi, Ghana, Kenya, Malawi, Tanzania, and Uganda introducing various education policies such as free compulsory basic education that have increased enrollment in schools. But many children of school-going age still remain uneducated.[96]

---

92. Peacefmonline.com, 2017.

93. Adjei, "Poverty in Ghana," 68.

94. Hope, *Poverty, Livelihoods, and Governance*, 155.

95. NAR refers to the "attendance rates of children at Primary, Junior High School (JHS) and Senior High School (SHS) is the number of children of official schooling age (as defined by Ghana Education Service) who are attending Primary, JHS and SHS as a percentage of the total children of the official school age population." Ghana Statistical Service, *Ghana Living Standards Survey*, 37.

96. Adjei, "Poverty in Ghana," 69.

Poverty in the education sector also manifests itself in inadequate infrastructure and facilities.[97] Schools under trees are still a reality in Africa. Many school buildings are so dilapidated that they have become death traps for occupants. There are many schools which have to close down whenever it rains because of serious leaks. Facilities such as Information Communication and Technology (ICT) laboratories and equipment and science laboratories are not available in many schools.[98] The result is that pupils learn without any practical exercises and so they are unable to put what they learn into any practical use after school, a situation that further worsens the unemployment rate and economic performance of countries.[99] Coupled with this is the lack of qualified teachers in some schools.[100] Some teachers handle more than one class in the basic school where each class ordinarily requires a teacher. Large class sizes also make monitoring and evaluation of student progress ineffective.

Other Socioeconomic Problems

There are a number of other socioeconomic challenges associated with poverty in Africa. Writing about the effect of poverty on the social life of the youth, D. C. Ononogbu avers that poverty makes the youths "hang on for some time, just whiling away the time but when they get tired of merely sitting on the wall, they tend to implode and fall into all sorts of anti-social behaviours and habits that the society may never be able to help them again".[101] This statement makes the point that most deviant behavior among the youth in Africa may be the result of their experience of poverty. "Child streetism" is one of such problems. Some poor parents send their children onto the street to search for money to supplement the family's income. Others are born on the street from teenage pregnancies and because they have no home, they live on the street. Still, some children move from rural areas to cities to look for greener pastures and end up becoming children of the street as porters and hawkers.

Another socioeconomic challenge of poverty is the high incidence of internet fraud.[102] This may take place anywhere, whether in the city or rural areas. Some youth also engage in the act of using juju (black powers) to mislead

---

97. Adjei, 69–71.
98. Adjei, 69.
99. Adjei, 69.
100. Adjei, 70.
101. Ononogbu, "Unemployment Among Youths," 134.
102. See Poku-Boansi and Afrane, "Magnitude and Impact of Youth," 74–76.

wealthy people (usually foreigners on the Internet) to send them huge sums of money. The rituals involved in the Internet fraud business may comprise one or more of the following activities, which are usually done by the young people looking to defraud others: carrying a coffin at midnight through one's neighborhood; using human parts or blood for a specified ritual; meeting and interacting with a spirit and/or a strange being at the cemetery at midnight.

The high incidence of prostitution and taking and sharing of nude pictures and videos among Africa's youth may also be the result of poverty.[103] Some youth use their naked pictures and videos to attract their foreign friends of the opposite sex to send them money. In the end, some of these pictures are leaked either by the people themselves or by their foreign counterparts, especially when there is misunderstanding between them.

Also, poverty can lead also to indebtedness. Some people are so poor that they are not able to support their life. Without having access to bank credit facilities, they resort to borrowing from friends and relatives (who charge far higher interest than the banks in some cases) to cater for their basic needs. As it turns out they are not able to pay because they have no gainful employment or have no source of income to settle these debts. In some cases people lose their farmlands to creditors when they cannot pay debts. The loss of land makes a bad situation worse because the poor are then deprived of what is often their last remaining means of getting food and making a living.

Conclusion

Beginning with the socioreligious and sociopolitical context of Africa and ending with an examination of the poverty situation and its effects in Africa, this chapter has maintained that poverty has been in Africa since precolonial times. The chapter has reviewed the African communal view of life, the African traditional understanding of poverty and wealth and the factors that contribute to Africa's poverty situation. With this foundation laid, I now proceed to a theological and exegetical study of selected texts in Scripture on the subject of poverty.

---

103. See Poku-Boansi and Afrane, 74.

3

Poverty in the Context of the Old Testament

This and the following chapters place the subjects of wealth and poverty in the biblical context, to enable us to appreciate what Scripture teaches about the subject. These chapters on the biblical teaching on poverty and the previous chapter on the context of poverty in Africa provide the contextual framework within which I formulate a theology of poverty in Africa. I have focused on four anchor passages, one each from the Law (Deut 15:1–11), the Prophets (Isa 10:1–4), the Gospels (Matt 6:19–34), and the Epistles (1 Tim 6:6–10). The choice of these passages was informed both by their relevance to the study subject and my desire to present a focused examination of passages from as many genres of Scripture as possible. The method used in studying these texts is the exegetical method which comprises the following: (a) contextual analysis; (b) literary analysis including a study of the form (genre), structure and movement of the text; (c) detailed analysis of key parts of the text involving lexicology (the meaning of words), morphology (the form of words), grammatical function of words (parts of speech), syntax (the relationships of words), figures of speech, and so on; (d) theological synthesis of the findings. I begin the chapter with a brief outline of key biblical terminologies associated with "poverty" and then proceed to analyze Deuteronomy 15:1–11 and Isaiah 10:1–4.

Key Biblical Terms for "Poor"

Of the many Hebrew and Greek terms used in reference to "the poor" in the Bible, I found seven, including *ānî*, *ānāwîm* (or *anaw*), *'ebyôn*, *dal*, *rush*, *miskēn* and *ptōchos*, which I consider most relevant to the study. I proceed to discuss each term briefly below. The term *ānî* has a wide range of meanings including "the poor, afflicted, oppressed, powerless, needy, helpless, humble, weak, distress, suffering, wretched."[1] According to James Hastings *ānî* originally meant one who bows down due to oppression or one who suffers some kind of social injustice.[2] In biblical terms, however, *ānî* may also refer to a person who is poor in the sense of being impoverished (cf. Exod 22:25; Lev 19:10; Deut 15:11; 24:14–22; Job 24:4–11; Ps 9:18; Prov 14:21; 31:20).[3]

William Domeris opines that the financial bankruptcy of *ānî* makes them socially defenseless, subject to oppression, and an occupant of a lowly position, looking up to someone higher than themselves for survival.[4] *Ānî* appears in the Psalms (together with the adjective *w̓ebyon*) to signify a state of inward lowliness rather than material poverty (cf. Pss 40:17; 70:5; 86:1). For example, in Psalm 109:22–24, the state of being "poor and needy" is associated with a "wounded heart," "an evening shadow," and being "shaken off like a locust."

Another Old Testament term for poverty is *anaw* which has Arabic origins and means "lowly," "submission," "obedient," "bow down" especially, in relation to a captive.[5] It can also mean humility, abasement (see Isa 31:4), or a situation of social inferiority, especially oppression. It is used three times in communal Psalms to describe the crisis of the entire nation (see Pss 76:10; 147:6; 149:4). Pleins regards *anaw* as "a political movement of the pious poor."[6] Domeris, however, avers that the term "pious" in the above expression should be understood as spiritual or religious rather than "false piety." From this perspective, *anaw* is to be understood as "social movements which combined a strong religious commitment with a clear social agenda."[7]

Anaw and *ānî* differ in that the former refers to one who is "humbled in disposition and character, 'humble-minded'" or one who considers themselves to be of little account before God, while the latter refers to one who is humble due to some external adverse condition.[8] Therefore, *anaw* has a more religious and moral connotation (that is, a person's attitude towards God) than material connotation (that is, lack of material needs).

---

1. Onyinyechukwu, "Old Testament Concept of Poverty," 67.
2. Hastings, *Dictionary*, 19.
3. Renn, *Expository Dictionary of Bible*, 742.
4. Domeris, *Touching Heart of God*, 18.
5. Hastings, *Dictionary*, 19.
6. Pleins cited in Domeris, *Touching Heart of God*, 19.
7. Domeris, 19.
8. Hastings, *Dictionary*, 20.

Ānāwîm (the plural of *anaw*) is used in the prophetic and wisdom literature in the context of oppression and injustice.[9] It appears thirteen times in the Psalms in reference to "hunger (Ps 22:26 [27]), suffering (69:32 [33]), landlessness (37:11) and . . . God's relationship with and rescue of the poor (e.g. 25:9; 34:2 [3])."[10] In this usage, *ānāwîm* signifies a body of poor people. In addition, *anaw* is used in Psalm 25:3 to designate a "motif of confidence": "My soul makes its boast in Yahweh; let the afflicted (*'ānāwîm*) hear and be glad."

The third term for poverty is *dal* which is an adjective signifying poor in the sense of "one that has become exhausted, low, wasted, and weak in substance or natural strength".[11] It derives from the root *dālal*, which means "to be low," "inferior" or "languish."[12] The Akkadian equivalence is *dalâlu* which means "to be weak," "to be humble."[13] Onyinyechukwu notes a different translation of *dal* including "poor," "weak," "haggard," "helpless," "humble," "needy," "scrawny." In addition, *dal* may connote social poverty or lowliness (see Lev 19:15).[14]

Dal commonly occurs in the Wisdom literature and poetry, occurring about fourteen times in Proverbs alone. In most cases, the people described as *dal* are objects of disgrace, whose lot God promises to restore (cf. 1 Sam 2:8; Ps 113:7). Other times, *dal* (the poor) are subjected to abuse and oppression by the wealthy (cf. Amos 2:7; 4:1; 5:11; 8:6).[15] To sum up, *dal* refers to helplessness that comes as a result of poverty.

The noun form *dallâ* occurs five times in reference to the "poorest people of the land" who remained in Judah after others were taken into exile in Babylon (e.g. Jer 40:7; 52:15–16).[16] Pleins also describes the "poor farm labourers" or the peasant farmers in Babylon as *dallâ* (2 Kgs 24:14; 25:12).[17]

A fourth term for poverty is *'ebyôn* which refers generally to the poor, the desirous, or the needy and derives from the root *'ābāh*, meaning "to lack," or "to be in need."[18] With the exception of Isaiah 29:19, where it refers to spiritual need, *'ebyôn* consistently means material need (e.g. see Exod 26:6; Deut

---

9. Domeris, *Touching Heart of God*, 19.
10. Domeris, 19.
11. Wilson, *Wilson's Old Testament*, 317.
12. Hastings, *Dictionary*, 19.
13. Hastings, 19.
14. Onyinyechukwu, "Old Testament Concept of Poverty," 67.
15. Renn, *Expository Dictionary of Bible*, 742.
16. Domeris, *Touching Heart of God*, 15.
17. As quoted by Domeris, 15.
18. See Onyinyechukwu, "Old Testament Concept of Poverty," 67.

15:4; 24:14; Pss 49:2; 112:9; Isa 25:4; Amos 2:6; 5:12).[19] Such material need is associated with lack of social standing which endangers one's life and makes it needful for a person to seek protection. '*Ebyôn* refers predominantly to one who lacks materially but also occasionally to a spiritually destitute person who has acknowledged the need for spiritual blessings. The terms *'ebyôn, ānî* and *dal* may be used synonymously.[20]

The verb *rush*, often translated "to be poor" (e.g. see Prov 10:4; 13:7; Eccl 4:14), is also one of the Old Testament terms used in reference to "the poor." When used in the nominal sense, *rush* refers to a poor person or the poor (cf. 1 Sam 18:23; 2 Sam 12:3; Prov 13:8; Eccl 5:8). Of its twenty-five appearances in the Old Testament, *rush* is found fifteen times in Proverbs where it relates directly to friendlessness (14:20; 19:4, 7), low-spiritedness (16:19), pleading (18:23) and stealing out of need (30:9), and being mocked (17:5); injustice (13:23; 31:9), oppression (14:31a; 22:16, 22; 28:3; 30:14), and even debt slavery (22:7).[21]

Rush never occurs in the Prophets. Amos 2:6 uses different words for poor but *rush* is not used: "Because they sell the righteous *(tsaddiq)* for money and the needy *('ebyôn)* for a pair of shoes; they that trample the head of the poor *(dallim)* and turn aside the way of the afflicted *(ānāwîm)*." Here, Amos compares the state of poverty to the state of being righteous. It is likely that the prophets did not use *rush* because of its neutral nature.

Furthermore, the word *miskēn* is a rare noun found only in Ecclesiastes with reference to a poor person. *Miskēnut*, a related term, occurs in Deuteronomy 8:9 to signify material lack. Domeris considers this term as connoting the idea of honor as against the word *mahsôr* which signifies being ashamed of a situation.[22] For Pleins, however, it means "poverty is better."[23] Domeris's view seems better with regards to the use of *miskēn* in Ecclesiastes. For example, Ecclesiastes 4:13 says it is better to be poor "but wise youth than an old but foolish king who no longer knows how to heed a warning" (NIV). In Ecclesiastes 9:15 and 16 too, the poor person is associated with great wisdom. The point is that one has to seek wisdom regardless of their economic class.

The Old Testament presents a very close correlation between various disadvantaged or oppressed groups. The list in Isaiah 58:6–7 includes the

---

19. Renn, *Expository Dictionary of Bible*, 742.
20. Renn, 743.
21. Renn, 743.
22. Domeris, *Touching Heart of God*, 16.
23. As cited by Domeris, *Touching Heart of God*, 16.

shattered, the hungry, the poor, and the naked; in Job 29:12–17, it includes the poor, orphans, widows, the blind, the lame, and the weak or powerless; Psalm 145:7–9 includes the shackled, the broken down, the blind, the righteous, the sojourner, the orphan, and the widow. Others are the deaf mute, the blind, the poor, and hopeless (Isa 29:18–20); the blind, the deaf mute, the lame, and the dumb (Isa 35:4–6); the blind, those who are bound, and those who are imprisoned (Isa 42:6–7). These lists reveal that the poor were among the marginalized in the community.

The most common word for "the poor" in the New Testament is *ptōchos*, which occurs about thirty-five times.[24] Two other terms for "the poor" in the New Testament are *penēs* (cf. 2 Cor 9:9, in reference to "the poor" who received divine giving) and *penichros* (cf. Luke 21:2, in reference to the "poor" widow).[25] Though not a beggar, *penēs* lacks money and has to work every day to make ends meet.

Ptōchos is generally understood as referring to the economically destitute (see Matt 11:5; 26:11; Mark 14:5; Luke 4:18; 16:20–22; John 12:5; Rom 15:26; Gal 2:10; Jas 2:2–3). It means resigning oneself to a life of having nothing. *Ptōchos* differs from *penēs* in that the former, unlike the latter, refers to extreme economic lack that leads to begging or dependence on others for support, such as the beggar Lazarus of Luke 16:20. However, Jesus used *ptōchos* metaphorically in Matthew 5:3 (in the expression "poor in spirit") to signify those who recognize their spiritual lack and hence their need for dependence on God (see also Luke 6:20).

Exegesis of Deuteronomy 15:1–11
Background to the Book of Deuteronomy

Deuteronomy is the last book of the Pentateuch (the first five books of the Bible). The title "Deuteronomy" derives from the Greek word *deuteronomion* which means "second law," "repetition of the law" or "second telling of the law."[26] For some one thousand and seven hundred years (before the period of critical scholarship), both Jewish and church traditions considered Moses to be the author of Deuteronomy.[27] Internal evidence in support of Mosaic authorship

---

24. Renn, *Expository Dictionary of Bible*, 742.
25. Renn, 743.
26. Deere, "Deuteronomy," 259; Lasor, Hubbard and Bush, *Old Testament Survey*, 111; Longman and Dillard, *Introduction to Old Testament*, 102.
27. Longman and Dillard, *Introduction to Old Testament*, 104.

of Deuteronomy includes passages where Moses is said to have written some document down (cf. Deut 1:1, 5; 27:3, 8; 28:58; 29:21, 29; 30:10, 19; 31:9, 24). However, from the nineteenth century, liberal scholars (such as W. M. L. de Wette) begun to argue that "the Book of the Law," which was found in the temple in Josiah's time (2 Kgs 22:8), was the book of Deuteronomy or part of it which had been composed in Moses's name for the reformation of the people.[28] Some of the reasons for this argument as given by Longman and Dillard are summarized below.[29] The first reason is the remarkable similarity between Deuteronomy's insistence that the people should make sacrifices to God at a God-chosen sanctuary, and Josiah's religious reforms with its insistence that all sanctuaries be closed except the one in Jerusalem (2 Kgs 22–23; cf. Deut 16:1–8). Second, Josiah's removal of mediums and spiritists in fulfilment of the requirements of the law book (2 Kgs 23:24) parallels the Deuteronomistic demand for the elimination of mediums, spiritists and diviners from the nation of Israel (Deut 18:14–22). Third, Josiah's rule according to the requirement of the law (2 Kgs 22:11; 23:2–3) seems to be the prescription in Deuteronomy 17:18–19. Since then, massive scholarship has gone into the authorship of Deuteronomy; yet no consensus has been built. I am of the view that Moses has a hand in the authorship of Deuteronomy but his work went through a process of redaction before reaching its present form.

The date of composition of the book of Deuteronomy depends on one's view about its authorship. Those who support Mosaic authorship argue that the book was composed not later than 1406 BC, (the year Moses died) but most critics place the date of composition in the seventh century.[30] A seventh century dating has wider acceptance.[31] The dynamics of the issue makes it difficult to settle on a particular date, and so the dating of Deuteronomy still remains a subject of debate.

Geographical Setting and Audience

The geographical setting of the events in Deuteronomy is the Plains of Moab (a place north of the Dead Sea and east of the River Jordan; see 1:5; 4:46), opposite the town of Jericho, where Israel camped in preparation for the crossing of the River Jordan to take possession of the promised land.[32] The events in

---

28. Longman and Dillard, 105.
29. Longman and Dillard, 105–106.
30. Merrill, "Deuteronomy," 449.
31. Lundbom, *Deuteronomy*, 7.
32. Merrill, "Deuteronomy," 449.

Deuteronomy took place at a time between the wildernesses experience to the conquering and occupation of the land of Canaan over about a two-month period of time (see, for example, 1:3; 34:5, 8; Josh 4:19). It was on the first day of the eleventh month of the fortieth year after leaving Egypt that Moses begun to talk to Israel about all that God had commanded him to tell them (1:3–5). Moses was 120 years old by this time (31:2) and was going to die soon (see ch. 34).

The addressees of the book are the second-generation Israelites from the Exodus; that is, those Israelites who, in obedience to and trust in the Lord, were going to enter the land of Canaan and take possession of it by conquest. The events that took place at Mt. Sinai serve as the historical backdrop to the book of Deuteronomy. At Mount Sinai (Exod 19–24), God called Moses and gave him the Decalogue. He inaugurated the nation, established his covenant with them, and instituted their religion. Most of the exodus generation died in the wilderness due to disobedience, and so most of the people who were going to occupy the land were ignorant about the relationship between God and Israel. It was therefore necessary for Moses to prepare the people for the task ahead and what God expected them to do in the Land, and so "Moses undertook to expound this law" (1:5).

Literary Context
Deuteronomy 15:1–11 consists basically of laws meant to guide the Israelites in their relationship with God and their fellow Israelites particularly regarding debts. The preceding immediate context (14:22–29) consists of laws about tithing. The Lord gave Israel stipulations regarding the payment of three tithes, Levitical tithe, festival tithe and charity tithe.[33] The laws on the last two tithes are found here. The festival tithe was contributed towards the celebration of the major Jewish festivals. The Lord promised to choose a place at which they will celebrate these festivals. Verses 28–29 then talk about God's social security for the poor (orphans, Levites, aliens, and widows), in the form of a tithe paid every three years. This is immediately followed by our text which deals with how Israelites are expected to relate to the poor living among them.

What follows our text is the law on release of slaves (vv. 12–18). God instituted this law so that those who sell themselves into slavery due to poverty could be freed. The freeing of slaves was to be done every seven years, that is, in the Sabbatical Year. They were to remember the difficulties they went through as slaves in Egypt and to appreciate the need to free their own slaves.

---

33. Amevenku and Boaheng, *Tithing*, 47.

In doing so, the Lord promised to bless their works (v. 18). We now proceed to read the text closely.

Close Reading of Deuteronomy 15:1–11

The Sabbatical Debt Release (Deut 15:1–3)

> Every seventh year you shall grant a remission of debts. And this is the manner of the remission: every creditor shall remit the claim that is held against a neighbor, not exacting it of a neighbor who is a member of the community, because the LORD's remission has been proclaimed. Of a foreigner you may exact it, but you must remit your claim on whatever any member of your community owes you.

The passage begins with the command "Every seventh year you shall grant a remission of debts." The expression "every seventh year" occurs also in Exodus 23:10–11 and Leviticus 25:1–7 and can be rendered "every Sabbath Year." The word s*e*mittah comes from *samat* and means "cancel debt," "release," "remission (of debt)."[34] It also means relinquishing one's rights, either temporarily or permanently. This term is unique to the book of Deuteronomy (where it occurs in 15:1, 2, 9; 31:10). A debt refers to borrowed money or property that the borrower is legally bound to pay back to the owner. Economic pressures could make one sell their land and even the family into slavery.[35]

The Deuteronomic *samat* law with its demand of a complete remission of debt in the Sabbath Year is a further development of the earlier seventh-year law which required that people cease from their labor in that year (see Exod 23:1–11; Lev 25:1–7). The poor were then to glean from the resting farms while the others survived on the six-year food savings. In addition, Hebrew slaves were to be released in the Sabbath Year (Exod 21:1–6). In the current passage, the people (in addition to resting in the Sabbath Year) are asked to cancel debts in every Sabbatical Year in order to ensure that a temporary misfortune (due to drought or sickness, for example) did not become a burden forever. God used this law to teach his people to be generous and to free themselves from the love of money and accumulation of material wealth (cf. Matt 6:19–34; 1 Tim 6:10). Foreigners were, however, required to repay their debts in the Sabbatical Year. Luciano Chianeque and Samuel Ngewa are of the opinion that foreigners were

---

34. Zodhiates and Baker, *NIV Key Word Study*, 1558.
35. Vogt, "Social Justice," 38.

exempted from enjoying the release of debt in the Sabbatical Year in order to prevent them from exploiting Israel due to their generosity.[36]

The key exegetical question in this passage is whether the debt remission is temporal or permanent. The view that the debt was not to be discharged permanently and absolutely, but passed over to the following year without demanding payment in the Sabbath Year, is supported by the contention that there was total suspension of agricultural activities in the Sabbath Year and so debtors could not have enough money for their basic needs, let alone the payment of debt.[37] It follows, therefore, that foreigners were required to pay their loans in the Sabbath Year because they, unlike the Israelites, did not observe any Sabbatical Year but engaged in their usual economic activities (v. 3).

Contrary to the above view, I contend that the passage calls for total and permanent cancellation of debt for the following reasons. First, such a position is consistent with the numerous biblical teachings of God's generosity towards the poor. Second, this view agrees with the immediate context of the text (see vv. 9–11). Third, the practice of permanent cancellation of debts is consonant with the requirement in the Jubilee Year, the fiftieth year (that is, the year following the seventh Sabbatical Year; see Lev 25:8–12). Leviticus 25:10 presents the concepts of liberty from "the burden of debt and bondage it may have entailed" and return of "both the ancestral property if it had been mortgaged to a creditor and to the family which may have been split up through debt-servitude."[38] Fourth, permanent cancellation of debt was required to ensure the attainment of the poverty-free community projected in verse 4.[39] Fifth, Israel's potential to acquire great wealth in the Promised Land also favors the permanent cancellation of debt (v. 5) without making the creditor poor. Sixth, this position finds extrabiblical support from the *misharum* decree of King Ammisaduqa of Babylon (1646–1626 BC) that demanded that creditors no longer pursue payment of debt.[40]

The Sabbatical Year release is grounded on "the divine ownership of the land" (Lev 25:23) and was described as "a Sabbath to the LORD" (Lev 25:4) and "the LORD's time for cancelling debts" (Deut 15:2)'" or "the LORD's release."[41] It is "the LORD's release" (v. 2 NKJV) because he requires it as the owner of all

---

36. Chianeque and Ngewa, "Deuteronomy," 232.
37. Deere, "Deuteronomy," 290.
38. Wright, *Old Testament Ethics*, 202.
39. Deere, "Deuteronomy," 290.
40. Walton, Matthews, and Chavalas, *IVP Background Commentary*, 185.
41. Wright, *Old Testament Ethics*, 296.

resources for ensuring that his divine (Sabbath) economic principles prevail. Therefore, while obedience to the Sabbath regulation was obedience to God, the regulation was made for the humanitarian goal of helping the poor and the needy (cf. Exod 23:11; Lev 26:6; Deut 15:2, 7–11).[42] The point then is that one cannot claim to worship God truly and yet practice injustice against others (especially against the poor) or ignore their responsibility of showing compassion to the needy. This is one of the mechanisms God established to ensure that neither poverty nor wealth developed to an extreme.

The Sabbath economy instituted by God needs a further examination in order to lay a solid foundation for the theology developed in the rest of the Bible. In Exodus 16, the people of Israel grumbled against God when there was a shortage of food in their camp. They compared the economy of Pharaoh in Egypt, characterized by hoarding and abundance under which they lived as slaves, with their current economy in which they seem to have little to eat. They even wished to return to Egyptian bondage (v. 3). In response to their complaints, God promised to rain manna from heaven for them (vv. 11–12).

The principles that guided the gathering of the manna were as follows. First, each family was required to gather just enough for their needs (vv. 16–18). The new economy was different from the Egyptian economy in that under the former, every family had their needs met without oppression while in the latter, Israel's needs were met through suffering oppression by Egypt. Again, the new economy, unlike the old, was devoid of people having "too much" or "too little"; everyone had enough, not more, not less (cf. 2 Cor 8:14–15).

Second, the manna was not to be "stored up" (vv. 19–20). The Israelites were not to build store houses and hoard the manna as the Egyptian economy did (see Exod 1:11). The prohibition of hoarding the excess manna was meant to teach the people to trust the Lord daily for their survival. Those who did not trust God's provision, and so stored up excess manna for the next day, found the stored manna infested with maggots (v. 20). This experience was intended to discourage greediness and establish the fact that tomorrow's life does not depend on today's accumulation but on God's daily provision for his people.

Third, the Israelites were required to gather manna only on six days and on the seventh day take a rest from the gathering (vv. 5, 26). It was this periodic rest for the land and from human labor, which, having been expanded in the social justice code (Exod 23:10–12), finally developed into the sabbatical release of Deuteronomy 15:1–3. The Sabbath rest teaches that it is wrong for humans to make attempts at controlling nature and maximizing profits. The earth is the

---

42. Wright, 296.

Lord's (Ps 24:1–2) and so its fruits are a gift which must be distributed justly to meet people's need rather than used selfishly and hoarded.

Fourth, the Lord's call on Israel to keep "the Sabbath" (Exod 16:29; 20:8) was meant to teach them to depend on him. The Sabbath rest involves a ceasing from the active pursuit of one's livelihood. If after ceasing from active work, one still gets food to eat, then it stands to reason that the supply of one's need comes primarily from the Lord (the ultimate Provider) and not from human toil. This principle is further developed by the Prophets (including Amos 5:7–12 and Isa 10:1–4), by Christ in Matthew 6:19–34, and by Paul in 1 Timothy 6:6–10, 17–19.

The Poor-Free Economy (Deut 15:4–6)

> There will, however, be no one in need among you, because the LORD is sure to bless you in the land that the LORD your God is giving you as a possession to occupy, if only you will obey the LORD your God by diligently observing this entire commandment that I command you today. When the LORD your God has blessed you, as he promised you, you will lend to many nations, but you will not borrow; you will rule over many nations, but they will not rule over you.

There are two key exegetical issues to address in this section. First, the opening of this verse poses some translation difficulties as to whether it is to be understood as a command or a statement. Is it saying that "There will . . . be no one in need," or that "there ought not ('must be . . . no poor' [NJB] or 'need be no poor' [NIV]) to be anyone in need"? The second issue has to do with the relationship between the above statement or command and what comes after it. Bullinger renders it, "that there be no poor among you."[43] This situation will be achieved because of the debt release in the Sabbatical Year. The loss incurred by the creditor will not lead to poverty because God will richly bless them. Bullinger reasons further that the continual presence of the poor among the people forecast in verse 11 will partly be due to sin and partly be a condition for teaching people to be compassionate by sharing.[44]

Vogt, on the other hand, argues that by use of the restrictive adverb *efes ki* (meaning "however" or "notwithstanding"), Moses is contrasting verses 1–3

---

43. Thomson, "Deuteronomy," 214.
44. Thomson, 214.

with verses 4–6.[45] Moses's argument is that in the Promised Land, the law on debt release (v. 1) will become unnecessary because God's blessing upon his people will make everyone have enough for their needs. This, however, Vogt argues, is dependent on the people's faithfulness to their covenant with the Lord.[46] He draws attention to the fact that the poverty-free community of verse 4 was predicated on Israel's obedience to "the whole command" God gave to them through Moses (v. 5), which included "the full integration of marginal groups and the poor into the life of the nation."[47] He reasons further that if Israel obeys the Lord and "care for one another, and . . . share the bounty of blessings with the entire community"[48] no one (including the Levites, aliens, orphans, and widows) is to be considered poor, because they will all have enough for their basic needs. Such care for the poor is not to be regarded as a charitable act but as a communal responsibility of sharing available resources with the needy. In such a situation there would be no need for debt-slavery or any year of release.

I find merit in Vogt's argument for the following reasons. The realization of such an ideal situation is dependent on the people's faithful obedience to God's law. The Lord is not saying that Israel will have no poor regardless of whether they obey or disobey his commandments and their obligation to showing brotherly kindness under his covenant with them. The covenant between the Lord and Israel was such that the benefits Israel was to derive were dependent upon Israel's faithfulness in obeying the covenant. Therefore, the text should be understood as follows: Israel's faithful obedience to all the commandments of the Lord (including their responsibility of sharing resources with the poor), will ensure that there is no poor among them. To ensure that there is abundance to share, the Lord will abundantly bless them (provided they obey all his commandments [v. 5]). The expression *raq im* (literally "only if" or "provided only") at the beginning of verse 5 seems to give support to this position.[49] The result of this situation is that Israel will not borrow from but lend to other nations (v. 6).

---

45. Vogt, "Social Justice," 40.
46. Vogt, 40.
47. Vogt, 40.
48. Vogt, 40.
49. Gleason, *New International Encyclopedia*, 150.

Generosity to the Poor (Deut 15:7–11)

> If there is among you anyone in need, a member of your community in any of your towns within the land that the LORD your God is giving you, do not be hard-hearted or tight-fisted toward your needy neighbor. You should rather open your hand, willingly lending enough to meet the need, whatever it may be. Be careful that you do not entertain a mean thought, thinking, "The seventh year, the year of remission, is near," and therefore view your needy neighbor with hostility and give nothing; your neighbor might cry to the LORD against you, and you would incur guilt. Give liberally and be ungrudging when you do so, for on this account the LORD your God will bless you in all your work and in all that you undertake. Since there will never cease to be some in need on the earth, I therefore command you, "Open your hand to the poor and needy neighbor in your land."

The economy, which promised wealth, also commanded the care of the poor. According to verse 7, the presence of the poor in the community should lead to free-will giving from the rich to help improve the poor's condition. The word translated "your neighbor" is to be understood generically as referring to one's siblings, kinsmen, allies, or fellow countrymen.[50] The verb meaning "to strengthen" or "to harden," is used to prohibit deliberate denial of one's help to the needy.[51] The heart is the seat of one's will and emotions, the part of the body with which one decides to give or not to give. The idioms "hard-hearted" and "tight-fisted" mean lack of compassion and stinginess. Therefore, a hard heart does not give generously but a soft heart does.

In verses 8–9, Moses warns the people not to let the year of release of debts become an obstacle to their generosity towards the poor. This point was necessary because of the tendency that many lenders might be unwilling to lend when the Sabbatical Year was approaching so that they could prevent a situation whereby their loan ends up becoming a gift to the poor. From the perspective of the Lord, lending to a brother is a form of ministry rather than a business transaction.[52] It follows, therefore, that the Sabbatical Year was not only instituted as a test of faith, but also as a test of love. Failing to lend to the poor because of an impending Sabbatical Year was failure to trust the Lord

---

50. Bratcher and Hatton, *Handbook on Deuteronomy*, electronic version.
51. Bratcher and Hatton.
52. Wiersbe, *Wiersbe Bible Commentary*, 339.

to bless. If the rich really loved God and their neighbors, they would give to them cheerfully (cf. 2 Cor 9:7).

In verse 10, Moses assures the people that their generosity towards the poor will be rewarded by the Lord in the form of abundant blessing upon their work. This sounds like Proverbs 11:25 which states, "The generous soul will be made rich, and he who waters will also be watered himself" (NKJV). Finally, Moses predicts that "There will always be poor people in the land" (v. 11 NIV). This statement, which is alluded to in Mark 14:7 (cf. Matt 26:11; John 12:8), seems contradictory to verse 4. How are we to reconcile verses 4 and 11?

Chianeque and Ngewa, and Wiersbe agree that the situation described in verse 4 is subject to total obedience of the law, but because Israel would not obey the Lord completely, there would always be poor people among them (v. 11).[53] Israel would have been the richest nation in the world if they had obeyed the Lord. Their adoption of foreign religious life led to the poor being with them always. Their failure to observe the Sabbath rest deprived the land the rest it needed. Their seventy-year captivity compensated for this (2 Chr 36:14–21).[54] Therefore, the situation in verse 4 is the ideal situation predicated on the perfect and consistent obedience to the holy standards of God[55] while that in verse 11 is the real situation. All in all, the text teaches the principle, "sharing is caring."[56]

Exegesis of Isaiah 10:1–4
Background to the Book of Isaiah

The traditional rabbinic and Christian view is that the prophet Isaiah wrote the book of Isaiah.[57] However, critical scholarship dating from the eighteenth century contends that the book of Isaiah is not a product of a single author.[58] From this perspective Isaiah is divided into two, chapters 1–39 (called proto/first Isaiah) and chapters 40–66 (called deutero/second Isaiah). Longman and Dillard assign at least three reasons for this division.[59] The first reason

---

53. Chianeque and Ngewa, "Deuteronomy," 232; Wiersbe, *Wiersbe Bible Commentary*, 339.
54. Wiersbe, *Wiersbe Bible Commentary*, 339.
55. Wiersbe, 339.
56. Christian Adom-Boaheng made this point in a personal conversation in Sunyani on September 22, 2019.
57. Lasor, Hubbard and Bush, *Old Testament Survey*, 281.
58. Baker, "Isaiah," 489.
59. Longman and Dillard, *Introduction to Old Testament*, 303–304.

concerns the setting of the book: the first part depicts a setting in eighth-century Jerusalem during the ascendancy of the Assyrian Empire while the second is addressed to Israelites already in Babylonian exile (48:20), who look forward to their immanent deliverance and return to Zion (40:9-11; 42:1-9; 43:1-7; 44:24-28; 48:12-22; 49:8-23; 51:11; 52:1-12) as well as a divine judgment against their captors (43:14-15; 47:1-15; 48:14; 49:24-26; 51:21-23) and the reconstruction of the city of Jerusalem and its temple (e.g. 45:13; 51:3; 54:11-14; 58:12; 60:10; 61:4). The second reason is theological: the first part stresses God's majesty, whereas the second stresses his sovereignty and infinitude. The third concerns language and style: "The second half of the book is often described as more 'lyric, flowing, impassioned, hymnic' than the first."[60]

Others (including Duhm, as cited by M. A. Sweeney)[61] divide it into three books: chapters 1-39, chapters 40-55, and chapters 56-66, with the last book referred to as trito/third Isaiah. By this partitioning of the book, the first is regarded as covering the preexilic time with the other two sections covering the exilic and postexilic periods, respectively. Differences in subject matter, and the different conception of God in chapters 40-55 and chapters 56-66, are some of the reasons for which some scholars divide chapters 40-66 into two to arrive at a threefold division of the book. Weighing the various sides of the argument, I find merit in the view that the prophet Isaiah wrote chapters 1-39, while the rest were written by an unknown person, probably his disciple. On the whole, events recorded in the book of Isaiah took place during the divided kingdom period, the time of the decline of Israel's nation, the exilic period and postexilic period.

Literary Context and Structure

Isaiah 10:1-4 belongs to the first part of the book (chs. 1-39). It fits within the so-called "Book of Immanuel" (chs. 7-12) and prophesies about the incursion of the king of Assyria into Immanuel's land (8:8). Isaiah 9:8-10:4 forms the immediate literary unit within which the text under consideration lies. The unit is structured by the repetition of a refrain in 9:12, 17, 21 and 10:4. The same refrain is found in 5:25 and this has led to the contention that these passages were originally connected.[62] The section 9:8-10:4 belongs to Isaiah's ministry to the northern kingdom of Israel, with Judah mentioned only in 9:21.

---

60. Longman and Dillard, *Introduction to Old Testament*, 304.
61. Sweeney, *Isaiah 40-66*, 14.
62. Mackay, *Isaiah Chapters 1-39*, 247.

I believe, however, that the message was relevant to the southern people too. The prophecies are basically a series of punishments that Yahweh was going to bring upon his people if they continued to be disloyal to him.

Structurally, Isaiah 9:8—10:4 divides into four strophes. The first (9:8–12) predicts the severe punishment that was about to be meted out on Israel. The second strophe (9:13–17) supplies the reason for severer punishment for Israel as its stubborn refusal to turn to God. In the third strophe (9:18–21), Isaiah gives pictures of the destructive power of evil in the society as a fire in the forest and its consequence as lawlessness and the violence of beasts in the forest. The fourth strophe (10:1–4) "marks the transition from the presentation of past events illustrating the sins and punishments of Ephraim to the present condition and threatened doom of Judah."[63]

The unit under consideration (10:1–4) can be divided into four parts. The first (v. 1) deals with an oracle against those who decree and those who write unjust decrees. In the second verse the prophet describes injustice in his community in four clauses, while the third verse has a series of rhetorical questions addressed to the oppressors in the community. The fourth verse concludes with a statement about God's wrath. Together, the unit under consideration deals with injustice and oppression in Isaiah's society, especially as manifested in the courts. The main theme of the text is sin and retribution. The section that follows the pericope under consideration (10:5–12:6) deals with Isaiah's contrast between the Assyrian empire and God's millennial rule. Here, Isaiah predicts the fall of Assyria, which will be followed by God's glorious empire.

Socioreligious and Economic Context

The socioreligious and economic situation that informs the understanding of Isaiah 10:1–4 is the moral and religious corruption that characterized Isaiah's community. The nation had turned to idolatry (2 Chr 28:22–24), taking Yahweh as one of the gods. At the same time evil had grown to its maturity in the form of personal immorality and political corruption, pride, luxury, selfishness, and oppression. The government, with the judges and courts, had become corrupt and unjust, for they had made decrees that were contrary to God's moral principles (10:2). Their laws were to the disadvantage of the widows and the orphans (10:2). The courts were against the needy as cases sent there for redress were decided in favor of the rich who paid bribes to the judges. The

---

63. Scott, *Interpreters Bible*, 238.

poor and the less privileged in the society were exploited for material gain and were also denied justice (10:2).

The pericope sets out to warn people to desist from their evil deeds or to expect God's wrath to be poured upon them. This warning to Israel sounds like that of Amos (see Amos 2:6–7; 5:11–12; 8:4–6). On this, Domeris has stated that in the biblical world, the ruling elite exploited the peasant majority through a variety of mechanisms, including rents, pledges and fines, interest on loans, taxes and labor obligations.[64] Isaiah's fight against the exploitation of the poor is deeply rooted in the law that states, "Do not pervert justice; do not show partiality to the poor or favoritism to the great, but judge your neighbor fairly" (Lev 19:15 NIV). The message of the text will be unraveled as we proceed to read it more closely.

Close Reading of Isaiah 10:1–4

Pronouncement of Woe (Isa 10:1)

> Ah, you who make iniquitous decrees,
> who write oppressive statutes.

The Hebrew word *hoy* (translated "woe," "doom," "ah") is a word of warning. It may be a prophetic adaptation of the lament over the dead. In the current context it is used to signify a condemnation of evil behavior which includes:

1. Decreeing unrighteous decrees (v. 1)
2. Issuing oppressive decrees – making oppressive laws for society (v. 1)
3. Turning aside the needy from fair trial (v. 2)
4. Taking away the rights of the poor (v. 2)
5. Preying on the widow (v. 2)
6. Plundering the orphan (v. 2)

Isaiah uses the expression "you who make iniquitous decrees" to point out the corruption in the judicial system of Judah. This phrase suggests that the leaders of Israel had instituted decrees that were contrary to the Mosaic standard. This was one of the reasons for the impending woe announced by the prophet. The use of power to the advantage of the governing authority at the expense of the

---

64. Domeris, *Touching Heart of God*, 103 and 108.

powerless underscores Domeris's assertion that "Power corrupts, and absolute power corrupts absolutely."[65]

The word *aven*, which is usually translated "iniquitous," has a wide range of meaning including "evil," "wicked," "sin," "wrong," "calamity," "false," "injustice," malice," or "unjust."[66] Here, it serves as an adjective describing the kind of laws and decrees the governing authority of Judah established. These decrees were contrary to God's laws in the Mosaic code against injustice (see Deut 15:7–8; 24:17–18).

The decrees were the result of careful thought among the leaders. Therefore, it was not ineffective leadership that Isaiah was dealing with but deliberate wickedness. Any attempt by the poor to improve their living could not succeed because of injustice against them. This idea of the vulnerability of the poor is well captured in the statement "The field of the poor may yield much food, but it is swept away through injustice" (Prov 13:23). Mackay notes further that the expression "unjust decrees" suggests that the leaders misused power to the disadvantage of others, probably through "deceit and cunning."[67] They passed laws that made their exploitative practices technically "lawful." How sad it is that the powerful in society could enact poverty by decree!

The second part of the text uses the term *amal* to describe the decrees written by scribes. *Amal* means severe "labouring" or "toiling."[68] The decrees written by magistrates were regarded as oppressive (burdensome) because they imposed elaborate and unpleasant restrictions on the poor, denied them justice and served as a source of trouble and suffering for the needy. The perversion of justice evident in this text is well captured in Habakkuk's lament "Therefore the law is paralyzed, and justice never prevails. The wicked hem in the righteous, so that justice is perverted" (1:2–4 NIV).

Reasons for Pronouncement of Doom (Isa 10:2)

> To turn aside the needy from justice and to rob the poor of my people of their right, that widows may be your spoil, and that you may make the orphans your prey!

The prophet uses this verse as a polemic against the leaders and lawmakers of his time who used their power to oppress the poor (see also Prov 28:3;

---

65. Domeris, 121.
66. Goodrick and Kohlenberger III, *NIV Exhaustive Concordance*, 1363.
67. Mackay, *Isaiah Chapters 1–39*, 259.
68. Wilson, *Wilson's Old Testament*, 455.

31:14). Four accusations are listed here against the rulers (in addition to two in v. 1). First, the leaders turn aside the helpless from fair trial (v. 2a). The term *dalim* translated "needy" or "helpless" derives from a root signifying "smallness" or "lack of importance," "lowly" and means people who are at "economic disadvantage" in their societies.[69] The leaders (especially judges and magistrates) ignored them probably because the needy could not offer a bribe. Some of the poor might have even refused to take their cases to court for redress because they viewed the system as unfair. This was a reality in Isaiah's context and in the Psalms (e.g. 94:20; 82) where the righteous poor person finds "no human redress in the society" and then, "appeals only to God."[70]

Second, the leaders rob the needy of God's people of justice (v. 2b). Israel's laws were meant to protect the needy, not exploit them. The term *ani* means "poor," "afflicted," "humble," "wretched," "needy" and "weak," "lowly" and so on (see word study above). In the present context it refers to "affliction suffered by the impoverished and the weak – either the disability arising from their economic deprivation or their distress arising from their exploitation by others."[71]

The word *ami* (meaning "my people") "expresses the affront of God's special relationship with the whole people that this evil legislation constituted."[72] Israel was a people God really loved and wished could live up to his expectation. *Ami* also expresses Isaiah's empathy for the people of Judah (cf. 9:21) to whom his prophecy was directed.

Third, the leaders make widows their prey (v. 2c). The term *almanot* corresponds to the Greek word *chera*, which refers to a person whose husband is dead and has not remarried. The root of this word means "unable to speak" and that of the Greek word *chera* means "left empty."[73] In the state of widowhood, women lost their social status, financial support, source of companionship, and property and became "empty." As people of low social class, widows often suffered oppression, exploitation, and mistreatment (cf. Jer 7:6; Ezek 22:7). The leaders of Isaiah's time took advantage of the widow because they were defenseless.

Isaiah pictures the leaders as hunters out to trap their prey, the widows (cf. Ps 10:9). The word *sh^elalam* comes from the root which means "to draw out,"

---

69. Mackay, *Isaiah Chapters 1–39*, 260.
70. Wright, *Old Testament Ethics*, 171.
71. Mackay, *Isaiah Chapters 1–39*, 261.
72. Grogan, "Isaiah," 78.
73. Renn, *Expository Dictionary of Bible*, 1043.

"to strip," "to spoil," "to plunder" or "to make [something] a prey."[74] Isaiah's use of this word underscores the seriousness of the leaders' attack on the widows.

Fourth, they plunder orphans (v. 2d). The term *yetomim* is the plural of *yatom*, which means an orphan or a fatherless person. Orphans were also among the poor in Isaiah's society. The leaders plundered orphans by taking from them their rightful inheritance. The prophet accuses the leaders of treating orphans like war plunder. The African society also has the fatherless to cater for. But unfortunately, most of them are ignored and left on their own to find their own means of living. They usually end up as school dropouts, street children, gangsters, and the like.

A brief analysis of God's attitude towards widows and orphans is relevant for a better understanding of this text. Throughout the Old Testament we find traces of God's compassion for widows and orphans. God is their defender and provider (Deut 10:18), and protector (Pss 68:5; 146:9) and forbids people from taking advantage of them (Exod 22:22). To oppress widows and orphans is tantamount to having no fear for God, and that attracts divine judgment (Mal 3:5). Mistreating widows and orphans attracts God's curses (Deut 27:19) while caring for them leads to God's blessings (Jer 7:5–7). God forbids his people from taking the widow's garment as a pledge (Deut 24:17). The triennial tithe (Deut 14:28–29; 26:12), the gleaning law (Lev 19:9–10; Deut 24:19–22), and the sabbatical rest for the land (Exod 23:10–11) are other means by which God ensured the social security of widows and orphans. The care for the poor continued in the intertestamental period where we read that some money belonged to the widow from the temple treasury (2 Macc 3:10).

The New Testament also advocates for the need to cater for widows (Acts 6). Paul asked the church to cater for widows who had devoted themselves to prayer and good works but had no family to cater for them (1 Tim 5:3–16). James defines pure religion in terms of one's care for widows and orphans (Jas 1:27). The foregoing is summarized in the statement "Whoever oppresses the poor shows contempt for the Maker, but whoever is kind to the needy honors God" (Prov 14:31 NIV).

Clearly, God's concern for the poor is not an afterthought but a central and pervasive theme in Scripture. It is the reason why he expected the leaders of Isaiah's time to care for and protect the widows and orphans rather than treating them like enemies to be looted. How the leaders treated the needy at that time was a violation of God's law. Against this backdrop, it is not surprising

---

74. Wilson, *Wilson's Old Testament*, 326.

that Isaiah considers the exploitation of the helpless as a grievous sin which deserves harsh divine punishment.

Three Rhetorical Questions (Isa 10:3)

> What will you do on the day of punishment, in the calamity that will come from far away? To whom will you flee for help, and where will you leave your wealth?

In the first two verses of this chapter, Isaiah speaks about the rulers, but now he speaks to them about the results of their sins which he formulates into three rhetorical questions illustrating how helpless and hopeless they (the leaders) will be in the day of the Lord's visitation.[75]

The first question is "What will you do on the day of punishment?" The word *yom* (translated "day") may refer to a twenty-four-hour day. In the present context, however, it refers to an unspecified duration of time within which the impending judgment will take place. In this sense it reminds us of the "day of the reckoning" (cf. Hos 5:9 NIV) which refers to the period of time of God's wrath.

The word *pequddah* (translated "of punishment") comes from a root (*paqad*) which denotes "an action of a superior with respect to an inferior."[76] *Paqad* has a wide range of meaning including "to count, to call into account, to look after,"[77] "custody," "mustering," or "punishment." It underscores the fact that God is going to ask the rulers to account for whatever he has entrusted into their care. The picture that comes to mind is that of stewardship and accountability illustrated by Jesus's parable of the Talents (Matt 25:14–30). From the foregoing, one may conclude that God requires good stewardship not only of power but also of every other resource he has given us, including time, money, wisdom, and others.

The question "To whom will you flee for help?" suggests that no power can deliver the people from the impending judgment. The false gods they worship cannot prevent the desolation; neither can their own power do so. The oppressors in the community will be shown no mercy on the day of reckoning. Presently, they feel secured and self-sufficient by their position and power, but on that day, they will feel the need to ask for help from others.[78]

---

75. Mackay, *Isaiah Chapters 1–39*, 261.
76. Mackay, 261.
77. Zodhiates and Baker, *NIV Key Word Study*, 1544.
78. Mackay, *Isaiah Chapters 1–39*, 261.

The question "Where will you leave your wealth?" draws attention to the fact that on the day of reckoning, the possession of ill-gotten wealth will make one an object of divine destruction. It underscores the fact that wealth without righteousness is useless: "Wealth is worthless in the day of wrath, but righteousness delivers from death" (Prov 11:4 NIV). While the majority of translators use "wealth" for *kebodkem*, the idea of "dignity" and "honor" are also possible and in this sense, it refers to the honored place the judges had in the society.[79] They receive glory because of their wealth but on that day, they will be objects of shame. Those who forced others to serve foreign gods will also not be left out.

God's Answer (Isa 10:4)

> . . . so as not to crouch among the prisoners or fall among the slain?
> For all this his anger has not turned away; his hand is stretched out still.

In the first part of the verse, God gives an answer to the rhetorical questions in verse three. He states, "Nothing remains but to crouch among the prisoners" (v. 4 ESV). This suggests that there is nothing the evil legislators can do but to submit to the impending punishment. The word *kâra* (translated "crouch") means to bow the knee or a position inbetween standing and kneeling.[80] It must be differentiated from *barak* which means to kneel or to bow. Isaiah used *kâra* to give a picture of these powerful leaders cringing along the way into exile, or trying to hide behind others to avoid being seen or killed.[81]

The word *naphal* means to "fall, lie, be cast down, fail, violent death, fall away, go away, fall out, turn out, waste away, be inferior to, throw down, knock out, to overthrow."[82] Those who perverted justice for the poor were to face God's judgment, in the form of captivity or death.

Conclusion

The exegetical analyses have established that poverty has been with humanity since human history began and that God has always been on the side of the poor. This chapter has revealed certain theological principles: God is the

---

79. Mackay, 262.
80. Mackay, 262.
81. Mackay, 262.
82. Wilson, *Wilson's Old Testament*, 155.

ultimate owner of all resources; God cares for his people, especially the poor; God's provision for our needs is enough for those who trust in him; our love for God should result in generosity to the poor; God abhors accumulation of resources at the expense of others; the poor will always be present due to our fallen nature (which makes it impossible for us to obey God completely). These principles will play a major role in formulating a suitable theology for poverty for the African continent.

4

Poverty in the Context of the New Testament

The last chapter provided a representation of what the Old Testament teaches about the subject of poverty. Since Jesus is God incarnate, it is crucial to consider his teachings before formulating any kind of theology. On the subject of poverty, he gave many teachings both by words and by deeds. I find Matthew 6:19–34 to be one of the key passages that portray Jesus's idea about how wealth should be handled and how the poor are to live. I also consider it necessary to examine Paul's teaching about wealth in the ongoing discussion. From the Pauline corpus I will examine 1 Timothy 6:6–10, a significant Bible text on the subjects of wealth and poverty.

Exegesis of Matthew 6:19–34
Background to the Gospel According to Matthew

The first gospel does not identify its author. However, from the early second century, the church has identified the Apostle Matthew (Levi, who was a tax collector) as its author.[1] This tradition began when Papias of Hierapolis (in about AD 150) attached the superscription "according to Matthew" to the first gospel. Relying on oral tradition, Papias also suggested that Matthew was the first gospel to have been written and that it was originally written in Hebrew or Aramaic, a position which was later found to be invalid.[2] Since the authenticity of such tradition cannot be established today for sure, the authorship of the first gospel still remains debatable.

---

1. Ayegboyin, *Synoptics*, 87.
2. Keener, *Commentary*.

The place of the composition of the Matthew's gospel cannot be known for certain because the text does not reveal it. A Palestinian origin is, however, virtually impossible because this gospel was originally written in Greek.[3] A Syrian origin, precisely (but not exclusively) Antioch, has a wider acceptance,[4] for reasons including its heavy influence on Ignatius and its strong emphasis on locations in Syria (4:24–25).

There is no scholarly consensus regarding the date of composition of the Matthean gospel. Two major proposed dates are the AD 80s and about AD 70. One argument in favor of the former date is that since Mark, the first written gospel account, was composed in about AD 70, it is unlikely that Matthew (who used Mark as a source) could have been written in the same year that its source, Mark, was written.[5] Another argument is that Matthew reflects a Jewish tradition that is closer to the rabbinic movement, which achieved prominence only after AD 70.[6] Proponents of the latter view claim support from the fact that Matthew reflects the religious and political context after AD 70. In view of all the evidence, I place the date of composition of the first gospel after AD 70, perhaps as late as AD 80.

Matthew's audience was mainly the Jewish Christian community which had just been formed, but integrated Gentile Christians over time.[7] It was not an isolated community but a community that was networked to other Jewish Christian communities who also encountered situations similar to the Matthean community.[8] The Matthean audience was also under persecution for their allegiance to Jesus.[9] There is an increasing recognition that the social context of the first gospel is closely related to the author's relationship with Judaism.[10]

The purpose of Mathew's gospel was to encourage Christians in their suffering of persecution, to warn them against apostasy and to strengthen them to proclaim the gospel in the midst of persecution.[11] It also purposes to

---

3. Ayegboyin, *Synoptics*, 92.
4. Ayegboyin, 92.
5. Keener, *Commentary*, 50.
6. Keener, 50.
7. Howell, "Examining Jewish Origins," 1.
8. Howell, 43.
9. Howell, 43.
10. Keener, *Commentary*, 51.
11. Picard and Habets, *Theology and Experience*.

establish the fact that Jesus was the Messiah the Old Testament promised, so that the Jews could accept him as their long-awaited Messiah.

Geographical Setting and Audience

Matthew 6:19–34 shares the same geographical setting with the Sermon on the Mount, of which it is a part. Matthean tradition holds that the Beatitudes were pronounced on a mountain in Galilee (see 4:23—5:2). Fenlon identifies this mountain as Karn Hatti (the Horns of Hattin), a mountain which receives its name from the little village at its northern base and from the two horns which crown its summit.[12] Karn Hattin is located in "Galilee in easy distance of Nazareth, Cana, and Mt. Tabor to the southwest, of Tiberia and Lake Gennesaret (the Sea of Galilee) to the east, and of Capharnaum to the northeast, in the center, therefore, of much of the ministry of Jesus."[13]

Jesus's original audience were people who came from all over the surrounding regions including Galilee, the Decapolis, Jerusalem, Judea, and the area across the Jordan River (cf. 4:23—5:2). They consisted of Jesus's disciples and a much larger group of people from the various places stated above. These people included Pharisees, tax collectors, Sadducees, Roman soldiers, farmers, day laborers, the marginalized, and so on. The majority of people in these localities experienced Roman control and oppression.[14] This probably informed Jesus's address to the poor in spirit, those who mourn, those who thirst for righteousness, and those who are persecuted (cf. 5:3–12).

According to Denzil Tryon Jesus also intended his message to be taken to the Roman and religious elites (particularly those in Jerusalem) who were not present at the time that he spoke to the crowd.[15] Tyron argues (convincingly, I think) that the economic hardship most of the audience present at the time were facing was caused by these elites who exploited others to amass wealth, and so it is unlikely that Jesus would deliver a message against the accumulation of wealth without having those who are the root cause of the economic problem in mind.[16] If so, then Jesus, while directly addressing the crowd, was also indirectly addressing the power-elite wherever they were.

---

12. Amevenku and Boaheng, "Theological Interpretations," 71.
13. Felon as cited by Amevenku and Boaheng, 71.
14. Picard and Habets, *Theology and Experience*.
15. Tryon, "Accounting for Anxiety."
16. Tryon, 171.

Literary Context and Structure

Similarities in theme and structure between Matthew 6:19–34 and 7:1–12 make some scholars consider 6:19–34 as part of the larger pericope of Matthew 6:19–7:12. The text under consideration falls within the section of the Sermon on the Mount dealing with social issues (6:19–7:11). The text that precedes it (6:1–18) deals with the private life of the disciple of Christ. Verses 1–4 deal with giving and has the main teaching that Christian giving must be done in secret so as not to attract public attention. Verses 5–15 deal with the proper attitude to prayers and contain a model prayer for believers. These verses are followed by teachings on fasting (vv. 16–18).

Our pericope (6:19–34) divides into two major sections: one on wealth (vv. 19–24) and the other on worry (vv. 25–34). The main thesis of the pericope is that Christians must detach themselves from anything that hinders their trust in God, and absolute submission to his will, because he will provide for all who seek the righteousness of his kingdom. The first section, which instructs believers to prioritize divine things, is made up of three parts: the contrast between two treasures (one on earth and the other in heaven [vv. 19–21]), the contrast between two bodily conditions (light and darkness [vv. 22–23]), and the contrasts between two masters (God and mammon [v. 24]). We may also consider the three parts in this section as emphasizing the first three petitions of the Lord's Prayer which emphasizes the glory and purpose of God as the ultimate priority of the disciples.

The second section (vv. 25–34) posits that believers should not value material possessions enough to worry about them. Verse 25 prohibits worrying about food, drink, and clothing, verses 26–30 supply the reason for such prohibition: since God cares for lesser forms, he will surely supply human needs. The thesis of the section, "do not worry," is reiterated in verse 31 by three rhetorical questions. Verses 32–33 give further rationale for why we can trust God: "your heavenly Father knows that you need all these things". Verse 34 repeats the initial command not to worry about life. Verses 25–34, with their emphasis on trusting in God's providence rather than living an anxious life, parallels the fourth petition of the Lord's Prayer for daily bread. There is no unified parallel passage in the gospel for the whole of this unit. However, verses 19–21 reappear in Luke 12:33–34; parts of verses 22–23 in Luke 11:34–36; verse 24 in Luke 16:13, and verse 25–34 in Luke 12:22–31.

Our text is followed by Jesus's teachings regarding the believer's public life in relation to questions of money, treasures, food, drink, clothing, and ambition. In effect Jesus is encouraging his audience to be different in two ways: "different from the hypocrisy of the religious (1–18) and now different also from the materialism of the irreligious (19–34)."[17] This is followed by 7:1–11 which deals with how to treat others (vv. 1–6), as well as asking, seeking, and knocking (vv. 7–11).

Socioeconomic Context

In the opinion of Mark Allan Powell, the world of Jesus's time was characterized by economic inequality.[18] The economic gap between the rich and the poor continued to widen as the rich took advantage of their social status to exploit the poor and to amass wealth for themselves.[19] The poor continued to lose their farmland due to high debt.

People's interest in accumulating wealth was whipped up by the teachings of some religious leaders that wealth is a sign of God's blessings and poverty a mark of divine displeasure.[20] Consequently, many people attached much importance to wealth and pursued whatever economic advancement was available. Powell describes the economic disparity in these words, "virtually everyone in the New Testament times believed that there was only so much 'stuff' to go around and that some people had less than they needed because other people had more than they needed."[21] Jesus's use of wisdom sayings and parables to speak against those with vested economic and political interests must be interpreted within this contextual framework.[22]

The Greco-Roman world was highly hierarchical with various classes. Scheffler has argued that any society in the Greco-Roman world that had a population of half a million or more people was not simply made up of only two main classes, such as the rich and poor, or patrons and clients.[23] He presents Friesen's seven-fold economic class system for the Greco-Roman world, which I show below.[24]

---

17. Stott, *Deeper Look*, 131.
18. Powell, *Introduction to New Testament*, 41.
19. Powell, 40–41.
20. Powell, 41.
21. Powell, 420.
22. Powell, *Introduction to New Testament*.
23. Scheffler, "Luke's View," 118–119.
24. Scheffler, 119.

Table 4.1: Friesen's sevenfold economic class system for the Greco-Roman world

Economic class	Class description	%
(1) Imperial elites	The imperial dynasty, Roman senatorial families, a few retainers, local royalty, a few freed persons	0.04
(2) Regional or provincial elites	Equestrian families, provincial officials, some retainers, some decurial families, some freed persons, some retired military officers	1.00
(3) Municipal elites	Most decurial families, wealthy men and women who do not hold office, some freed persons, some retainers, some veterans, some merchants	1.76
(4) Moderate surplus resources	Some merchants, some traders, some freed persons, some artisans (especially those who employ others), military veterans	7.00
(5) Stable near subsistence level (with hope of remaining above the minimal level)	Many merchants and traders, regular wage earners, artisans, large shop owners, freed persons, some farm families	22.00
(6) At subsistence level (and often below minimum level to sustain life)	Small farm families, laborers (skilled and unskilled), artisans (especially those employed by others), wage earners, most merchants and traders, small shop or tavern owners	40.00
(7) Below subsistence level	Some farm families, unattached widows, orphans, beggars, disabled, unskilled day laborers, prisoners	28.00

The table indicates that the population of lower-class citizens (5–7) was more than 80 percent. This means that the Greco-Roman society had a very high dependency ratio. The rich took advantage of their status to set their own standard of evaluating human dignity.

Some philosophers in Jesus's time, with the perception that material wealth is inherently evil, encouraged contentment and modest living, and condemned wealth.[25] Keener notes further that Jews viewed wealth positively, as a sign of blessing (as noted earlier) or negatively according to how people used it.[26] This view was based on the Deuteronomistic tradition that God's blessing in terms of abundance will be experienced by the obedient and that the disobedient

---

25. Keener, *Commentary*, 232.
26. Keener, 233.

will experience loss and lack (Deut 28). Some of the Jewish writers, however, recognized the spiritual dangers of wealth (See 1 Enoch 63:10; 94:8; 96:4; 97:8; 1QS 10:18–19; 11:2). With this background, I now proceed to look at the text more closely.

Close Reading of Matthew 6:19–34
Two Treasures (Matt 6:19–21)

> Do not store up for yourselves treasures on earth, where moth and rust consume and where thieves break in and steal; but store up for yourselves treasures in heaven, where neither moth nor rust consumes and where thieves do not break in and steal. For where your treasure is, there your heart will be also.

This unit comprises a negative command (v. 19) and a positive command (v. 20) followed by a proverbial justification of the commands (v. 21). It shows the contrast between two treasures (one on earth and the other in heaven) and propounds that what one treasures is informed by what he or she values.

The opening verse (v. 19) begins with the expression *me thesaurizete* which could be rendered "stop storing up" or "stop treasuring," rather than "do not store up."[27] The present tense of the verb underlines the fact that the time has come for the people to take a decisive break in their act of storing up treasures on earth.[28] I indicated earlier that most of Jesus's physical audience ranked very low on the socioeconomic ladder and worked from hand to mouth. The elites on the other hand were accumulating wealth "through the mechanisms of taxation, control of land, control of labour and manipulation of money."[29] Against this backdrop, one may deduce that the command "Stop storing up treasures" had the few elites who were physically present and those absent as primary targets. However, it also served as a caution for the poor who might later enjoy economic advancement and begin to store up earthly treasures. The message was that those currently busily treasuring earthly treasures must stop and those contemplating a similar or same practice in future should not try it at all.

The verb *thesaurizete* ("storing up") derives from *thesaurizo* and refers to the act of keeping one's treasures in a safe place.[30] For Renn, the noun form *thesauros* (treasure) occurs about twenty times in the New Testament in the

---

27. Blomberg, "On Wealth and Worry," 76.
28. Carson, "Matthew," 177.
29. Tryon, "Accounting for Anxiety," 171.
30. Liddell and Scott, *Greek-English Lexicon*, 45.

sense of "valuables" (cf. Matt 2:11; 6:19; 13:44; Heb 11:26), "treasures" of the heart (cf. Matt 12:35; Luke 6:45; 12:34), or heavenly "treasures" (cf. Matt 6:20; Mark 10:21; Luke 18:22; 2 Cor 4:7).[31] The earthly treasures to which Jesus refers include clothes, precious metals (gold, silver, bronze, and so on), expensive or valuable things, mansions or wealth that people can own, and anything that is perishable. *Thesauros* derives from *thesauro*, a term which was used by ancient Jews to refer to "a place for storing valuables" or a storage room.[32] This term corresponds to the Hebrew word *osar*, which refers to the treasury or storehouse of the temple (see Josh 6:19). Usually what we keep in the storeroom is not something we really need for everyday life. Against the background of the foregoing discussion, I am of the opinion that Jesus was speaking to those who had kept certain things they really did not need whilst others lacked the basic necessities of life.

The personal pronoun *humin* ("for yourselves") underscores the fact that the wealthy in Jesus's community considered wealth as belonging to them alone.[33] They did not have the traditional communal sense of wealth held by Africans. Neither did they regard themselves as stewards of what ultimately belongs to God. As stated earlier, the wealthy used every available opportunity to get more wealth without considering the plight of the poor. They systematically stripped the country of its surpluses and hid them in the fortified cites and in their homes to increase their wealth.[34] This was a mark of greediness and selfishness in that a large amount of the national wealth went to a few people while the majority struggled to survive on virtually nothing. (Recall that the lower-class citizens of a typical Greco-Roman community were more than 80 percent.)

The principle Jesus teaches is that wealth should be used for the benefit of the entire community. Generosity (sharing with others) as opposed to selfish accumulation (storing up "for yourselves") is the Christian model. This does not mean that one cannot save money. Kingdom ethics require that one makes and saves money (not at the expense of others), and use it in a generous way to help others improve their lives.[35]

---

31. Renn, *Expository Dictionary of Bible*, 985.
32. See Liddell and Scott, *Greek-English Lexicon*, 1274.
33. Tryon, "Accounting for Anxiety," 172–173.
34. Tryon, 172–173.
35. Tryon, 173.

The word *brosis* translated "rust" actually refers to "[t]hat which eats," "the act of eating food" (Rom 14:17), or food itself (see John 4:32; 6:27, 55).[36] In the present context, however, it signifies the corrosive effect on metals as well as the possibly destructive effect of burrowers like woodworm or insects.[37] Ancient people were aware of the corruptible nature of wealth. For example, Ben Sirach encouraged his people to give freely to the needy rather than let money rust, for in sharing with others, one would be storing up treasures according to God's commandments (Sir 29:10–11; cf. 34:5; Pirke Abot 2:8). This text teaches that wealth is perishable but can be used in a way to attract God's blessings.

Treasures that could not easily corrupt could be stolen by thieves who could break in or "dig through" (*dioryssousin*). Typical first-century Palestinian houses, like most rural settlements in Africa, were made of mud through which thieves could easily bore holes and enter.[38] It was a common practice for people to hide their money in strongboxes in their own homes or in holes beneath their floor. Gold, silver, and costly garments were common signs of wealth in the Greco-Roman world (cf. 1 Tim 2:9) because they were the means by which people stored excess wealth.[39] While these items were not easily corruptible, they could easily be stolen from the owner. The point then is that earthly treasures are transient, vulnerable, and have no eternal value. Here too, one finds that the message is most suitable for the wealthy elites because they were the only people whose homes contained the commodities mentioned in the text. As in our time and in much of Africa today, the rural peasant farmers and other poor people of the Greco-Roman Jewish society did not have the commodities that attracted thieves and so were not easy targets for thieves.

The word *de* (rendered "but" or "instead") at the beginning of verse 20 shows a contrast between the previous verse and the present one. Instead of accumulating earthly treasures, Jesus urges his audience to accumulate heavenly treasures because these are free from the effect of decay and theft (cf. Luke 12:33).

A key exegetical issue is to define "treasures in heaven" and determine "how to store them." The expression "treasures in heaven" is of Jewish origin. It refers to all that results from our earthly activities that have eternal significance or persist beyond the grave.[40] The way to store up heavenly treasure includes

---

36. See Liddell and Scott, *Greek-English Lexicon*, 332; Vincent, *Vincent's Word Studies*, 46.
37. Carson, "Matthew," 318–319.
38. Vincent, *Vincent's Word Studies*, 46; Carson, "Matthew," 318.
39. Tryon, "Accounting for Anxiety," 173.
40. Carson, "Matthew," 177.

"doing righteous deeds, suffering for Christ's sake, forgiving one another."[41] I am of the opinion that within the context of the Sermon on the Mount, suffering persecution for Jesus's sake (Matt 5:12), loving one's enemies (Matt 5:46), generosity to the poor (Matt 6:2–4), earnest and sincere prayer (Matt 6:5–6), and true fasting (Matt 6:16–18) are possible ways of accumulating heavenly wealth. I agree with Frederick M. Amevenku that "people who are ready for the Kingdom would do their acts of piety in such a way as to store up their treasures in heaven, not on earth because their cherished treasures (which in that culture included clothing) are perishable and insecure (thieves could enter the storehouse to steal them)."[42]

Is material poverty a sign of spiritual wealth? Jesus's view about wealth and poverty was different from the philosophic view that wealth is inherently evil. For Jesus, even though possession of wealth is not inherently evil, one should not accumulate wealth when others in the society have too little for life. In other words, one's material possessions should be used to serve others (Matt 19:21; cf. Luke 3:11; 12:33–34). That wealth should be used in promoting the kingdom of God underlines Jesus's demand that the rich ruler sells his possessions and give to the poor before following him (Luke 18:22). This advice to the rich ruler should not be understood as Jesus endorsement of material poverty.

It was people's misplaced priorities due to materialism that prompted Jesus to teach against accumulation of riches; it was not the mere possession of wealth that he opposed. In the wider context of Scripture, wealth is not inherently evil because the Scriptures require that we care for our families (1 Tim 5:8), commends us to work hard and to invest prudently to provide for the future (Gen 41; Prov 6:6–8), encourages us to enjoy the good things God has given us (1 Tim 4:3–4; 6:17), which obviously includes wealth. Paul teaches the same truth by contending that it is not money itself but the love of money that is evil (1 Tim 6:10, 17–19). The love of money is evil because it leads to social, economic and religious problems that contribute to the poverty of others in the society. Therefore, "what Jesus forbids is the selfish accumulation of goods; extravagant and luxurious living; the hardheartedness which does not feel the colossal need of the world's under-privileged."[43] The foregoing analysis leads to the conclusion that it unbiblical to equate material poverty to spirituality as some people mistakenly do.

---

41. Carson, 177.
42. Amevenku, "Reinterpretation of Law," 152–153.
43. Stott, *Deeper Look*, 131.

The radical financial principle set by Jesus in the two previous verses is rooted in the fact that "where your treasure is, there your heart will be also" (v. 21). The term *kardia* corresponds to the Hebrew nouns *leb* and *lebab* and can mean physical heart (cf. 1 Cor 14:25).[44] However, in the present context, I believe Jesus uses *kardia* metaphorically to refer to one's inner-self, will, interests, concerns, and feelings. A person's heart (or real interest) lies where they have invested. Jesus encourages the accumulation of heavenly wealth not only because of its eternal value but also because "a heart that sets its affection on [earthly] wealth will be a life lived in contrast to the demands of obedience in God's Kingdom."[45]

The parable of the Rich Fool (Luke 12:16–21) provides a useful commentary on this verse as well as a link between verses 19–20 and verse 21. This parable is Jesus's response to someone who asked him to order his (the person's) brother to divide their inheritance with him (v. 13). Jesus could have used existing Jewish laws on inheritance to solve the problem at stake. However, he chose to tackle the root cause of the problem (that is, greed) which the Jewish law was not meant to deal with. In other words, Jesus, like a radical prophet, dealt with the root of the issue, which is greed or covetousness. This is evident in his warning, "Watch out! Be on your guard against all kinds of greed; life does not consist in an abundance of possessions" (v. 15 NIV). S. Calef observes that the "word, *pleonexia*, translated 'greed,' means literally 'the desire for more,' and in the Greek 'the abundance of possessions' (*en tō perisseuein*) suggests 'more than is enough.'"[46] This means that Jesus was not speaking about the mere possession of possessions, but rather the unquenchable desire for more than what is sufficient for one's basic needs.[47] Jesus used the rich fool to explain the kind of greed he was talking about.

The rich man had a bumper harvest from his land, which according to biblical tradition was the result of God's blessings. It is clear from the story that the man's barns were full, and yet he decided to tear them down and put up bigger ones in which to store his new surplus. The man put his trust in his wealth without thinking of God's priorities, and so thought to himself, "I will say to my soul, Soul, you have ample goods laid up for many years; relax, eat, drink, be merry" (v. 19). Obviously, the man considered his stored-up food as a security for the years to come. The result was that he lost everything he had,

---

44. Liddell and Scott, *Greek-English Lexicon*, 887.
45. O'Donoghue, "Biblical-Theological Analysis," 44.
46. Calef, "Prophet Margins," 114.
47. Calef, 114.

not through corruption or robbery but through death. In the words of Calef, the man did not recognize "the fact that his 'soul' or 'self' (Greek, *psychē*) is not a property over which he has ultimate control; for it belongs to God, is simply on loan, and can be 'demanded' back at any moment."[48] This story underscores both the dangers associated with, and the right use of, riches as well as human mortality and the destructible nature of earthly wealth.

The Sound and Bad Eyes (Matt 6:22–23)

> The eye is the lamp of the body. So, if your eye is healthy, your whole body will be full of light; but if your eye is unhealthy, your whole body will be full of darkness. If then the light in you is darkness, how great is the darkness!

The main thesis of this section is that just as good eyesight is required for the functioning of the body, so right perception of reality is required for earthly life. The opening statement is "The eye is the lamp of the body." Literally, it is through the eye that the body finds its way. A good eye will illuminate the body but a bad one will put the body in darkness (v. 23). The eye may be a metaphor for the heart: "The heart set on God as to hold to his commands (Ps 119:10) is equivalent to the eye fastened on God's law (Ps 119:18, 148; cf. Ps 119:36–37)."[49] In the metaphorical sense, the expressions to "set the heart" and to "fix the eye" on something are interchangeable (see Ps 119:10, 37).

The term *aplous* usually translated good can be rendered "single," "straightforward," "simple," "innocent," "clear," or "healthy."[50] It carries the impression of "a piece of cloth or material, neatly folded once and without variety of complicated folds."[51] A single-eyed person never covets his neighbor but follows Christ, doing what is good in simplicity of the spirit.[52] Bonhoeffer is of the opinion that "the singleness of the eye and the heart corresponds to that 'hiddenness' which knows nothing but the call and word of Christ, and which consists in perfect fellowship with him."[53] Such an eye has no darkness because it is illuminated by Christ. The expression is used to make the point

---

48. Calef, 114.
49. Carson, "Matthew," 178.
50. See Vincent, *Vincent's Word Studies*, 46.
51. Vincent, 46.
52. Bonhoeffer, *Cost of Discipleship*, 118.
53. Bonhoeffer, 118–119.

that the spiritually healthy person is not double-minded or indecisive (v. 24, cf. Jas 1:7–8) about their loyalty to God.

The word *poneros* (translated "bad" or "unhealthy") could mean "evil" (cf. Rom 12:9).[54] Therefore, the expression *ophthalmos sou poneros* could be rendered "evil eye." "Evil eye" may be understood variously. For example, it may be understood as wicked intention (cf. 1 Sam 18:9) but such a view does not fit the present context. It may also refer to "grudging, selfish character (cf. Matt 20:15)."[55] The Jews used the expression "evil eye" to signify stinginess, jealousy, miserliness and selfishness (see Prov 23:6; 28:22; Sir 14:8–10) and good eyes for generosity.[56] An example of this usage is found in Deuteronomy 15:9 which says, ". . . and your eye be evil against your poor brother and you give him nothing" (NKJV). The context of this text, as we discovered, was God's instruction to Israel to be generous in releasing each other from debts. Here, and also in Matthew 20:15, the expression "evil eye" means "greedy." Jesus's use of "evil eye" in the present text seems similar to its usage in Deuteronomy 15:9 and Matthew 20:15. Carson, however, proposes two interpretations: "Jesus is saying either that (1) the [person] who 'divides his [or her] interest and tries to focus on both God and possession . . . has no clear vision, and will live without clear orientation or direction' . . . or (2) that the [person] who is stingy and selfish cannot really see where he[or she] is going; he [or she] is morally and spiritually blind."[57] In my opinion, the first interpretation is compatible with verse 24 while the second is compatible with verses 19–21.

Two Masters (Matt 6:24)

> No one can serve two masters; for a slave will either hate the one and love the other, or be devoted to the one and despise the other. You cannot serve God and wealth.

Verse 24 begins with the assertion that "No one can serve two masters." The verb behind "serve" is not *diakoneo* ("to serve"), but *douleuo* ("to be enslaved to").[58] The corresponding nouns are *diakonos* and *doulos* respectively. Therefore, Jesus is talking about slavery, not just service. In the ancient world, every *doulos*

---

54. Liddell and Scott, *Greek-English Lexicon*, 1447.
55. Johnson, *Interpreters Bible*, 319.
56. Grogan, "Isaiah," 178.
57. Carson, "Matthew," 178.
58. Zodhiates and Baker, *NIV Key Word Study*, 1612.

was a *diakonos*, but not every *diakonos* was a *doulos*.[59] That is to say, every slave rendered services but not all who rendered services were slaves. According to Longenecker, slavery was prevalent in the Greco-Roman world and the lives of the middle and upper classes were dependent on the services of slaves.[60] He estimates the number of slaves in the Roman Empire was as much as one-third of the Italian population.

The slave-master relationship in the Greco-Roman world was such that the slave belonged entirely to the master, the master sharing this right with no one.[61] This situation made it impossible for one slave to belong to two different masters at the same time. He would have belonged absolutely to one, but could not have belonged to two owners simultaneously. The Ghanaian proverb, *wontumi mfa w'ani mmienu nhwɛ toa baako mu* ("You cannot look into a bottle with two eyes [at the same time]") expresses this fact. Therefore, just as it is not possible for one to devote all their services to two different people at the same time, so a slave could not be owned entirely by two masters at the same time.

The next part begins with *gar* ("for") which signifies that the reason for the first part is about to be supplied. The reason why "no one can serve two masters" is that a "slave will either hate the one and love the other, or be devoted to the one and despise the other." Jesus's use of "love" and "hate" are not to be taken absolutely. From the context of the text, one must understand the expression "to hate someone" as showing preference for one as against the other rather than active dislike. The verb *agapesei* (from *agapao*) should be understood as valuing something greatly.[62] Therefore, no one can have two masters because such a situation will inevitably lead the person to show greater value and preference for one master over the other.

The application of the above fact is that "you cannot serve God and mammon" (NKJV). The word *mamona* (translated "mammon") derives from the Aramaic term which refers to possessions, wealth or property.[63] Both the Hebrew and Aramaic roots of this term connote something that one places their trust in rather than God.[64] The verse demands a mutually exclusive choice

---

59. Zodhiates and Baker, 1612.

60. Longenecker, *New Testament Social Ethics*, 48.

61. Zodhiates and Baker, *NIV Key Word Study*, 1612.

62. See Blomberg, "On Wealth and Worry," 79; Zodhiates and Baker, *NIV Key Word Study*, 1571.

63. Blomberg, "On Wealth and Worry," 79; Liddell and Scott, *Greek-English Lexicon*, 1078; Youngblood, *New Illustrated Bible Dictionary*, 794.

64. Carson, "Matthew," 178.

between God and mammon. Since it is not possible to be a slave to both God and mammon simultaneously, one has to make a choice between them. In the view of Stott, "anybody who divides his allegiance between God and mammon has already given it to mammon, since God can be served only with an entire and exclusive devotion."[65] God cannot be served with a divided loyalty because we are to serve him with all our heart, with all our soul and with all our strength (Deut 6:5; cf. Matt 19:22–23). This service to God requires that we show concern for others in terms of providing for their needs. I conclude that one's disposition is set in accordance with who or what they are serving, God or mammon.

Prohibition of Worry (Matt 6:25–32)

> Therefore I tell you, do not worry about your life, what you will eat or what you will drink, or about your body, what you will wear. Is not life more than food, and the body more than clothing? Look at the birds of the air; they neither sow nor reap nor gather into barns, and yet your heavenly Father feeds them. Are you not of more value than they? And can any of you by worrying add a single hour to your span of life? And why do you worry about clothing? Consider the lilies of the field, how they grow; they neither toil nor spin, yet I tell you, even Solomon in all his glory was not clothed like one of these. But if God so clothes the grass of the field, which is alive today and tomorrow is thrown into the oven, will he not much more clothe you – you of little faith? Therefore do not worry, saying, "What will we eat?" or "What will we drink?" or "What will we wear?" For it is the Gentiles who strive for all these things; and indeed your heavenly Father knows that you need all these things.

Verse 25 introduces the second major part of the unit we are considering. This part begins with a prohibition of worry (25a) and it is then followed by four reasons for the prohibition (25b–30). The opening expression is "Therefore I say to you". The use of *dia touto*, "therefore" or "this is why," highlights the fact that what follows is deducible from what has been said (vv. 19–24, but particularly v. 24).[66] What forms the basis of verse 25a is the contention that believers must detach themselves from whatever hinders their complete loyalty

---

65. Stott, *Deeper Look*, 132.
66. O'Donoghue, "Biblical-Theological Analysis," 53.

to God and absolute submission to his will.[67] The expression "I say to you" affirms the authority behind Jesus's teaching.[68] Jesus used this expression very often in the six antitheses of Matthew 5:21–48 to show that his words carry the same authority as those of the Father.

The word *merimnate* (translated "to worry") means "[to] be distracted by cares."[69] The command not to worry is again appropriately understood as a command to stop an action in progress.[70] Believers are not to worry but to trust God's power to provide for their real needs (6:25–34).

The reasons for the prohibition of worry as evident in verses 25b–32 could be summarized as follows.[71] First, human calculations are mostly defeated by the "intricacies and inviolabilities" of life because we do not own the world, neither do we understand how it works. That is the reason why Jesus asked, "can any of you by worrying add a single hour to your span of life?" (v. 27) Second, since God has given us life freely, it is fair to believe that he will cater for us. To make this point, Jesus asked, "Is not life more than food, and the body more than clothing?" (v. 25) Third, since God provides for creatures such as birds, and for flowers and grass as they fulfil their nature, it stands to reason that if human beings fulfil their nature ("not idleness, but trustful work"),[72] God will not disappoint them. Fourth, taking calculated care for garments and clothing makes one behave like a pagan whose mind is set on earthly things: "For. . . Gentiles strive for all these things" (v. 32).

Jesus makes the point that there is overwhelming evidence in God's creation to teach us of God's providence so that it is only those of little faith who will fail to trust him to supply all their needs (Matt 6:30–31). Is Jesus asking believers to remain idle and be fed by God? A careful reflection on the passage shows that Jesus is not saying that Christians must sit aloof and wait for God to feed and clothe them. The KJV translation of verse 31 "take no thought" seems inaccurate and misleading because there are times when Jesus's own thought reflected prudence (Luke 14:28–32).[73] Carson notes that the command not to worry "can be falsely absolutized by neglecting the limitations the context imposes and the curses on carelessness, apathy, indifference, laziness, and self-

---

67. O'Donoghue, 53.
68. Hagner as cited by O'Donoghue, 53.
69. Newman and Stine, *Handbook on Matthew*, electronic edition.
70. Blomberg, "On Wealth and Worry," 79.
71. See Johnson, *Interpreters Bible*, 320–321.
72. Lathem, *Our Father . . . I Believe*, 68.
73. Johnson, *Interpreters Bible*, 320.

indulgence expressed elsewhere."⁷⁴ The context within which Jesus ministered defined necessity quite differently from our modern society. Jesus asked them not to worry about even the basic necessities, let alone luxuries, because by so doing they portray that their existence is dependent on such things. One reason why Christians do not have to be distracted by cares is that their life, which is freely given by God, is far more important than food or drink. Therefore, if God has given a greater gift of life, he will definitely give a lesser gift of sustenance.[75]

Worry can be both appropriate and sinful. Worry understood as merely "concern" may not be wrong most of the time. One's concern (worry) about inability to take part in the Christian Lenten season may not be wrong. However, worry that leads to misplaced priorities is sinful. The worry about basic life necessities has the tendency of obscuring one's priority of seeking God's kingdom and his righteousness (Matt 6:33). Jesus also prohibits worry because "anxiety or calculated care in regards to such items as food and clothing is egocentricity."[76] In my view, the prohibition of worry must be understood in this light.

Kingdom of God and His Righteousness (Matt 6:33–34)

> But strive first for the kingdom of God and his righteousness, and all these things will be given to you as well. So do not worry about tomorrow, for tomorrow will bring worries of its own. Today's trouble is enough for today.

The previous section ended on the note that believers must not worry about the basic needs of life because their Father in heaven is aware of these needs and will provide them (these things) as long as he lends them breath. The question that comes to mind is "If we are to not worry, what are we to do?" Jesus answers this question by saying, "But strive first for the kingdom of God and his righteousness." (v. 33). The verse begins with *de* (translated "but") which could be also translated "instead" or "rather" to show what believers ought to do rather than worry about life and its necessities. The Greek term *proton* (rendered "first") means primacy or "above all else."[77] Believers must put the kingdom of God and his righteousness first on their list of preferences.

---

74. Carson, "Matthew," 179.
75. Blomberg, "On Wealth and Worry," 80.
76. Johnson, *Interpreters Bible*, 320.
77. Newman and Stine, *Handbook on Matthew*, electronic edition.

The expression *basileian tou theou* (kingdom of God) needs to be examined. The term *basileian*, kingdom, refers to both concrete ideas such as realm, territory, domain, or people over whom a king reigns, and abstract ideas such as sovereign authority, royal power or dominion.[78] When applied to God, the term kingdom comprises "God's overall reign in the universe, His present spiritual reign in His people, and His future messianic reign on earth."[79] This kingdom has a future aspect (see Matt 24) as well as a present aspect (see Matt 12:28; Mark 1:5; Matt 10:7; Luke 17:20).

The term *dikaiosune* (righteousness) occurs seven times in Matthew's Gospel, with five of the seven appearing in the Sermon on the Mount; two in the Beatitudes (Matt 5:6, 10, 20; 6:1, 33).[80] *Dikaiosune* also means "justice," "fulfilment of Law"[81] or "holy and upright living, in accordance with God's standards."[82] The Old Testament uses *saddiq* (righteous) to define the relationship between the people of God and himself (see Gen 6:9; 7:1).[83] The one who meets God's requirement is said to be righteous (see Matt 3:15). In the present context where *dikaiosune* applies to the person of God, it refers to his essential attribute.[84] See also Romans 1:17; 3:5, 21–22; 2 Corinthians 9:9; Ephesians 4:24 for such usage of *dikaiosune*. Jesus is exhorting his audience to pursue holy living according to the holy character of God.

Those who serve God and unrighteous mammon at the same time will have their wealth destroyed by moth and rust and eventually learn how vain it is to treasure up their treasure on earth (Matt 6:19–21). If so, then it is better for people to serve God alone, striving first for the kingdom and God's righteousness (Matt 6:34). For Jesus, those who seek God's kingdom and his righteousness are those who recognize the worth of human beings and hence work not only towards their own survival but towards the survival of others as well.[85] The point is that God's provision for the needs of the needy will come (from him) through the wealth of wealthy. Getz rightly states that, "situations occur where people's needs are not met because followers of Christ have not

---

78. Geisler, *Systematic Theology*, 1347–1348.
79. Geisler, 1347.
80. Boaheng, "Christian Discipleship," 18.
81. Liddell and Scott, *Greek-English Lexicon*, 429.
82. Youngblood, *New Illustrated Bible Dictionary*, 1089.
83. Renn, *Expository Dictionary*, 825–826.
84. Renn, 829.
85. Tryon, "Accounting for Anxiety," 183.

been obedient in applying the principles that God has outlined in His Word."[86] The early church practiced this principle by selling their possessions and giving to the needy (Acts 2:44–45). Later, Paul encouraged the believers in Corinth to give in order to provide for the needy (2 Cor 8:12–15).

The passage concludes on a restatement of the prohibition on worry. Worrying is future-oriented, meaning we worry about what is going to happen to us in the next moment or later. However, the future is not under the worrier's control, but under that of a loving heavenly Father. Therefore, all we must be concerned with is the circumstance of the present day, for tomorrow will worry about itself (v. 34). The one-day-at-a-time mentality taught in this verse alludes to the petition in the Lord's Prayer, "Give us this day our daily bread" (Matt 6:11). God promises to satisfy our needs, not our greed. The whole point is that instead of worrying about life, humans should do their best to serve God faithfully, and leave the rest to him.

Exegesis of 1 Timothy 6:6–10
Background to 1 Timothy

The letters to Timothy and Titus are classified as pastoral letters of the Apostle Paul because of their concern for the pastoral responsibilities of their two primary recipients. First Paul indicates that Timothy was in Ephesus (1:3) at the time the letter was written. Timothy was born to a Jewish mother (Eunice, see 2 Tim 1:5) and a Greek father at Lystra (Acts 16:1). There is no mention of his father's faith in Christ, but his mother and grandmother, Lois, are said to have sincere faith (2 Tim 1:5). Paul adopted him as a companion (Acts 16:2) and set him apart for ministry through the laying on of hands. He became one of Paul's companions (during Paul's second missionary journey), a faithful messenger and representative (Acts 19:22; 1 Cor 16:10; Phil 2:19-22; 1 Thess 3:2, 6). Paul included Timothy in the salutations of six of his letters (see 2 Cor 1:1; Phil 1:1; Col 1:1; 1 Thess 1:1; 2 Thess 1:1; Phlm 1).

No scholarly consensus has been reached regarding the date of composition of 1 Timothy. One could, however, gather from Daniel Arichea and Howard Hatton that this epistle was known to the Christian community at least by the middle of the second century.[87] This is because the epistle appears in the Muratorian Canon which contains a list of New Testament books likely

---

86. As cited by Blomberg, "On Wealth and Worry," 84.
87. Arichea and Hatton, *Handbook*, electronic edition.

to have been penned at the end of the second century.[88] First Timothy was occasioned by the presence of false teachers in the church (see 1 Tim 1:4; 4:7). Paul therefore instructs Timothy urging him to oppose these false teachings by giving sound teaching and conducting himself properly.

Literary Context

1 Timothy 6:6–10 is part of a larger unit which deals with the causes and antidotes for false teachings (vv. 3–10). The preceding pericope (6:3–5) is a summary and restatement of Paul's indictment of the false teachers of his day. These teachers taught what was completely in contrast with orthodoxy. Paul contends that the corrupted mind of these teachers produces all kinds of jealousy and strife. Earlier, Paul had described false teachings as "things taught by demons" (4:1b NIV) and listed some of the characteristics of these teachings (4:1b–3). In this section (that is vv. 3–5), however, he focuses on warning against those who are contemplating introducing such teachings into the Christian community. He identifies ignorance and greed as some of the causes of false teachings (see vv. 4–5). False teachers are egocentric, and think only of their own interests (v. 4), not those of other people. They are motivated also by their unhealthy desire for material wealth (v. 5).

Paul then moves on to give the antidote to this kind of behavior (vv. 6–10). The key to dealing with greed which results in false teachings is to develop the virtue of contentment. Paul avows that people must be content with having the basic necessities of life, namely food, clothing and shelter, met. This is the Christian way of dealing with the human insatiable desire for wealth. This does not mean Paul is asking people to be poor. Rather, he is making the point that those who are content with what they have live happier and are in a better position to serve God than those who desire to become rich.

This section is then followed by verses 11–16 where Paul writes about the Christian virtues of righteousness, godliness, faith, love, endurance and gentleness. Paul believes that these virtues will also make one safe from the dangers associated with the love for material things. He exhorts his spiritual son to live blamelessly (v. 14) while waiting for the appearing of Jesus, the Christ of God (v. 15). Having briefly outlined the background and context of the text, I now proceed to examine it closely.

---

88. Arichea and Hatton.

Close Reading of 1 Timothy 6:6–10
Contentment (1 Tim 6:6–8)

> Of course, there is great gain in godliness combined with contentment; for we brought nothing into the world, so that we can take nothing out of it; but if we have food and clothing, we will be content with these.

Paul says, "But godliness with contentment is great gain" (v. 6 NIV). There were false teachers who were teaching that one should take advantage of their godly life to make financial gains (v. 5). Paul combines the words godliness and gain to shift attention from the erroneous view of wealth to the truth. For Paul, godliness is not a means to financial gain (see v. 5); rather godliness itself, when combined with contentment, is gain. The word contentment (*autarkeias*) appears in the Bible only in this verse and in 2 Corinthian 9:8. According to Marvin Vincent, *autarkeia* refers to "an inward self-sufficiency, as opposed to the lack or the desire of outward things."[89] The point then is that the one who lives according to God's will becomes inwardly self-sufficient with life in that the goal of such a life is not to consume what the flesh lusts after but to acquire treasures that have eternal significance. The word contentment was used by Stoic philosophers to indicate self-sufficiency, referring to people who "need nothing except what Nature has given them."[90] Paul uses contentment in a different way to signify self-sufficiency that is dependent upon Christ's sufficiency (cf. Phil 4:11; 2 Cor 9:8). The "great gain" which results from the combination of godliness and contentment (v. 6) far exceeds the limited financial "gain" of Paul's opponents (v. 5).

In verse 7 Paul uses two proverbs to support his contention in the previous verse. The first, "For we brought nothing into this world, and we can take nothing out of it" (NIV), echoes a common Jewish and Christian idea that material things are absolutely temporary (cf. Job 1:21; Ps 49:16; Eccl 5:15; Luke 12:16–21). This view is also found in Diaspora literature and among other Greco-Roman writers.[91] The point is that the human condition is a gift from God and cannot be improved significantly materially, else "we would have arrived better equipped."[92] As humans, our lives in this world are too brief to focus on worldly possessions (cf. Jas 4:14). God knew we would need the things

---

89. Vincent, *Vincent's Word Studies*, 275.
90. Keener, *IVP Bible Background Commentary*, 613.
91. Keener, 613.
92. Towner, "Letters to Timothy," 400.

of the world to sustain us during our stay here; he did not put them there to become the focus of our life. People must therefore enjoy material things to the glory of God, but should not consider them as contributing to their godliness.[93]

In a second proverb, Paul avows that when Christians "have food and clothing, [they] will be content with that" (v. 8 NIV). According to Keener, food (*diatrophas*) and clothing (*skepasmata*) were the basic needs identifiable in ancient literature.[94] However, the noun *skepasmata* comes from the verb *skepazo* which means "to cover" and so could mean both clothing and shelter.[95] Paul's point is that the Lord takes care of his people, and so they must trust him to provide their needs (Matt 6:25–34; Phil 4:11).

The concept of contentment needs further examination together with materialism. The attitude of contentment is characterized by focusing on what God has given us already, disregarding what we do not have, and avoiding being covetous of what belongs to others and thanking God for the gifts he has given us. What God has given us may include good health, material wealth, fertility, and other things. However, the most important gift he has given us, which must be our focus, is the salvation we have in Christ through the forgiveness of sins (Eph 1:6–8; cf. Rom 5:10). We cannot have all that we want because human wants are insatiable. No matter how rich or poor we are there are things we will lack. It may be difficult for people to be content with meeting the basic needs of life when others are enjoying great wealth. However, those who realize that no material treasure can add anything to their being can develop contentedness without difficulty. The apostle is exhorting us not to focus on what we do not have but what we have instead. Focusing on what one has rather than what others have is a panacea to covetousness. The word covetousness means desiring more of what one already has enough of or desiring to possess what others have. Avoiding covetousness and becoming content with what we have will lead us to magnify, praise, and thank God for his goodness.

Those who are not content with what they have tend to be materialistic. Materialism is, therefore, the opposite of contentment. Materialism may be defined as a preoccupation with the possession of material things (especially luxury goods and wealth) and the tendency to equate material wealth to happiness and fulfilment. For Paul, this misconception must be avoided.

---

93. Litfin, "1 Timothy," 746.
94. Keener, *IVP Bible Background Commentary*, 613.
95. Vincent, *Vincent's Word Studies*, 276.

Money and Evil (1 Tim 6:9–10)

> But those who want to be rich fall into temptation and are trapped by many senseless and harmful desires that plunge people into ruin and destruction. For the love of money is a root of all kinds of evil, and in their eagerness to be rich some have wandered away from the faith and pierced themselves with many pains.

In verses 9 and 10 Paul contrasts the proper attitude of contentment with desiring to get rich (v. 9) and the love of money (v. 10) in order to bring out the dangers associated with wealth. Here, "Paul addresses those seeking to accumulate wealth (cf. Prov 28:20) rather than those who had already become wealthy through inheritance or industry (6:17)."[96] The expression "People who want to get rich" refers to all those who deliberately desire more than having food, clothing and shelter.[97] Those who have the basic necessities and yet desire to acquire more riches and store them up as possessions, as land, or as money against adverse situations belong to this category. According to Paul, those desiring to be rich or those who lose their contentment with the basic necessities of life "fall into temptation and a trap and into many foolish and harmful desires that plunge people into ruin and destruction" (v. 9 NIV). Here, Paul is not speaking about wealth gained by evil means (such as theft, robbery, oppression and extortion) but about the desire for wealth by whatever means, be it godly or evil. Paul speaks against such perpetual desire because it does not promote the kingdom of God (cf. Matt 6:19–34).

Paul then concludes with a well know dictum "the love of money is a root of all kinds evil." To be sure, the text does not say money is inherently evil. Money may be used in the service of God with good results. As John Wesley points out, money "is an excellent gift of God answering the noblest ends. In the hands of his children, it is food for the hungry, drink for the thirst, raiment for the naked. It gives the traveler and the stranger where to lay his head. By it we supply the place of a husband to the widow, and of a father to the fatherless."[98] The rich "may be a defense for the oppressed, a means of health to the sick, of ease to them that are in pain; it may be eyes to the blind, as feet to the lame; yea, a lifter up from the gates of death!"[99] This means that wealth possessed by

---

96. Keener, *IVP Bible Background Commentary*, 613.
97. Moltmann et al., *Economy of Salvation*, 100.
98. Wesley as cited in Moody and Breeze, *Philanthropy Reader*, 177.
99. Wesley as cited in Moody and Breeze, 177.

Christians has the tendency of solving most problems common in societies, and hence the possession of wealth is not inherently evil.

What is wrong about money then is the love of it. The writer of Hebrews echoes this thought in the admonishment "Keep your lives free from the love of money" (Heb 13:5). In Matthew 6:24, we realized that one cannot love two masters equally at the same time and consequently one cannot serve both God and riches. Here, Paul is condemning love of money because of the danger of putting one's trust in wealth as in the parable of the Rich Fool who builds new barns and sits back to enjoy his life (Luke 12:16–21), or in the story of the rich ruler who found it difficult to let go of riches and follow Christ. Another reason is that the love of money has the tendency of making people measure human worth and success of life (status) by material possessions rather than by the status of a person's relationship with God. More so, the love of money may lead people to focus their energies on making money rather than serving God through godly industry. In other words, the love of money can make one neglect spiritual things and eventually wander from the Christian faith (v. 10). The end of such a person is sorrow or "tragedy of wasted life."[100] The following quote by John Ryle summarizes my discussion so far: "Money, in truth, is one of the most *unsatisfying* of possessions. It takes away some cares, no doubt; but it brings with it quite as many cares as it takes away."[101] He continues, "There is trouble in the getting of it. There is anxiety in the keeping of it. There is temptation in the use of it. There is guilt in the abuse of it. There is sorrow in the losing of it. There is perplexity in the disposing of it."[102] This confirms the assertion that "Human beings generally fall prey to a sense of false security when they become wealthy and live comfortably. Their way of life insulates them from the real issues of life"[103]

While Paul does not mean every kind of evil in the universe is the result of the love of money, he contends that the love of money can lead to any kind of evil. For example, the love of money can lead to murder, hatred, envy, selfishness, corruption, backbiting, forgetfulness of God, theft, strife, dishonesty, covetousness and the like. I join Fairbairn in his assertion that "The sentiment is, that there is no kind of evil to which the love of money may not lead men, when once it fairly takes hold of them."[104] To conclude, Paul's main

---

100. Guthrie, "1 Timothy," 2101.
101. As cited in Guthrie, 2101.
102. As cited in Guthrie, 2101.
103. Bitrus, "Amos," 1063.
104. As cited in Ralph, "1 Timothy," 385.

contention in this section is that godliness with contentment is great gain while desiring to be wealthy and loving money leads to all kinds of evil. Christians must trust God to supply their needs and be generous to others. Paul does not condone asceticism but simplicity.

Theological Synthesis of Exegetical Analyses

After the exegetical studies of the above four key passages, it is important to outline systematically what the Bible teaches about wealth and poverty based on the outcome of the exegeses. The present section is an attempt to give a systematic formulation of the biblical view on wealth and poverty as found in the exegeses.

A Biblical Concept of Poverty

My discussion so far reveals that many terms are used to describe "poverty" and each of them has a range of meanings depending on the context in which it is used. Furthermore, the term "poverty" refers not only to lack of economic resources and economic goods (a condition of having "less than enough"), but also to political and legal powerlessness, oppression, and lack of good health. With regards to its economic dimension, poverty may be considered an individual's inability to meet their basic needs. Included in this category are the sick, widows, slaves, physically disabled, orphans, children, elderly, beggars, debt slaves, village dwellers and prisoners. Poverty has a communal and social dimension, whereby the society may be considered a poor one. The health and wealth of the community are closely related. A society may be considered healthy and rich if it exhibits the following features: justice, mercy or loyalty, and compassion (Zech 7:9–10). Injustice, oppression, exploitation, and disloyalty are some of the marks of an unhealthy and poor society.

The following quote by Domeris outlines the common understanding of poverty in both ancient Israel and today in terms of its social classification:

> To be poor means more than just experiencing an absence of wealth or possessions. It is to occupy a specific place within the social ordering of society. To call someone "poor" is to make a value judgment: it is to create two groups, us and them; to say, that they (the poor) are somehow different from us (the non-poor) and because there is such a small step between difference and value, to imply that they are therefore inferior, lacking in certain values and

deviant. Poverty labels signal areas of possible exploitation within the economic domain, by separating out those with economic power (non-poor) from those without. No group identity or class-consciousness binds the poor together. They are unified only by virtue of their place within the thinking and perspective of the dominant class.[105]

Because of the multifaceted nature of poverty, one has to avoid the narrow definitions I discussed earlier in this book, which were based on economic dimensions. An acceptable definition of poverty must necessarily include social, economic, religious, health, and cultural dimensions. The Old Testament gives various causes of poverty namely: oppression and fraud (Prov 14:31; 22:7; 28:15), misfortune, persecution, or judgment (Job 1:12–19), laziness, neglect, or gluttony (Prov 10:14; 13:4; 19:15; 20:13; 23:21), short-sightedness (Matt 7:24–27), selfishness (Prov 11:24; Jer 6:12–13), or the culture of poverty (Prov 10:15).

Wealth in God's Sight

Wealth in the biblical tradition is not in itself a wicked thing, or necessarily either the result or sign of sinful living. The Matthean passage underscores the principle that the attainment of material success is not a measure of godliness. Therefore, it is wrong for us to think that the poor are under God's curse and the rich deserve their wealth because it is the result of their supposedly righteous life.

On the other hand, poverty is also not necessarily a virtue in itself. As Domeris puts it, the poor "are not, by virtue of their situation, somehow closer to God than are the rich."[106] The poor may not necessarily refer to people with a spiritual attitude of dependence on God. In fact, poverty can sometimes be a temptation to distrust God or to be dishonest. The right balance between wealth and poverty is probably best stated by Agur in Proverbs: "Give me neither poverty nor riches – Feed me with the food allotted to me; Lest I be full and deny you, and say, 'Who is the LORD?' Or lest I be poor and steal, and profane the name of my God" (30:8b-9 NKJV).

God is the source of wealth and all other good things. He promised to bless Abram (Gen 12:1–3) and he made Abram really rich (Gen 13:2). He also

---

105. Domeris, *Touching Heart of God*, 13.
106. Domeris, 2.

blessed other people materially, including Job and Solomon. In our exegesis of Deuteronomy 15:1–11 we came across God's promise to bless his people abundantly such that they will have no poor among them and lend to, rather than borrow from, other nations. Throughout the Old Testament there are many other Scriptures (e.g. Deut 28–30) that are clear that material possessions are a sign of God's blessings. God's promises of abundant wealth are, however, predicated on faithful obedience to his word. But this does not mean that anyone who is poor is under God's curse. God may allow someone to become poor for his glory to be manifested in his life (e.g. Job). To be precise, God's concern is with the relative value a person places on wealth.

Materialism/Wealth Accumulation

Materialism has to do with a preoccupation with material things or the insatiable desire for more and more luxuries. Materialism has to do with one's attitude towards wealth and its importance. All four passages we considered touched on materialism. Both the Sabbath economy of Deuteronomy 15:1–11 and Jesus's kingdom ethics in Matthew 6:19–34 and 1 Timothy 6:6–10 oppose hoarding of material goods. In the Sabbath economy, God taught his people that he is the primary provider of life resources when he made Israel engage in no activities on the Sabbath, in the Sabbatical Year and in the Jubilee Year, and yet ensured that they had enough food to eat during these periods of rest. The Sabbath economy demanded cancellation of debts every Sabbatical Year so that the poor could be relieved of suffering and begin life again without any debt.

Jesus also drew attention to the fact that life characterized by hoarding of material things cannot bring one into the kingdom of God because kingdom living requires that each citizen shares what they have with others. Solomon's economy, characterized by wealth accumulation, did not make him better than the lilies of the field which keep nothing in store (Matt 6:29). Rather than accumulating wealth, believers must use wealth to ease the financial burdens of others.

The passages in Deuteronomy and Matthew underscore the fact that God has abundant resources for the world but the scarcity we are experiencing is due to materialistic human behavior which has led to the hoarding and selfish use of goods. These teachings about materialism sharply contrast two principal suppositions of classical economics, namely the natural condition of scarcity and the human propensity for unlimited appetite. The kingdom or Sabbath economy teaches that God's gift is natural abundance, and our response should be self-restraint.

Materialism has to be avoided for at least the following reasons. First, accumulation of wealth erects barriers, and leads to pride and envy which set a person apart from others. The fact that excessive wealth can make one insensitive to the realities in life and even erect barriers has been noted earlier. Yancey makes this point when he states that "Affluence had a strangely distancing effect. It created barriers."[107]

In addition, (accumulated) wealth threatens one's devotion to God because one cannot have allegiance to both affluence and God. Any preoccupation or obsession with anything other than God is sinful and is displeasing to God. He alone deserves our total attention, love and service. In view of Deuteronomy 6:5, it is idolatrous to be preoccupied with materialistic thoughts. Pope Francis, confirming that materialism takes the place of God, stated, "It is true that nowadays, to some extent, everyone including our young people feels attracted by the many idols which take the place of God and appear to offer hope: money, success, power, and pleasure."[108] The foregoing is the reason why wealth can actually prevent people from entering the kingdom of God (Matt 19:24; Mark 10:25; Luke 18:25).

Further, materialism leads to selfishness, exploitation of others and unnecessary popularity. Due to a fixation of the mind on material possessions, people try to maintain their wealth through whichever means are available, but mostly through the exploitation of others, especially the poor and vulnerable. For example, legislators sometimes enact laws that legalize their exploitative activities due to their materialistic mindset (Isa 10:1–4).

Anxiety and Worry

Materialistic thinking leads to anxiety and unhappiness. Money and possessions require a constant worry about their acquisition, increase, and preservation. Wealthy people are always anxious to get more and more wealth in order to maintain their social status. The parable of the Rich Fool teaches us that people who are seriously amassing wealth are likely to be obsessed by it to the extent of losing their life in the end. The continual, selfish search for happiness through material wealth more often than not leads to misery. Wealth gives the illusion of security.

---

107. As cited in Strickland, "Money Matters," 8.
108. As cited in Umoh, "Prosperity Gospel," 658.

Aside from the rich, the poor also worry about their basic needs. Some make calculated attempts to maximize profit and so on. This book points to the fact that while worry may have some positive effects in some cases, in a majority of cases, it tends to obscure our view of God and his power. Worry and anxiety must be avoided because they are not kingdom values and they lead to reversal of priorities (Matt 6:25), and they make people fail to see things as they really are (Matt 6:26). More so, worry and anxiety are anti-Christian because they are a waste of energy (Matt 6:27) and acts of unbelief (Matt 6:28–30), which characterize unbelievers (Matt 6:32).

Generosity

We have established that there is nothing wrong with acquiring wealth. However, riches come with the responsibility of sharing our resources with others and guarding against finding in them a false sense of security (1 Tim 6:17). The individualistic view of wealth is unbiblical; a communal view of it is encouraged. Wealth is like manna that falls from heaven and belongs not to the one who gathers it but to God. It is the responsibility of the gatherer to ensure that those who did not have a chance to gather it also get a share of the manna. The ideal situation, which we must strive for, is that there be no poor people in our communities. However, because there are still many poor among us then it is imperative for us to open our hands to them and share what we have been given with them. This thought is in line with Moses's exhortation to the Israelites to be generous towards the poor (Deut 15:7–11). In Matthew 6, Jesus also teaches the need to be generous towards the needy. God has abundant resources for all but, in most cases, these resources are found in the hands of a few people. Jesus requires that we consider ourselves as stewards of God's possessions and as responsible to God for the things he has entrusted to us. Jesus requires that Christians share their resources from a pure heart rather than a legalistic mindset, as a way of alleviating poverty. This kind of giving is reflected by a willingness and readiness to help others with our resources through generous giving. Ultimately, it is not equality that we hope to achieve but that everyone will have what is enough for life.

There are two lords for everyone, mammon and God. The two cannot be served simultaneously, because no slave can belong legitimately to two masters at the same time. Whichever of the two masters one submits to determines their attitude towards riches. The one who serves God has their disposition towards generosity and sharing their material goods with the needy. On the other hand, the person who serves mammon has their disposition towards the selfish accumulation of wealth, and an inevitable meanness towards the needy.

The Kingdom of Heaven and His Righteousness

Whereas our Old Testament passages use laws and judgment to rebuke the rich and rulers who oppress the poor, Jesus teaches that seeking worldly possessions, material wealth, and exercise of power over others have no place in the kingdom of Heaven. In the Matthean passage, Jesus draws attention to the need to prioritize the kingdom of God and his righteousness over the pursuit of wealth. As kingdom seekers, believers are expected to exhibit a lifestyle of a distinctive value-system, ethical standards, religious devotion, and an attitude towards money and ambition that clashes with the world and nominal religion. This demand is strange to man in the twenty-first-century church which is characterized by the error conforming to worldly standards, particularly in matters of wealth.

Jesus preaches to the wealthy because, as Hoppe asserts, "people of means are at risk precisely because their social, religious, and economic circumstances can make them unresponsive to Jesus's proclamation of the kingdom."[109] Rather than tirelessly seeking wealth, which humans believe is the source of happiness, the Lord is asking us to seek first the kingdom of God and his righteousness. Many Christians, especially in Africa, seem to spend their whole lives seeking happiness and blessedness: they go round from one revival meeting to another and from one convention to another with the hope that they are going to experience a financial breakthrough. But they do not find or experience this joy because their priorities are misplaced. The passages we have looked at in this book remind us that, as Christians, our heavenly citizenship requires that we focus more on obtaining spiritual wealth than physical material riches.

Oppression, Injustice and Poverty

God is concerned about justice and right relationships among people. He created human beings as social beings responsible for ensuring the preservation of each person's dignity for the common good. According to Domeris, "Justice is understood, as so often in the ANE [Ancient Near East], as not taking advantage of the powerless, including using violent behaviour (spilling innocent blood). . . . The Hebrew says literally 'to do justice,' which has the

---

109. Hope, *Poverty, Livelihoods, and Governance*, 151.

double implication of acting justly and doing away with injustice."[110] Among the various causes of poverty, injustice, and oppression seem to receive much attention in the Scriptures. The word "oppression" in this context must be understood as the abuse of power in line with another's disadvantage.

The exegesis of Isaiah 10:1–4 brought to the fore how injustice and oppression could entrench the poor state of people. Sometimes, the wealthy use their power (social status) to oppress and exploit the poor, making them poorer. Domeris rightly points out that "Power, rather than wealth, is the major distinction between the oppressors and the oppressed, between the rich (strong) and the poor."[111] This means that the wealth of the wealthy makes them acquire power with which they treat the poor unfairly. This power allows them to formulate policies that end up legitimizing their bad deeds. His study reveals various nuances of "oppression" including to "take by extortion," "to reduce to slavery; to enslave," "to crush," and "pulverise."[112] Oppression has the effect of making the oppressed lose their human dignity and degrading them to an animal-like existence. The poor may be regarded as anything but human; oppression humiliates.

That oppression is cyclical can be inferred from Ecclesiastes 4:1. Domeris understands the repetition of the phrase "and they have no comforter" as underscoring "the absence of hope for both oppressed and oppressor, drawing both into the cycle of oppression."[113] He argues further, "Oppression, like violence, is a process in which the oppressors become trapped within their role as the oppressed oppressors who also need to be liberated, not least from their own fears."[114]

Isaiah 10:1–4 also underlines the fact that oppression involves injustice (see also Eccl 5:8). Domeris identifies three kinds of injustice, namely, injustice in the markets, for instance the use of false scales (Prov 11:1; 16:11; 20:10, 23; Hos 12:7; Amos 8:5); injustice in the courts, for instance making unjust decrees and ruling in favor of the rich because of their status (Amos 2:6c; Isa 1:23; 5:23; 10:1; 33:15; Mic 3:11), and unfair labor practices, for instance forced labor (1 Kgs 22:13; Mal 3:5).[115] Throughout history God has condemned social injustice. He continues to condemn it today.

---

110. Domeris, *Touching Heart of God*, 118, 120.
111. Domeris, 95.
112. Domeris, 96.
113. Domeris, 97.
114. Domeris, 97–98.
115. Domeris, 110–112.

God's Concern for the Poor

All four passages and the rest of Scripture show that God is a God of the poor. In most cases the poor find themselves rejected by their communities. Their conditions of life are so abhorrent that many would not like to relate with them. That poverty leads to social exclusion is evident in the text that says, "The poor are shunned even by their neighbors, but the rich have many friends" (Prov 14:20 NIV). The poor do not have the favor of the masses.

Poverty can lead one to a state where the person loses dignity as a human being. Due to poverty people become slaves, sometimes together with their whole families, and serve others for the rest of their (the poor people's) lives. Even in that situation where the poor have become social outcasts, they still bear God's image and so God still values them just like he does the well-to-do. God identifies with the poor in their repulsive existence. In the Law, God's concern for the poor is seen in the institution of the triennial tithe for the poor, the gleaning laws, and his opposition to the exploitation of the poor. The fact that God identifies with the downtrodden, who are experiencing oppression and hardship, is seen also in the Psalmist's description of God as "A father of the fatherless, a defender of widows, Is God in His Holy habitation" (68:5 NKJV). God is intimately connected to those who are vulnerable to exploitation and abuse by the powerful.

God sides with the disadvantaged when they are oppressed. "The point is rather that the poor are the first, though not the only ones, on which God's attention focuses and that, therefore, the church has no choice but to demonstrate solidarity with the poor."[116] God is the one who authenticates their struggle against poverty and orchestrates their freedom.

> He raises the poor out of the dust,
> *And* lifts the needy out of the ash heap,
> That He may seat *him* with princes –
> With the princes of His people. (Ps 113:7–8 NKJV).

God's concern for the poor is strongly articulated by the prophets. The exegesis of Isaiah 10:1–4 demonstrated God's opposition to those who take advantage of the poor, deny them injustice, or oppress them. Here, and in many other passages, justice is measured in terms of care for needy. At times, as in the case of Isaiah, the Lord visits the people who treat the poor unjustly with his wrath. Clearly, the suffering of the poor in no way escapes God's attention and scrutiny. The poor can rest assured that in their struggles and afflictions,

---

116. Bosch, *Transforming Mission*, 436.

God is with them. The social message of the prophets and the Old Testament description of the nature of a healthy community may be summarized as "Administer true justice; show mercy and compassion to one another. Do not oppress the widow or the fatherless, the foreigner or the poor. Do not plot evil against each other" (Zech 7: 9–10 NIV).

Conclusion

This chapter shows that "poverty" refers not only to lack of economic resources and having "less than enough" material goods, but also to political and legal powerlessness, oppression, and poor health. Poverty has both an individual and a communal and social dimension because the well-being of individuals and the community are closely related. Societies that exhibit justice, mercy, loyalty, and compassion can be considered wealthy compared to other poor societies that are dominated by injustice, oppression, exploitation, and disloyalty.

Extreme poverty can deprive people of their human dignity and many who experience such poverty often end up as slaves trapped in cycles that affect their, and their families, lives in the long-term. But the poor regardless of their status are bearers of God's image and are valued in his sight. He cares about the disadvantaged and the oppressed and because of this, Christians everywhere should care about the plight of the poor. Like God, we should use our resources and goods to elevate the status of the poor.

5

Prosperity Theology in Africa

The African religious landscape shows different theological approaches for understanding and alleviating poverty. The four main approaches are viewing poverty as a requirement for entering the kingdom of God, espousing the prosperity theology, living a modest life as a solution for poverty, and proper stewardship of resources as a way of tackling poverty. Of these approaches, the prosperity theology model is the most influential in Africa. But many people have questioned its appropriateness and theological foundations as a Christian approach to poverty alleviation. The controversies surrounding prosperity theology and its huge impact on Christianity in the continent make it necessary to evaluate this approach to poverty alleviation in the light of biblical, theological and cultural contexts to determine how biblically, theologically and culturally appropriate it is for Africa.

What Is Prosperity Theology?

According to Kasera the term prosperity may refer to "literal wealth, success, and honour" or an upward movement "in something desirable: the state of succeeding or flourishing, [especially] financially."[1] Paul Gifford defines prosperity theology as the belief that "God has met all the needs of human beings in the suffering and death of Christ and every Christian should now share the victory of Christ over sin, sickness and poverty" and that one can have access to these blessings through "a positive confession of faith."[2] I propose a working definition of prosperity theology as the Christian belief that material prosperity and physical health are always the will of God for every believer and

---

1. Kasera, "Biblical and Theological Examination," 25.
2. Gifford, "Prosperity Gospel in Africa," 20.

that these were accomplished by the Christ-Event and can now be activated through donations made to church leaders (a practice known as seed-sowing) and the positive confession of faith. Having outlined what prosperity theology is, I now proceed to examine how prosperity theology emerged and developed.

The Rise of the Prosperity Gospel

McConnell has shown with irrefutable scholarship that the roots of prosperity theology in all its manifestations can be traced to Kenneth Hagin.[3] While this view may not be considered as unanimous, there is consensus that he was the one who popularized what came to be termed the "word-faith" teachings. As explained below, Hagin's belief in the word-faith teachings was based on his life experience. Born with a deformed heart and an incurable blood disease, Hagin experienced ill health throughout his childhood and teenage years until he got this condition miraculously corrected at age seventeen, in August of 1934.[4] Having been healed of this chronic disease, Hagin devoted himself to preaching the word of God for three years even though he had no theological education.[5]

In 1937 Hagin decided to join the Full Gospel Tabernacle in McKinney, a Pentecostal church affiliated with the Assemblies of God, because he shared their beliefs.[6] After serving as an ordained minister of the Assemblies of God church for the next twelve years, Hagin, in 1949, joined the ranks of healing luminaries (such as William Branham, Oral Roberts, A.A. Allen, Jack Coe, T.L. Osborne, Tommy Hicks and the Northern Albertan, Lorne Fox) who worked in the United States during the fifteen years that followed the Second World War. Without making much impact in this field, Hagin transitioned to other avenues of evangelism and initiated a radio ministry in 1966.[7] In 1968, Hagin began to publish *The Word of Faith*, a monthly magazine that was highly patronized.[8] Through his activities, the word-faith theology began to attract followers. Later, Hagin launched the Rhema Bible Training Center in Tulsa

---

3. McConnell, *Promise of Health*, 1–21. Other major proponents include Fred Price, Kenneth and Gloria Copeland, John Avanzini, Charles Capps, and Benny Hinn.
4. Hagin, *Believer's Authority*, xiv.
5. McConnell, *Different Gospel*, 58.
6. Hagin, *Believer's Authority*, xix.
7. Hagin, xxix.
8. Hagin, xxx.

in 1974[9] which gave him the necessary platform to project his ideas. Hagin's word-faith theology had two principal components, namely, divine healing and God's irrevocable desire to bless every believer materially. As time went on, the second aspect of word-faith theology metamorphosed into what is known today as the prosperity theology.

The Planting of Prosperity Theology in Africa

Certain factors contributed to the planting and spread of prosperity theology in Africa. I outline some of these factors briefly below. First, in many parts of Africa (e.g. Nigeria) the introduction of this kind of teaching coincided with the emergence of the charismatic movement and the circulation of books and cassettes of foreign prosperity preachers like Oral Roberts, Kenneth Hagin, Kenneth Copeland, Reinhard Bonnke and later on Benny Hinn. Most African preachers, with the exception of a few (such as Pastor Mensah Otabil of Ghana), drew ideas from and even copied the dress code of their American counterparts. During this period, Hagin's publications such as *The Name of Jesus* (1979), *Words* (1979), *Redeemed from Poverty and Spiritual Death* (1983) and *How to Write Your Own Ticket with God* (1979) influenced the thoughts of many Africans.[10] Oral Roberts had a television program which also made prosperity preaching become popular in Africa.[11] The interactions between African Pentecostal or charismatic leaders and ideas of foreign prosperity preachers became a channel for the acceptance and spread of prosperity preaching. It also cemented the idea of prosperity preaching, which some local pastors already knew about.

The second factor has to do with the economic situation that prevailed in the continent at that time. I noted in chapter 2 that the post-independent history of many African countries was characterized by political and economic instability. The planting of prosperity theology coincided with the experience of economic hardship in many parts of the continent in the 1970s and 1980s. This made Africa fertile ground for planting the seeds of prosperity teaching. The slogan for Roberts's weekly program (Abundant Life), "Something good is going to happen to you," and Hagin's slogan, "You can have what you say," according to Emmanuel Larbi, "became sources of comfort and hope for many,

---

9. Hagin, xxv.
10. Larbi, *Pentecostalism*, 297.
11. Larbi, 297.

as people battled with the economic and social realities of the time."[12] Many Africans felt that the new teaching was the "messiah" sent to deliver them from their economic woes.

One of the foremost promoters of prosperity theology in Africa was the late Archbishop Benson Idahosa of Church of God Mission, Nigeria. His life changed dramatically in 1971 during a crusade organized by American evangelist Gordon Lindsay, in Nigeria. Idahosa received his ministerial training from the Rhema Bible College of Kenneth Hagin in Oklahoma.[13] Idahosa then returned to Nigeria and established his own Bible school and subsequently his church, the "Church of God Mission International" with its headquarters in Benin City.[14] Through his Bible school and church, Idahosa spread the prosperity ideology that he acquired from the Rhema Bible College. His "Redemption Hour" TV program was highly patronized by many Africans. His messages about wealth, health, and freedom from evil powers became very attractive to many people who in turn spread it to other believers. He encouraged the establishment of new churches to expand God's kingdom and also trained many charismatic pastors including the Archbishop Duncan Williams of the Action Faith Chapel International and Bishop Charles Agyin-Asare of Perez Chapel. His training shaped the theology of these people and then helped spread his prosperity ideas throughout the continent.

Bishop David Oyedepo who established the "Living Faith World Outreach" or "Winners' Chapel" in Lagos in 1983 also contributed to the spread of prosperity theology in Africa. The motto of his church – "I am a winner" – is found on stickers adorning cars, shops, and houses in many countries in Africa. This slogan not only attracts people who are in hardship and aspire to succeed in the future, but also those who have already succeeded in one way or the other. According to the bishop, the slogan identifies who is a Christian, meaning the Christian is born to win. He puts it this way: "It gives you an identity . . . it gives you a sense of conviction, that you are heading for something positive."[15] Oyedepo's teachings became famous through publications such as *Anointing for Breakthrough* (1992), *Breaking Financial Hardship* (1995), *Fulfilling Your Days* (1998), *Understanding Your Covenant Right* (2003), *Winning the War against Poverty* (2007), and *I Choose to Change* (2007).

---

12. Larbi, *Pentecostalism*, 297.
13. Anderson, *Introduction to Pentecostalism*, 66.
14. Anderson, 133.
15. Maier, *This House Has Fallen*, 264.

The case of South Africa is a bit different in that this theology was planted during their preindependence era. According to Ilana van Wyk, prosperity theology was planted in South Africa in the late 1970s (when the country was under colonial rule) through the activities of churches like Rhema Bible Church of televangelist Ray McCauley.[16] The impact of prosperity theology at that time was limited because of the apartheid restrictions on the movements of Blacks. However, since the country's independence in 1994, this theology has become increasingly popular as numerous pastors have moved across the length and breadth of the country to propagate it.[17]

Major Teachings of Prosperity Theology

Material Prosperity

Prosperity preachers contend that God wills the financial prosperity of every Christian and that God's favor (blessing) upon the faithful is manifested in terms of material prosperity, particularly financial assets such as personal and business success.[18] Pastor Oyedepo, for instance, declares that poverty is completely outside God's divine will for the believer.[19] He reasons as follows: "Why . . . do you think that your lack excites God? Which father is excited to see his children begging all around? Have you ever heard somebody give a testimony, saying, 'I thank God, two of my sons are beggars?'"[20] Upon this premise he declares, "Your children's children will never beg! I want you to know that the prosperity God has planned for you has nothing to do with your profession, your career or your family background."[21] Pastor Joel Osteen adds his voice, saying, "It's God's will for you [the believer] to live in prosperity instead of poverty. It's God's will for you to pay your bills and not be in debt. It's God's will for you to live in health and not in sickness all the days of your life."[22] According to these preachers any believer who lives in poverty is living outside God's will. I will later demonstrate that this view is not biblically grounded.

In a recent study on prosperity theology among neo-Pentecostals in Accra, Ghana, James Kwateng-Yeboah identified four major causes of poverty according

---

16. Van Wyk, "Look at the 'Prosperity Gospel,'" n.p.
17. Van Wyk, n.p.
18. Goliama, "Gospel of Prosperity," 143.
19. Oyedepo, *Understanding Financial Prosperity*, 7.
20. Oyedepo, 7.
21. Oyedepo, 7.
22. Osteen, *Your Best Life Now*, 41.

to neo-Pentecostal theology, namely, supernatural causes, witches, demons, and generational curses.[23] His study also identified laziness, institutional failure, corruption and poor parenting as minor causes of poverty.[24] Though the study was conducted in neo-Pentecostal churches in Ghana, similar views are likely to found in Pentecostal and newer prophetic movements and other countries in the continent. Against this backdrop, Pentecostal or charismatic preachers believe that the solution to poverty in Africa lies in the breaking the power of the spiritual forces that hinder people's progress in life.

Prosperity preachers cite a number of Scriptures to support their position on material prosperity. For example, they say that God's promise of generosity to Abram (Gen 12:1–3) and its fulfilment (Gen 13:2) is available for every believing Christian on earth today. They deduce from Galatians 3:13–14, 29 that the death of Christ on the cross has made believers heirs of the Abrahamic covenant with its promises of wealth and health. Pastor Mensah Otabil contends that, it is simply not possible "for the person that operates under the blessing of Abraham" to get poorer.[25] Thus, each believer has the ability to access this blessing, claim it, and possess it. Archbishop Nicholas Duncan-Williams argues that "God never planned for (us) or any of mankind to have sickness, fear, inferiority, defeat or failure."[26] He refers to Genesis 1:29–30 and adds "[t]he Word of God is a tree of life that will produce riches, honor, promotion and joy."[27] He also connects the *imago Dei* (Gen 1:26), the fact that humans were created in the image of God, to material success.[28]

Prosperity preachers also deduce the promise of material success from Jesus's promise of abundant life (John 10:10), the freedom he promises his disciples (John 8:31–32), Paul's assertion that Jesus became poor so that we may be rich (2 Cor 8:9), James's encouragement to his audience that they should ask freely from God (Jas 4:2), and John's prayer for Gaius (3 John 2).

Faith Healing

Salvation in the hermeneutic and praxis of prosperity preachers is expected to yield a visible transformative and empowering effect not only in terms of the material wealth but also in terms of the physical healing of believers. Bowler

---

23. Kwateng-Yeboah, "Re-appraisal of Prosperity Gospel," 45.
24. Kwateng-Yeboah, 49.
25. Otabil, *Beyond Rivers of Ethiopia*, 24.
26. Duncan-Williams, *You Are Destined to Succeed*, 58 and 102.
27. Duncan-Williams, 58.
28. Duncan-Williams, 58 and102.

describes faith as "a force that reaches through the boundaries of materiality and into the spiritual realm, as if plucking objects from there and drawing them back into space and time" and by this she means, faith is the agent that makes what one wants become real in the real world, "transcending the separation between two universes for the sake of each believer."[29]

Like poverty, ill health, according to prosperity preachers, is the work of the devil. No illness occurs in accordance with the will of God: "It is the plan of our Father God in His great love and His great mercy that no believer should ever be sick, that every believer should live his full life span down here on earth and that every believer should finally just fall asleep in Jesus," says Hagin.[30] Based on this view, most faith healers do not accept even the nonobservance of basic personal hygiene as a legitimate cause of ailments.[31] Faith healers also "find it difficult to accept medical science intervention in dealing with the problem of ailment as an example of God's providential goodness."[32] Their belief is that all diseases have spiritual antecedents and are therefore best cured through exorcism.

Based on Isaiah 53:5, faith healers teach that the atonement of Christ brought physical healing to each believer. According to Copeland, "the basic principle of the Christian life is to know that God put our sin, sickness, disease, sorrow, grief, poverty on Jesus at Calvary."[33] Other texts considered as supporting faith healing include James 5:13–18 and 3 John 2. This understanding of these texts, as I demonstrate later, is not in line with the broader teaching of Scripture.

"Sowing Seeds" of Prosperity

Prosperity preachers contend that the believer's right to enjoy God's blessing is enacted through the sowing of "seeds of faith" to a spiritual leader who then reveals God's plan for the giver's prosperity to them.[34] To sow seeds of faith, according to prosperity teachers, is the act of making financial donations or other gifts to church leaders, thereby sowing seeds in their ministry. This is quite different from the act of telling people about Christ which is taught as seed-sowing in the parable of the Sower (see Mark 4:1–20). Prosperity preachers urge their disciples to give generously to their church in order to receive

---

29. Bowler, *History of American Prosperity*, 141.
30. Hagin, *Seven Things*, 21.
31. Amevenku, "Faith Healing," 87.
32. Amevenku, 87.
33. As cited by Lavender, *Are You Full Gospel*, 88.
34. Okosun, "Poverty, Illiteracy," 83.

abundantly. Oyedepo contends that God's covenant with believers through (generous) giving bestows on the giver the right to economic empowerment.[35] He argues further that sacrificial giving is the only way to obtain "enduring wealth, as every other means of acquiring riches is time-tagged."[36]

Prosperity preachers use the analogy of sowing and reaping in 2 Corinthians 9:6–11 (cf. Luke 6:38) to emphasize faithful and generous giving. On this, Bishop Dag Heward-Mills writes, "prosperity in its basic form consists of someone sowing a seed and later harvesting the returns."[37] The mathematical principle behind the practice of "sowing and reaping" is deducible from the following quote by Copeland (based on Mark 10:29–30): "You can give $1 for the Gospel's sake and $100 belongs to you; give $10 and receive $1000; give $1000 and receive $100,000."[38] Here, one finds a hundredfold financial return in one's giving, aside from other forms of blessings, such as good health. Meyer also supports the hundredfold material returns on the believer's giving. She says, "Whatever you give up now will come back to you one-hundred-fold in this lifetime (Mark 10:29–30). If you want to have everything God has for you, then I encourage you to ask Him to help you live generously."[39] Otabil states it this way: "God blesses us according to our deposits. If you have not deposited anything, you have no right to ask for anything."[40] He continues, "People think that you should give so that the Church has money. No. The main purpose is that you enter into a Covenant" with God so that he "will meet all your needs."[41] This kind of message with a "No giving, no material blessing" motif, fuels people's desire to donate huge sums of money to the church in order to have abundant wealth in return.

Tithing is a very big issue for prosperity preachers. An African US-based prosperity preacher is quoted to have ridiculed non-tithing members of his church, that they are "useless in the vineyard!"[42] Most pastors of this kind use Malachi 3 as their basis to threaten their followers with curses for failure to tithe "faithfully." For Adeboye tithe-paying is the believer's passport to heaven. He writes, "Anybody who is not paying his or her tithe is not going to heaven.

---

35. Oyedepo, *Possessing your Possession*, 75.
36. Oyedepo, 76.
37. Heward-Mills, *Why Non-Tithing Christians*, 1.
38. As cited by Cotterell, *Prosperity Theology*.
39. Joyce Meyer, "Living in Financial Freedom," https://joycemeyer.org/everydayanswers/ea-teachings/living-in-financial-freedom, accessed 19 May 2020.
40. Gifford, *African Christianity*, 80.
41. As cited in Gifford, 80.
42. Amevenku and Boaheng, *Tithing*, 26.

Some people have taught you that if you do not pay your tithes, God will not give you blessings. This is true, but a little more serious, you do not pay your tithes, and you do not go to heaven."[43] Tithing then, as prosperity preachers assume, is both the key to material prosperity and the passport to heaven.

The principle of sowing and reaping applies to tithing just as it applies to other forms of giving. Heward-Mills contends, "[n]ot paying your tithes separates you from [the] most basic principle of sowing and reaping. When you do not pay your tithes, you harm your finances because you take away the foundations of your prosperity."[44] Heward-Mills further argues that though hard work is a good step towards a successful life, without fulfilling the tithing obligation one's hard work may be in vain because the wealth of non-tithers is constantly eaten by devourers.[45] With such teachings people are made to calculate ten percent of their income and give to the church with the expectation that they will receive abundantly in return.

Positive Confession of Faith

Prosperity preachers assert that to "name it and claim it" one has to exercise a positive confession of faith.[46] They further teach that prayer becomes efficacious only when it is said appropriately through faith because "faith begins with desire and when it is confessed then it is substantiated."[47] Prosperity preachers encourage their members to have positive thinking about themselves and their lives. The law of "positive confession" is based on the fact that humans, being God's image bearers, have dominion over creation (see Gen 1:26–28). Positive confession is the means by which believers can exercise this dominion over both their soul and the environment. It involves having positive thoughts about one's self and all aspects of their life. This point of view is evident in the following quote by Osteen: "God wants us to have healthy, positive self-images, to see ourselves as priceless treasures. He wants us to feel good about ourselves . . . God sees you as a champion . . . He regards you as a strong, courageous, successful, overcoming person."[48] This sounds very positive and uplifting to the human ego; yet, it is not supported by the overall teaching of the Bible.

---

43. Adeboye, *Behold He Cometh*, 44.
44. Heward-Mills, *Why Non-Tithing Christians*, 1.
45. Heward-Mills, 1–5.
46. Goliama, "The Gospel of Prosperity," 145.
47. Goliama, 145.
48. Osteen, *Your Best Life Now*, 57–58.

Based on their reading of Romans 10:8, prosperity theology preachers contend that the "spoken word has power to bring desire into space-time existence."[49] Therefore, once a person says something and believes it is true, they can claim it. Osteen writes, "God works by faith. You must believe first, and then you'll receive . . . We receive what we believe. Unfortunately, this principle works as strongly in the negative as it does in the positive."[50] He continues, "God will help you, but you cast the deciding vote . . . [we must] get into agreement with God . . . It's our faith that activates the power of God."

Positive confession of faith is also based on the prosperity theology's reading of Mark 11: 22–24. From verse 22, prosperity preachers exhort their followers to "have the faith of God."[51] It is taught that, with the faith which God used in creating the universe out of nothing, the believer can also speak and it will manifest. Based on this teaching Hagin contends that "It is unscriptural to pray, 'If it is the will of God'" because "When you put an 'if' in your prayer, you are praying in doubt."[52] All the believer needs to do is to profess what they desire with faith and possess it, to name it by faith and claim it.

Factors that Sustain Prosperity Theology in Africa

The prosperity theology appeals to many people because of economics reasons. Chapter 2 brought to the fore Africa's economic difficulties including a high rate of unemployment, high dependency ratio, low living standards, and lack of social amenities, that make prosperity theology appealing to its people. Many Africans are struggling day in, day out to get over their predicaments and most of them would do anything to solve their economic problems, especially if the remedy is offered by a minister of the gospel because, as I noted in chapter 1, the African worldview is intensively and pervasively religious.

Prosperity preachers usually buttress their sermons with testimonies to make them practical and real. A preacher may cite their personal material acquisition as an example to show the audience how the principle of sowing and reaping has worked in their life.[53] Testimonies from members are also given either in the course of the sermon or at a different time. Asamoah-Gyadu cites the case of a woman who pledged five hundred cedis at Action Chapel's

---

49. Goliama, "The Gospel of Prosperity," 145.
50. Osteen, *Your Best Life Now*, 33, 72, 74, and 306.
51. Morris and Lioy, "Historical and Theological Framework," 103.
52. As cited by Morris and Lioy, 103.
53. Asamoah-Gyadu, *Sighs and Signs*, 163.

"Jericho Hour" and later came back with the testimony of her returns including: receiving a thousand cedis; spending a holiday in Cape Town, South Africa; going back to law school and passing an examination in which more than half of her mates failed and were withdrawn; having the opportunity to study in the United Kingdom; having twenty-five thousand dollars as a donation to start a nongovernmental organization (NGO); and receiving a divine promise of forty thousand dollars in two months' time.[54]

The principles of financial freedom preached, coupled with the testimonies from people claiming to have experienced the freedom preached, gives others (especially the underprivileged) the belief that once they give generously, their returns will be overwhelming. Therefore, in my opinion, though this theology prevails in most parts of the world, as long as poverty remains rooted in Africa, prosperity theology is likely to have an increasing number of adherents because of its ideology which appeals to the poor. The prosperity preachers are likely to continue finding opportunities for exploiting the desperate life situations of the poor to offer them an ineffective approach of dealing with poverty.

The next reason for the high patronage of prosperity theology among Africans is its appeal to emotion. Emotionalism is very appealing to Africans because it touches the very heart of the traditional religious roots of the African.[55] In prosperity-preaching churches, emotion serves as a test for truth: as people are made to feel emotionally good, "they deduce that what they are busy with is true, for if it were wrong, they would not have felt good in the first place."[56]

At a church service, someone may be so enthused by a sermon about principles of prosperity that they end up jumping and shouting, "I receive it," "I claim it," or "preach on" as a way of responding to the message being preached. Others may be touched so much that they shed tears of joy. Still others may walk to the front and lie on the floor to show how the message has touched their heart, or walk to the preacher and touch their feet or throw money on the ground in response to the sermon. The emotional effect in prosperity-preaching churches attracts many people because they feel good at church services.

Yet many Africans follow the prosperity theology because of spiritual reasons. Indigenous African religiosity and spirituality cherish the power of a

---

54. Asamoah-Gyadu, *Contemporary Pentecostal Christianity*, 93.
55. Asamoah-Gyadu.
56. Kasera, "Biblical and Theological Examination," 65.

spoken word in shaping social relations.⁵⁷ Once the word has been expressed, verbally or through gestures or merely by intention, then it can create or destroy. The spirituality proclaimed by prosperity teachers puts human beings on a supernatural platform. For Oyedepo, Psalm 82:6 "is the basis for the supernatural: you are no longer human, but superhuman. You are a son of God, so you are a god."⁵⁸ This spiritual upliftment preached by prosperity theologians makes the movement attractive to its adherents because people feel that they are on top of all circumstances of their lives. No longer do they have to wait upon God but they can demand of God what they desire and they can call upon any circumstance to change in their favor. However, such a teaching, though popular, has no biblical warrant.

Prosperity theology also thrives in Africa because it promises to provide good health to its adherents. Freedom from evil powers is very important because many Africans maintain that every challenge in life is the work of the devil, be it witchcraft, ancestral curses, or other problems. This is portrayed in the Akan saying "If you pull a rope and it does not come then something is holding it." African Christians expect healing to accompany their salvation experience: "healing and deliverance provide the ritual context for articulating a response to the inevitable shortfalls existing in the 'redemptive uplift' expected to accompany new life in Christ."⁵⁹ The deliverance ministry is therefore required to expel any of these powers that work against people's well-being.

Two kinds of deliverance may be identified in contemporary African Christianity, namely, personal deliverance which is administered to an individual by deliverance worker(s) or by the person through specific directions given by a spiritual leader, and collective deliverance which usually happens to a group of people at a deliverance service.⁶⁰ Prophetic directions towards deliverance take various forms. People may be asked to repeat certain words after a spiritual leader and then clap while praying with the belief that the clapping will send weapons to the spirits affecting their lives.⁶¹ After they have been blessed by a spiritual leader, liturgical substances such as anointing oil, soap, stickers, calendars, armbands, pomades, handkerchiefs, and holy water are believed to have potency in exorcising demons. This is what prosperity preachers teach, not what the Bible teaches. The Bible gives evidence of the use

---

57. Kasera, 66–68.
58. See Kasera, "Biblical and Theological Examination," 67.
59. Asamoah-Gyadu, *African Charismatics*, 164.
60. Ampong and Benyah, "Imposition of Hands," 91.
61. Ampong and Benyah, 91.

of liturgical objects in healing and deliverance; however, it does not consider any of these as the source of the power for healing and deliverance.

Quite recently, a pastor requested that his congregation bring their underwear to him to burn at night as part of the process of cleansing them and breaking any force that might be working against their well-being.[62] These and other exercises geared towards breaking the power of the devil against people's success are very welcoming to most underprivileged Africans who believe or have been made to think that the solution to their plight is their deliverance from the dominion of evil powers.

Prosperity theology is widespread because of ignorance and the lack of critical thinking on the part of many of its adherents.[63] Even though the Christian faith is firmly planted in Africa, most Christians have poor knowledge of the Bible and how to interpret it correctly. It is a common practice for believers to attend church on Sundays and listen to their pastor's sermon, which they usually take in hook, line, and sinker. Even among the clergy, there are many who are parroting other people's theology, especially in matters whose understanding requires critical and intellectual analyses. Many people want "cheap theology," already cooked and ready for consumption.

In such an environment, the popularity of one's teaching becomes a yardstick for its authenticity. Most prosperity preachers have their own TV and radio stations through which their teachings spread easily and appear to the ignorant as "authentic" doctrine. More so, many adherents of prosperity theology refuse to assess critically the teachings and practices that their leaders encourage them to consider. It seems people are made to believe that critical thinking cannot be applied to matters of religion and so people involve themselves in many unreasonable acts all in the name of Christianity. This state of affairs has made the work of prosperity preachers a relatively simple and easy task as their teachings are easily accepted because of their popularity.[64]

---

62. M. Quarshie, "'Angel' Obinim sets his congregation's underwear ablaze as part of deliverance," https://yen.com.gh/101014-angel-obinim-sets-congregations-underwear-ablaze-part-deliverance.html.

63. Temitope, "Prosperity Gospel Preaching," 317.

64. Temitope, 317.

Critique of Prosperity Theology
On Personal, Societal and National Development

Prosperity-preaching churches contribute their quota to the economic development of the nation through the provision of amenities such as microfinance companies, lodging facilities, portable drinking water, and road networks.[65] The operations of these and other facilities owned by prosperity-preaching churches create employment for many people and hence contribute to a reduction of Africa's unemployment rate. It is interesting to note, however, that some prosperity-preaching churches seek aid from foreign donors to fund some of the developmental projects they undertake.[66] The lives of many people have improved through these means. The nation also receives revenue (through, for instance, taxation) from these facilities for national development.

In addition, prosperity preachers encourage entrepreneurship.[67] Some prosperity preachers organize entrepreneurial workshops for people whereby lectures on topics such as job creation, writing a business proposal, seeking financial assistance, among others, are given. To help young entrepreneurs start their own enterprises, financial assistance (in the form of loan or a gift) is given to members. Through this work, many people have acquired financial freedom and have employed others. One adherent of prosperity theology stated (in an interview) that she became successful through prophetic guidance and working capital received from her pastor.[68]

Further, some prosperity preachers make donations to institutions such as prisons, orphanages, schools and others. Gifford records that the NGO Central aid of the International Central Gospel Church (ICGC, Ghana) has, since the 1990s, "been assisting good causes—for a cardio-thoracic unit, the physically handicapped, breast cancer, the blind and . . . the *Trokosi* women."[69] These donations not only ease the plight of the people in these institutions, but also make it possible for these institutions to have additional funds to attend to other pressing needs. More so, there are churches that offer free medical screening, diagnosis and treatment of ailment for their members or chosen communities. Certainly, by attending to the health needs of the community prosperity theology is contributing to people's socioeconomic development.

The contribution of prosperity preachers in the education sector is also very commendable. Many prosperity preaching churches have established

---

65. Gifford, *Ghana's New Christianity*.
66. Kwateng-Yeboah, "Re-appraisal of Prosperity Gospel," 82.
67. Kwateng-Yeboah, 84.
68. Kwateng-Yeboah, 85.
69. Gifford, *Ghana's New Christianity*, 115.

educational institutions in order to make education accessible to as many people as possible. These institutions are not established to just educate people but also to raise people of integrity and character who can take up leadership roles in the future. In most of these schools, the mode of payment of fees and other charges is flexible allowing the poor to complete their education. Some of these education institutions and the churches that establish them buy school uniforms for, and provide meals and housing to, underprivileged students.

Some churches also award scholarships. Pastor Otabil, for instance, has instituted a nondiscriminatory scholarship scheme to help gifted but needy students in secondary, technical, and vocational institutions in Ghana. According to Gifford, this scheme offered scholarships totaling 200 million cedis to about 500 gifted but needy students from the 1990s to the 2000s. In Africa, poverty is a major barrier to education. Therefore, by offering scholarships to needy students, the ICGC founder is helping the nation reduce illiteracy and improve people's living standards, which ultimately contributes to national development.

Despite these positive contributions to socioeconomic development, there are flaws in the attempts by prosperity teachers to improve people's living standards. In many cases these enterprises and initiatives fail to identify and deal with certain causes of poverty such as environmental destruction, poor agricultural practices, poor road networks, bad government policies, corruption and mismanagement of funds, expensive funerals, and large family sizes, which are major causes of poverty in Africa. They also do not address other causes of poverty such as injustice and oppression by the wealthy that can entrench the poor state of people. Often, the wealthy use their power (social status) to oppress and exploit the poor, making them poorer.

Prosperity preachers overemphasize the evil causes of poverty so much so that they tend to pay virtually no attention to economic theories or factors that contribute to poverty. The Lausanne Group rightly observes that factors such as social injustice, exploitation, oppression, and unjust trade practices that have been identified as causes of poverty are of no or little importance to prosperity preachers.[70] The result of this kind of theology is the rise in use of imprecatory prayers in contemporary African Christianity. Every believer has an imaginary enemy who is considered as the agent of the devil working against their material and health progress.[71] Consequently, people spend countless hours of productive time at prayer centers, leaving their work unattended to

---

70. Lausanne Theology Working Group, "Statement on Prosperity Gospel."
71. Amevenku and Boaheng, "Use of Imprecatory Prayers," 88–89.

with the hope that their lives will improve through some miraculous act of God. Unless prosperity preachers interrogate the structural injustice that causes poverty in Africa and formulate a model to deal with it, their fight against poverty will not achieve much success. This point, however, does not take away the fact that prosperity theology contributes positively to the socioeconomic well-being of some of its followers and countries in general. Rather, it means that the efficiency of prosperity theology towards poverty alleviation would be enhanced if prosperity teachers tackle causes such as corruption and mismanagement of state resources, structural injustice, and others.

In addition, prosperity theology has the tendency of impoverishing some of its adherents, despite the economic progress it offers to others.[72] As members are made to believe that their returns will be a hundred times their giving, some people give excessively. People may even go for bank loans to support their church with the hope of reaping a hundredfold. People may also donate just to prevent themselves from being considered as people of weak faith because their pastors teach that if one has faith and sows, they will receive material gain. Eventually when the expected return does not come, the person involved needs to pay the bank loan with other resources to be gathered. This may lead to falling into debt and bankruptcy.

Furthermore, prosperity theology widens the economic gap between poor church members and their spiritual leader.[73] We find these pastors having so much wealth in stock in churches where some members cannot afford three square meals a day. Kwateng-Yeboah gives this report about a certain prosperity preaching church in Accra: "Comparatively, while the prophet seems enriched by receiving money from believers as seed sowing, the majority of the church members experience insignificant change in their economic conditions."[74] Prosperity preachers afford the latest car, or any fashionable thing and surround themselves with security agents whose salaries are paid through the offering of the poor members.

On Promoting a Positive Mindset

A careful assessment of prosperity preachers and their messages shows that some of them promote a positive mindset that addresses inferiority complexes, non-achievement and backwardness in Africa. Such pastors combine prosperity

---

72. Kasera, "Biblical and Theological Examination," 119.
73. Asamoah-Gyadu, *Sighs and Signs*, 163–176.
74. Kwateng-Yeboah, "Re-appraisal of Prosperity Gospel," 87.

theology with Afrocentric nationalism and professionalism. Pastor Otabil of the ICGC belongs to this category. Otabil differs from other prosperity preachers in that he does not consider evil spirits, curses and the like as major causes of poverty. For Otabil, irresponsible living, ignorance, lack of creativity, and others are the major causes of poverty. He is of the view that God has created humans in his image and that we must be creative and hard-working like God in order to succeed. He does not see the solution to poverty in anointing oil, healing and deliverance, giving and miracles. In this sense, Otabil is more in line with what wider Christian theology teaches.

Otabil identifies two factors that keeps Africans poor: their inferiority complex and those cultural practices that militate against socioeconomic progress.[75] Otabil's *Beyond the Rivers of Ethiopia* corrects the misconception that Black people are cursed and hence not part of God's plan of salvation.[76] He considers the Western perception that Africans are poor because we are descendants of Canaan who was cursed by Noah, as a means of holding back Black people. In his view, Whites have distorted the Bible to arrive at such a conclusion. Referring to Genesis 9:25, he asks, "Is the Black race cursed?" He answers, "No, Ham was blessed" (Gen 9:1). The contention is that God blessed Noah and his sons (Gen 9:1) and so Ham carries that blessing. He argues further that Noah knew that once God had blessed Ham already, he could not curse Ham; that is the reason why he cursed Canaan, the yet-to-be-born son of Ham (Gen 9:25).

The principle that the one who God has blessed cannot be cursed by anyone is biblical (cf. Num 23:20). Otabil traces the Black race to Cush, the son of Ham, and contends that Cush was never cursed but received a double blessing as the firstborn (see Gen 9:25 and 10:6).[77] For Otabil, the truth must be told that Blacks are not cursed; neither are they descendants of Canaan.[78] Otabil then makes a case for the presence and impact of Black (African) personalities in God's salvific history for mankind. He cites a number of Black people, or people who were brought up on African soil, who played significant roles in God's plan in human history to advance his argument. For example, he says, Moses, the person God used in delivering his people from Egypt, was brought up in Egypt and was well versed in Egyptian civilization (Acts 7:22). Otabil then urges Blacks to rediscover their role and place in God's salvific history,

---

75. Goliama, "Gospel of Prosperity," 320.
76. I have gleaned what follows from Otabil, *Beyond Rivers of Ethiopia*, 16–80.
77. Otabil, *Beyond Rivers of Ethiopia*, 38.
78. Otabil, 10.

consider themselves as central to this plan, and do away with any mindset that hinders their economic development. For Otabil, without a liberation of the African mind, there can be no socioeconomic improvement: "We have to break these mental barriers to development."[79] Based on this assumption, he challenges Blacks to "take control of their own churches, and stop subscribing to [W]hite stereotypes of [B]lacks".[80]

At the same time, prosperity theology has the potential of having negative psychological effects on the poor, though we have also established earlier that it is a theology which is very welcoming to the poor. In any given prosperity-preaching church there may exist two classes of Christians, the first group made up of those of little or no faith evident in their persistent state of poverty and the second those with sufficient faith demonstrated by their material success.[81] That is to say, the poor are seen as either tight fisted or having little faith. If so, then they are to blame for their plight. This dichotomy eventually leads to a situation whereby the poor become disappointed because their lack of prosperity is seen as their own fault; consequently the poor are likely to think that God has "cursed or neglected" them.[82] The second group may feel proud because they may think that it is through their own efforts that they have expressed faith in God to deserve his material blessings, a thought which Deuteronomy 8:17 prohibits.

Since prosperity preachers keep on telling their congregation that the principles of prosperity ought to work for everyone, the materially poor are sometimes overtaken by feelings of failure and guilt for not exercising appropriate faith to succeed.[83] As the Lausanne Group observes, prosperity theology tends to victimize the poor by making them feel accountable for their penury, while at the same time failing to deal with the real causes of poverty.[84] This psychological anomaly and the inferiority complex that may result from this condition, demotivates people who are sincerely and eagerly working towards escaping the grip of poverty.

---

79. Otabil, 72.
80. Otabil, 87.
81. Kasera, "Biblical and Theological Examination," 118.
82. Asamoah-Gyadu, *Sighs and Signs*, 176.
83. Kasera, "Biblical and Theological Examination," 118.
84. Lausanne Theology Working Group, "Statement on Prosperity Gospel."

On Cultural Transformation

Some prosperity preachers promote positive transformations in the African culture. Otabil, for instance, is of the view that old, antiquated, unusable, unworkable traditions in African societies also contribute to the pain and suffering in the continent. He argues that structural adjustment does not bring as much change as "cultural understanding adjustment".[85] In this context, one may understand structural adjustment as economic measures that a country must put in place to qualify for foreign loans. Otabil further argues that Africa is underdeveloped because of the failure by Africans to modify some of their cultural practices.[86] He acknowledges the positive values in African traditions but opposes those that tend to dehumanize people, and fight against economic and spiritual progress. Otabil labels such "cultural strongholds".[87]

Otabil identifies inferiority complex as a major stronghold that prevents Africans from discovering their own greatness.[88] Another stronghold is tribalism.[89] Tribalism leads people to fight about their traditions and interests which eventually leads to loss of lives and underdevelopment. It also breeds ethnocentrism and makes people treat those of other tribes unfairly. Cultural stagnation, that is, living by the same old method even when time changes demand a change in way of life, is another stronghold.[90] For example, a twenty-first century country that still relies on rainfall for its agricultural activities or relies on labor-intensive methods of production rather than using machines is bound to remain underdeveloped. Another stronghold comprises fetishism and idolatry which is rooted in the African Traditional Religion. Otabil argues that these cannot bring about development; hard work can.[91]

A "village mentality" is another stronghold that, according to Otabil, hinders development.[92] He opines that every society in the world started as a village and so there is nothing wrong with having villages in Africa or elsewhere.[93] However, once villages have turned into towns and cities or once people have migrated from villages to cities, they must live as a people in

---

85. Otabil as cited in De Witte, *Spirit Media*, 109.
86. As cited in De Witte, 109.
87. Otabil as cited in Gifford, *Ghana's New Christianity*, 126.
88. Gifford, 126.
89. Gifford, 126.
90. Gifford, *Ghana's New Christianity*, 127.
91. As cited in Gifford, 127.
92. As cited in Gifford, 127.
93. Otabil cited in Gifford, 128.

the city and not as if they were still in the village. Another stronghold is bad leadership, a challenge to most African countries.[94] Otabil contends that leaders have the responsibility of making sure that everyone gets a fair share of the nation's resources.[95] If leaders do otherwise, then people are bound to suffer. For Otabil, a good leader is a servant, not a dictator.[96] It therefore follows that leaders can contribute to the socioeconomic development of the country through selfless and dedicated service.

The final stronghold, according to Otabil, is apathy.[97] Otabil calls his audience to stand against what is wrong and not sit unconcerned. People must be bold to speak against how leaders care less about the plight of the populace.[98] Otabil also notes that some people wrongly assume that they were created as poor people and based on this assumption fail to work hard to improve their lives.[99] In all, Otabil calls upon Africans to design a new roadmap for the journey to socioeconomic development. By these teachings, Otabil aims to emancipate his audience from an inferiority complex and cultural practices that hinder their socioeconomic progress.

On Church Growth

Through its great emphasis on pneumatological soteriology, prosperity theology has contributed to the rapid numerical growth of Christianity in Africa. The reasons for this observation are not far-fetched. First, prosperity preachers tap into African religiosity and spirituality to contextualize Christianity for Africans and make them feel at home during worship services.[100] Second, the healing and deliverance ministry of Pentecostal has solved health and spiritual as well as financial problems of many people. Prosperity theology has shown that God's material and physical care and provision for his people are very real aspects of his love toward us, because in the Bible we have so many instances of God making his faithful prosper. Pentecostals are also mission-minded and so they tend to be aggressive in their task of evangelism, the result of which is the winning of souls, while older churches do not evangelize or do not do so

---

94. Otabil cited in Gifford, 128.
95. As cited in Gifford, 129.
96. As cited in Gifford, 128.
97. As cited in Gifford, 129.
98. Otabil cited in Gifford, 129.
99. As cited in Gifford, *Ghana's New Christianity*, 129.
100. Asamoah-Gyadu, *Contemporary Pentecostal Christianity*.

effectively.[101] In addition, prosperity preachers usually organize large crusades and revival meetings which may result in soul winning. The huge donations of adherents of prosperity theology to their churches make it possible for churches to pay salaries of pastors on time, purchase modern equipment for services, propagate the gospel through the electronic media and establish good welfare packages for members; all of which tend to attract people to the church.[102]

On Wealth and Its Accumulation

According to the teachings of the Bible, riches are gifts from God to his people (Deut 8:11–18; Eccl 5:19; Hos 2:8).[103] Wealth is not inherently evil; it may become an evil thing depending on one's use of it. On the other hand, poverty is also not necessarily a virtue in itself. God is the source of wealth and all other good things. In the exegesis of Deuteronomy 15:1–11 earlier, we came across God's promise to bless his people abundantly such that they will have no poor among them and lend to rather than borrow from other nations. Throughout the Old Testament there are many other Scriptures (e.g. Deut 28–30) that are clear that material possessions may be a sign of God's blessings. God's promises of abundant wealth are, however, predicated on faithful obedience to his word (Deut 15:4–5). But this does not mean that the poor person is under God's curse or that the wealth of every person comes from God. Some people acquire wealth through evil means, such as ritual money. People can also be poor for God's own purpose (for example Job). Therefore, the mere fact that one is poor or rich does not necessarily indicate their status before God.

The exegesis touched on wealth accumulation. Both the Sabbath economy of Deuteronomy 15:1–11 (cf. Exod 16) and Jesus's kingdom ethics in Matthew 6:19–34 diametrically oppose the hoarding of material goods. In the Sabbath economy, God taught his people that he is the primary provider of life's resources.

In Matthew 6:19–34, Jesus draws our attention to the fact that life characterized by hoarding of material things cannot take one into the kingdom of God because kingdom living requires that each citizen shares what they have been given with others. Rather than accumulating wealth we ought to use it to ease the financial burdens of others. Both passages underscore the fact that

---

101. Asamoah-Gyadu.
102. Asamoah-Gyadu, *Sighs and Signs*, 165–166.
103. God blessed many biblical characters with wealth, including Abram (Gen 13:1–2); Isaac (Gen 26:12–13), and Solomon (2 Chron 9:13–22).

God has abundant resources for the world, but people's materialistic behavior and the hoarding of goods for themselves lead to scarcity.

Wealth accumulation should be avoided for at least three reasons. First, accumulation of wealth erects barriers and leads to pride and envy which sets a person apart from others. This happens because it is common for people to forget their roots after they have "made it" in life and are now living comfortably. Second, (accumulated) wealth threatens one's devotion to God (Matt 6:24). Third, wealth accumulation leads to selfishness and exploitation of others as the rich seek to maintain their wealth mostly by exploiting the poor and vulnerable.

The dangers of wealth and its accumulation (as I demonstrate below) are rarely included in the teachings of prosperity theology. Prosperity theology promotes a spirit of materialism at the expense of spirituality. Teachers of prosperity theology teach accumulation of wealth rather than sharing of resources with the underprivileged.[104] Prosperity theology fails to promote a sharing of resources because the context within which it was originally formulated (in the West) holds an individualistic, rather than a communal, view of life. The materialistic nature of prosperity theology makes its adherents so preoccupied by money and wealth that their focus in life becomes the accumulation of wealth.

The members follow the examples of their materialistic-minded pastors. Gone are the days when pastors adopted a detached and very moderate lifestyle.[105] In those days, minister toiled selflessly and wore themselves out for their church members at the expense of their own personal material gain and comfort.[106] Today, instead of living modestly, prosperity preachers live luxuriously and support their lifestyles with donations from the flock.[107] I do not see anything wrong with church members helping the pastor to improve their standard of living. The problem, however, as Asamoah-Gyadu notes, is that many of these pastors "take things far beyond merely making pastors comfortable" to hoarding of material goods.[108]

Many contemporary prosperity preachers live flamboyantly, evident in their outfits, residential facilities, electronic gadgets (like phones, iPads, laptop computers), and vehicles, among other things. The resultant effect of the

---

104. Goliama, "Gospel of Prosperity," 336.
105. Asamoah-Gyadu, *Sighs and Signs*, 165.
106. Asamoah-Gyadu, 164–165.
107. Asamoah-Gyadu, 165.
108. Asamoah-Gyadu, 165.

materialistic lifestyle of prosperity preachers is unhealthy competition among themselves or among their wealthy followers.[109] Some prosperity preachers constantly use their material wealth, the success of their spouses and children, and other personal gain as illustrations of success and God's blessing in their sermons. Some even go to the extent of filming their wealth and showing it on TV. While there is nothing wrong with testifying about God's goodness, these preachers overdo it and eventually use such sermon illustrations to show off or to brag about their wealth. By promoting the accumulation of wealth, prosperity theology threatens the Christian values of contentment, kindness, and charity. The writer of Hebrew exhorts his readers, "Keep your lives free from the love of money, and be content with what you have; for he has said, 'I will never leave you or forsake you'" (13:5). Jesus prohibited the love of money when he told his audience that they could not serve two masters (Matt 6:24). Paul spoke bluntly about the dangers associated with the love of money and prohibited it (1 Tim 6:10). Kindness and charity are clearly taught in Deuteronomy 15:7–11 where Moses appeals to the rich to be generous to the needy as a form of service, not as a way of making profit.

On Voluntary Giving and Tithing

Prosperity preachers both teach and practice generous giving. However, the principles of giving advocated by prosperity preachers have some flaws. First, most giving under prosperity theology is egocentric (centered on the giver).[110] A pastor who wants to buy a car may give a prophetic declaration that all his congregants should "sow" in his ministry by making an appreciable donation. For the one (pastor) who already has a car but wants a new one, the prophetic direction may be that the pastor gives his own car to a poor member first.[111] Later, when the pastor buys a new car from the wealth he has already accumulated, it becomes an evidence of God blessings to those who give generously. The pastor gave away his car and God has given him a better one. From this point, members are encouraged to give generously towards the pastor's ministry so that they will receive in abundance.[112]

This egocentric approach to giving contradicts our findings from the exegesis of Deuteronomy 15:1–11 and Matthew 6:19–34. In Deuteronomy

---

109. Asamoah-Gyadu, *Sighs and Signs*, 165.
110. Kyle, *Evangelicalism*, 291.
111. Asamoah-Gyadu, "Did Jesus Wear Designer?"
112. Kyle, *Evangelicalism*, 291.

15:1–11, God asked Israel to cancel people's debt at the end of every seven years (v. 1). At the same time, he prohibited the rich from refusing to lend to the poor when a year of debt remission was approaching. Also, we can deduce from a study of Matthew 6:19 that God requires the rich to be generous to the poor, in order for the rich to store heavenly treasures. In my opinion, the reason why God wants the rich to give to the poor is not primarily that the rich will receive their money in return but that the poor will be relieved of their stress.

Second, while acknowledging that donations by prosperity-preaching churches help to improve the lives of some people, it must be noted also that much of the donations given by adherents of this theology end up being kept by the church leader as their property. We noted earlier that prosperity theology requires that one gives to a "man of God" through whom God reveals success plans to the donor. The resultant effect of this teaching is that most donations in prosperity preaching churches go to the "man of God." Members are not given much encouragement to give directly to the poor who are in real dire need of basic life necessities; donations must come to the church, which in turn is expected to give to the poor.[113] Prosperity preachers hardly urge their members to give "to the needy on the street or sick in their homes and hospitals or prisoners in the cells."[114] After a long time of wealth accumulation, the pastor goes to an orphanage and makes a relatively small donation which they broadcasts through the media with the effect of encouraging followers to donate more and more to him in subsequent meetings. What the preacher receives from followers in return for this benevolence far outweighs what he or she donated.[115] The point is that the prosperity theology model of poverty alleviation could have greater impact on people's live if adherents were encouraged to give directly to the needy in their societies rather than bringing their donations to the church leader who ends up hoarding the majority of these donations.

Third, some prosperity preachers manipulate their members rather than allowing them to give freely and cheerfully. They use statements like "[t]rue prosperity is the ability to use God's power to meet the needs of mankind in any realm of life" or "[w]e have been called to finance the gospel to the ends of the world."[116] Further, some pastors may invite their members to come forward and drop their donation at their (the pastors') feet in order to ensure that no one

---

113. Temitope, "Prosperity Gospel Preaching," 319.
114. Temitope, 319.
115. See Temitope, 319.
116. Temitope, "Prosperity Gospel Preaching," 319.

gives a "small" amount as no one likes to be regarded as the one with the least offering.[117] This is against the principle of free-will, secret, proportionate, and cheerful giving (cf. Matt 6:1–4; 2 Cor 9:7). Christian giving should be rooted in one's love for God, not in one's desire to become rich (Deut 15:1, 7–9).

Fourth, by teaching that material prosperity is preconditioned on giving, prosperity theology makes giving a business transaction: "If our giving is just an exchange involvement with God where we give so [h]e can respond to the giving in return" as prosperity preachers make us understand, "then that is a commercial (business) transaction."[118] This transactional understanding of giving makes acts of kindness an investment rather than a Christian service and limits blessings that flow from this service to material prosperity. It also fails to recognize the working of God's grace in human lives and circumstances. It amounts to a reduction of God to an object to be manipulated by those who give to him.

This practice contradicts the biblical view that giving is a form of ministry rather than business transaction (cf. Deut 15:7–11).[119] We have established that riches come with the responsibility of sharing with others and the need to guard against finding in them a false sense of security (1 Tim 6:17). The individualistic view of wealth is therefore unbiblical, whereas the communal view of it is in line with biblical teaching. Wealth, like manna in the Old Testament, is a gift belonging not to the one who owns it but to God who gives it (see Exod 16). It is the responsibility of the rich person to ensure that the needy also receive a share of the wealth God has given. The ideal situation to strive for is that there be no poor (Deut 15:4). However, since we are surrounded by poor people in our communities in Africa, it is imperative for every believer to open their hands to them (John 12:8; Deut 15:7–9). In Matthew 6, Jesus also emphasized the need to be generous towards the needy. He says believers should consider themselves stewards of God's possessions and responsible to God for the resources he has entrusted to them (Matt 6:19; 25:14–30). God requires sharing of resources as a way of alleviating poverty in the society (Deut 15:7–9).

Furthermore, the approach of prosperity preachers to tithing needs some consideration. Tithing was an Old Testament requirement for the people of God under the law. In the New Testament, where believers are under the covenant of grace, God does not demand a specific percentage of one's income before blessing a person. Rather, he requires a sacrificial, systematic, proportionate,

---

117. Amevenku and Boaheng, *Tithing*, 98.
118. Oluoch, *Concerning Prosperity Gospel*, 162.
119. Wiersbe, *Wiersbe Bible Commentary*, 338–339.

cheerful, consistent and enthusiastic giving towards the advancement of the kingdom of God (cf. Matt 6:1–4; 1 Cor 16:1–2; 2 Cor 8).[120] Though tithing was not abolished by Christ, most of its purposes have been fulfilled in the life and ministry of Christ which culminated in his death and resurrection.[121] Three types of tithes, namely, Levitical, charity, and festival tithes are identified in the Bible.[122] Amevenku and Boaheng find the fulfillment of the priesthood in the priesthood of all believers. The New Testament describes believers as a "holy nation" and "royal priesthood" (1 Pet 2:9) who offer "spiritual sacrifices" (1 Pet 2:5) to God. The tithe received by the Levites as inheritance instead of the land in the Old Testament has been fulfilled in the sense that all believers receive an inheritance, that is salvation, in the new covenant (Acts 20:32; 26:18; Gal 3:18; Eph 1:11–12,14; 5:5; Col 1:12; 3:24; Heb 9:15; 1 Pet 1:4). The fulfilment of the Festival tithe is found in Christ, for example, when Paul describes him as our Passover lamb (1 Cor 5:7). Of the three tithes, only the principle behind the charity tithe remains in the New Testament; and even for that one, there has been a change in the practice. They argue further that one can encourage the payment of a tithe, provided "it is understood as the believer returning thanks to God's providence."[123] The legalistic demand for tithe by prosperity preachers with their threats of curses must be rejected on the ground that it has no biblical support.[124] What the Bible demands is that the church uses a greater part of its tithes (paid as a form of giving thanks to God) to care for the needy.

On Anxiety, Worry and Greed

Scripture is against anxiety, worry and greed. One of the rules that governed the gathering of manna was that no one was to gather more than was needed for the family for the day (Exod 16:16). This principle is found in the petition "Give us this day our daily bread" (Matt 6:11) in the Lord's prayer. Christ's model of life, as explained in our exegesis, is to be content with God's provision for our necessities and not to worry about wants to the extent of getting one's priorities displaced (Matt 6:25). These and other passages in the Bible teach the need for contentment. No matter one's economic status there is a need to pursue higher goals which have eternal values.

---

120. Amevenku and Boaheng, *Tithing*, 99–100.
121. Amevenku and Boaheng.
122. Amevenku and Boaheng, 45–50.
123. Amevenku and Boaheng, 107.
124. Amevenku and Boaheng, *Tithing*, 107.

Contrary to Scripture, prosperity theology directly or indirectly breeds anxiety and worry. For instance, the accumulated wealth of the adherents of prosperity theology is itself a source of worry in terms of losing it or maintaining it. Instead of having "one-day-at-a-time" mentality (Matt 6:34), disciples of prosperity theology expend much energy towards becoming wealthy and keeping many possessions for their material life. But the parable of the Rich Fool warns the adherents of prosperity theology against thinking that material increase gives us control over the future and guarantees a long life (cf. Luke 12:16–21).

Oyedepo teaches that prosperity is a believer's identity without which "one is a misfit in the Kingdom."[125] In this worldview, the poor are of lesser worth than the wealthy in the kingdom of God. Such teachings increase people's desire to acquire wealth by all means; a desire that makes people tight-fisted and greedy. Wariboko serves us well with this quote: "The more prosperity preachers can connect savory religious visions to the social and aesthetic values of the society, the more the idea of the divine is transformed into a drive-by window that fulfils orders."[126] He adds that "After months and years of this kind of production of desires and dreams, consumerism and greed take their abodes in their victims' deep unconscious, where they are very difficult to control."[127]

Materialistic thinking leads to anxiety and unhappiness. Money and possessions require a constant worry about their acquisition, increase, and preservation. The continual, selfish search for happiness through material wealth, more often than not, leads to misery. Wealth also gives the illusion of security.

But we have established that while worry may have some positive effects in some cases, it mostly tends to obscure one's view of God and his power. Worry and anxiety must be avoided because they overshadow kingdom values, alter our priorities, and make us fail to see things as they really are (Matt 6:25–26). More so, worry and anxiety are anti-Christian because they are a waste of the opportunities we have been given by God and acts of unbelief (Matt 6:27–30), which characterize unbelievers (Matt 6:32). Surprisingly, some followers of the prosperity theology believe that their material blessings come from their pastors. J. Moyo, for instance, observes that in Zimbabwe, there are Christians who hold that the wealth they have acquired comes from the pastor, not God, and therefore they will continue to donate to their pastor so long as he will

---

125. Oyedepo, *Possessing Your Possession*, 16.
126. As cited by Asamoah-Gyadu, *Contemporary Pentecostal Christianity*, 95.
127. As cited by Asamoah-Gyadu, *Contemporary Pentecostal Christianity*, 95.

continue to bless them.[128] This belief, though unfortunate, is not limited to Zimbabwe but is also found in other parts of Africa.

A Defective Biblical Hermeneutics Foundation

Prosperity theology is based on defective biblical hermeneutics. Hermeneutics refers to the study of the interpretation of texts.[129] Almost all the troubles associated with prosperity preaching are rooted in the methodology employed in interpreting Scriptures. In some cases (as I will demonstrate shortly), prosperity preachers quote isolated "proof" texts and treat them almost exclusively as propositional truths or promises without taking the contextual issues of the biblical passages into consideration. Three examples are given below.

The Hundredfold Return Principle in Mark 10:29–30

The prosperity theology's belief that God promises material wealth and health based on Mark 10:29–30 needs a closer examination. The context of the passage suggests that the reward for leaving our families to follow Christ is mostly the fellowship believers will enjoy with hundreds and thousands of other believers, not a hundredfold return on wealth (cf. Mark 3:11–13; 1 Tim 5:1–2). The gaining of homes seems to suggest that believers will have some material wealth in the form of shared houses and goods (inherited through wealthy believers, cf. Acts 2:42–47; 4:32–35). One thing most prosperity preachers fail to mention is that these verses also promise that believers will inherit persecution. Pastor White, however, recognizes that the text also talks about persecution but she argues that the persecution Jesus is talking about is the devil who does not want us to enjoy God's blessings.[130] Exegetical fidelity in interpreting the passage requires that the "persecution" be treated the same way the other part of the text is treated. By ignoring the promised persecution or treating the persecution as symbolizing the devil betrays the prosperity preachers' use of illegitimate means to propagate their teachings.

The Threefold Prosperity Promise in 3 John 2

Prosperity preachers use 3 John 2 to support their teachings. The text reads, "Beloved, I pray that all may go well with you and that you may be in good health, just as it is well with your soul." They claim that this verse means that

---

128. Moyo, "Preaching the Gospel."
129. Osborne, *Hermeneutical Spiral*.
130. White, *Living Abundant Life*, 13.

God desires that everyone prospers materially. I find this teaching to be in error on two grounds: the first contextual and the second grammatical. First, the context of the text reveals that John used 3 John 1 as a form of greeting rather than a doctrinal passage. Even though doctrines can be formed from a non-doctrinal passage (because all Scripture is profitable for doctrine [2 Tim 3:16–17]), John's original intent as shown by the context is not primarily doctrinal. Second, the term *euchomai* translated "pray" means a desire or a wish rather than a promise John is giving to his fellow believer.[131] The term *euodousthai* means "to journey successfully," "to succeed," "to be led along a good road," or "to get along well."[132]

Therefore, what John prays for is a good and safe journey throughout one's life (cf. Rom 1:10), rather than the enjoyment of material prosperity. Both the NRSV and the NIV bring out this meaning well by translating this expression as "all may go well with you." The text does no more than express John's wish for Gaius. John's wish, however, does not guarantee that Gaius will experience what he wishes for him. It is therefore not sound exegesis to derive any universal principle of material prosperity from this text.[133]

The Principle of Sowing and Reaping in 2 Corinthians 8:9

We noted earlier that prosperity preachers teach that all Christians are supposed to be materially rich based on passages such as 2 Corinthians 8:9 (cf. 2 Cor 6:10), which reads, "For you know the grace of our Lord Jesus Christ, that though he was rich, yet for your sake he became poor, so that you through his poverty might become rich" (NIV). Prosperity preachers assume that Paul was preaching about or advocating for an increase in material wealth. However, a careful examination of the context of the text indicates that the meaning of believers' riches must be determined by the meaning of Christ's riches before the incarnation. The word *plousios* rendered "rich" is used to refer to the original state (that is, divine existence) of Christ before his incarnation.[134] The word *eptocheusen* rendered "became poor" signifies his incarnation.[135] Christ voluntarily left his heavenly riches and glory for earthly poverty shown in his birth, ministry, and death on the cross.

---

131. See Lieu, *I, II & III John*, 268–270.
132. Lieu, *I, II & III John*, 268.
133. Johnson, "1, 2 & 3 John," electronic edition.
134. Omanson and Ellington, *Handbook on Paul's Second Letter*, electronic edition.
135. Omanson and Ellington.

The riches of believers therefore have to do with their eternal glory rather than earthly possessions. Based on this fact, Omanson and Ellington caution translators concerning this issue: "While this is clearly not intended to refer to material wealth, readers in many languages will easily understand the figurative sense in this context. If, however, there is any danger of this expression being taken literally, it may be necessary to clarify the meaning by saying something like 'rich in the eyes of God.'"[136] Clearly, what Paul is teaching here is opposite of the interpretation of prosperity preachers. Following the example of Jesus, Paul asks believers to empty themselves of earthly riches so that they can have heavenly riches (1 Tim 6:18–19; Matt 6:19). That is the reason why Paul exhorts the Corinthians to give their wealth away to their needy brothers saying "now at this time your abundance may supply their lack" (2 Cor 8:14 NKJV; read v. 15 as well). Paul's point is that "true wealth is of the spirit," consisting "in faith, in love, in peace with God."[137] The material prosperity teaching that is based on this text is certainly inaccurate.

Our analyses underscore the fact that prosperity preachers sometimes twist Scriptures to support their theology. As Temitope rightly points out, for prosperity preachers "It does not matter whether that interpretation is actually the mind of the [biblical] author or matches its contemporary interpretation following the authentic hermeneutic principles or not, as long as this interpretation suits the purpose of gaining the desired goal."[138] Prosperity preachers' selective use of Scripture to support materialism, in my view, is the most serious problem prosperity theology poses to contemporary Christianity.

On Work Ethics

In Africa, a negative work ethic (such as is seen in idleness and/or laziness) is a major contributor to people's poverty. Any theology of poverty for Africa needs to address this problem in addition to others. Earlier, we discovered that some prosperity preachers engage in human empowerment programs through entrepreneurship to the extent of giving initial capital to followers to start their own businesses. However, on the whole, prosperity theology tends to make hard work and striving towards a proven means of earning a living unnecessary because one's donations and faithful tithing to the church, as prosperity preachers claim, are the most crucial determinants of success in life, not hard work.[139]

---

136. Omanson and Ellington.
137. Filson, *Interpreters Bible*, 368.
138. Temitope, "Prosperity Gospel Preaching," 317.
139. Kasera, "Biblical and Theological Examination," 66.

In almost all cases, prosperity preachers illustrate their sermons with the experiences of people who gave generously and were blessed abundantly. They rarely take illustrations from people who studied hard at the feet of others, struggled in life, and became successful due to hard work, determination, perseverance and God's grace. Thus, prosperity theology fails to prepare believers adequately to develop endurance through hard work, suffering, and taking responsibility for their actions.[140] No wonder disciples of prosperity theology tend to look for quick ways of escaping economic hardships rather than enduring and working at it gradually. This theology's simplistic approach to living a successful life overnight has led to the paradigm shift in people's orientation and inclination, from hard labor with determination to idleness.[141]

On Combating Corruption (Sin)

Earlier in this book, I identified corruption as a major cause of poverty in Africa. It is therefore important that any model proposed for poverty reduction deals adequately with the issue of corruption, which is widespread in the continent. In his recent study on revival meetings in Pentecostal churches, Abamfo Atiemo wondered how the level of corruption in Ghana could be rising at the same time that the country was experiencing unprecedented Pentecostal revival activities.[142] He noted that the numerous Pentecostal revival meetings had failed to promote individual and societal moral transformation, especially in terms of "concrete acts of justice, obedience, mercy, compassion, honesty and loving deeds."[143] One of the main causes for this situation, according to him, is the Pentecostals' overemphasis on the ministry of healing and exorcism, and miracles at the expense of discipleship which makes them lose focus on teachings about repentance from sin, saving faith in Christ, accountability, honesty, public morality, and the hope for eternal life.[144]

In addition, most contemporary revival meetings tend to focus on fundraising rather than spiritual renewal. The choice of the speaker is informed by the speaker's ability to draw a crowd and to raise money. Most of these crowd-pullers and fundraising "commandos" are "self-proclaimed" prophets with inadequate knowledge about hermeneutics and the exposition of Scriptures. Unlike Old Testament prophets, these "prophetic" figures do not confront corrupt leaders to curb injustice. What they like doing instead is to prophecy

---

140. Kasera, "Biblical and Theological Examination," 66.
141. Temitope, "Prosperity Gospel Preaching," 232; Soboyejo, "Prosperity Gospel," 8.
142. Atiemo, "Crowds That Bring," 7.
143. Atiemo, 7.
144. Atiemo, 16.

the success of leaders to win their favor. They minor in teaching and preaching and major in enticing people to donate to the church. Their ministration is usually characterized by dancing, jostling, whistling, and shouting. They preach for a very short time or just read a passage without any exposition. The rest of the preaching time centers on how powerful their ministry has been over the years. After this, they spend several hours raising money and promising people that once they give to God, all their problems, no matter how hard they are, will be solved by God instantly. Prayers are offered for people depending on the amount donated.

The drama exhibited during these fundraising sessions is often interesting. In my ministerial work, I have encountered a fundraiser who would tie a rope around his neck and ask one of his associates to drag him around the congregation. He interpreted this activity as follows: "Every human being is like an animal tied to a rope and being dragged around. The one who takes active part in fundraising will have their neck untied." In other words, people need to partake in every fundraising activity in order to have their lives freed from the manipulation of evil powers. Through such and similar methods these fundraisers use socio-psychological manipulation to induce the audience to give to the church.[145] The time and energy spent on the fundraising as compared to the preaching leaves no doubt about the focus of most revival meetings, which are organized to give money, not spiritual renewal. As long as revival meetings are geared towards fundraising rather than spiritual renewal, the church will lose the fight against sin, particularly corruption, because the massive gatherings of believers will always be like crowds that gather and give hope of rains but bring no rains in the end.[146]

Another dimension of prosperity theology which needs attention has to do with the situation whereby corrupt people (especially politicians) donate huge sums of money (made through disreputable means) to their churches as freewill offerings or tithes as a way of wanting to appear "godly," or to "cleanse their money," or to curry favor with believers in our largely "Christian" countries in Africa. Since some of these people are usually connected to national corruption scandals, their acts can also be interpreted as a way of "preempting" prosecution for their actions by showing themselves as generous to God and church activities. This situation also alludes to the fact that prosperity theology cannot be a panacea to fighting corruption.

---

145. Lausanne Theology Working Group, "Statement on Prosperity Gospel."
146. Atiemo, "Crowds That Bring," 6.

On Self-Denial, Pain and Suffering

One of the major mandates of the church is to nurture disciples to become like Christ. The process involved in this task is what we refer to as discipleship. Since God's blessings according to prosperity theology is predominantly seen in terms of material possessions, followers of prosperity theology usually derive freedom, happiness, and worth from money and possessions. As such, its adherents prioritize material possessions, which contradicts Jesus's injunction that believers seek first the kingdom of God and his righteousness (Matt 6:33). The process of discipleship requires self-denial. Unfortunately, while Jesus teaches self-denial (Matt 16:24; Mark 9:34; Luke 14:26), prosperity theology teaches self-fulfillment.[147] Today, self-denial has become unpopular in African Christianity due to the influence of prosperity teaching. Prosperity theology fuels people's desires to become rich at all cost, thereby planting in them the evil of loving money (1 Tim 6:10). Since adherents of prosperity theology treat wealth as an end in itself rather than a means to an end, people may use all means including corruption, oppression, and social injustice to gain riches. With its strong emphasis on "material formation" rather than "spiritual formation," prosperity theology undermines Christian discipleship.[148]

Prosperity teachers have zero tolerance for hardship and any form of suffering.[149] Even some prosperity-preaching churches refuse to celebrate Good Friday because of its associated pain and suffering.[150] Contrary to this opinion, we find in the book of Job that the sovereign God (in his own wisdom) may work in unexplained and unexplainable ways to allow the righteous to suffer – in view of theodicy, to show his divine goodness and providence in a fallen world. God may elect people to suffer for his purpose just as some Old Testament saints faced challenges such as being flogged, chained, put in prison, stoned, sawed in two, put to death by the sword and so on (Heb 11:36–40). These believers obviously experienced great financial need and privation not because they did not know about God's promise of prosperity or lacked faith to claim it. I reason this way because they were people whose faith is commended in Scripture.

In the New Testament, one finds many people suffering for the sake of the gospel. Christ went through suffering of the highest kind. He also taught that people can pass through pain and suffering in order for God to use their

---

147. Soboyejo, "Prosperity Gospel," 8.
148. Soboyejo, 8.
149. Asamoah-Gyadu, "Did Jesus Wear Designer?"
150. Asamoah-Gyadu.

situation to achieve his purpose (John 9:3). Paul's exhortation for believers to endure suffering came from his own experience. He became poor and endured a lot of difficulties. He knew what it was like to be in need and what it was like to live in plenty (Phil 4:11–13). He, however, boasted in his poverty and saw it as establishing his credibility as a servant of God (2 Cor 6:3–10; see also 1 Cor 4:8–16). Interestingly, Paul's secret for getting along in "need" was not exercising a special kind of "faith" that changed his circumstances, but learning to be "content" (1 Tim 6:6–8).

It is therefore unbiblical to portray Christianity as a suffering-free religion. There cannot be a crown without a cross, as the prosperity preacher would want us to believe. Prosperity teachers' views about pain and suffering in the lives of believers are therefore to be rejected based on biblical revelation. J. O. Soboyejo corroborates this view when he says that prosperity preachers, with their zero tolerance for hardship, suffering, brokenness, or delay in life, undermine "the formation of Christian character."[151]

On the African Communal Worldview

The African philosophy of life is shaped by a survival mechanism in which people depend on one another. This interdependence among people is expressed in the statement "I am related by blood, therefore, I exist" or "I exist because I belong to a family." Earlier, I established that in Africa one's welfare is the responsibility of the whole family. People spend huge sums of money on their extended family to ensure that each member of the family has a means of living. This is not only cultural but biblical as well. Christ's example of self-emptying teaches that one has to look not only at their interest but also that of others (Phil 2:4–11). Prosperity theology, with its individualistic view of material success, militates against the interdependence of human beings.[152] It fuels, in the individual, the hunger to gather as much wealth as possible and makes people become so preoccupied with wealth that they forget about friends and relatives. This contention is buttressed by the Lausanne Group of theologians who state that prosperity theology "has stressed individual wealth and success, without the need for community accountability, and has thus actually damaged a traditional feature of African society, which was commitment to care within the extended family and wider social community."[153]

---

151. Soboyejo, "Prosperity Gospel," 8.
152. Goliama, "Gospel of Prosperity," 226.
153. Lausanne Theology Working Group, "Statement on Prosperity Gospel."

Kwateng-Yeboah also observes that in prosperity-preaching churches, the primary aim of giving is not "generosity of a Christian social responsibility" but "the individual's search for his [or her] own wealth and success without any awareness of communal sharing of resources."[154] Thus, because money is a priority and the factor that controls the life and feeling of adherents of prosperity theology, there is a neglect of people's needs. This, in my view, is the reason why it is not uncommon to find disciples of prosperity theology living comfortably in poor communities without feeling the need to help their poor neighbors. Since prosperity theology fights against the idea of interdependence that sustains African societies, it will be very difficult to achieve any sustainable success using prosperity theology as the antidote to Africa's poverty.

On Eschatology

In essence and approach, prosperity theology is solely this-worldly. So much emphasis is placed on this world that prosperity preachers tend to ignore teachings on the second coming and related subjects. Prosperity theology, whether explicitly stated or not, contends that all the benefits of the kingdom of God can be enjoyed by all believers here and now.[155] However, the Bible teaches that though the kingdom of God was inaugurated by Jesus in the first Advent, it will not be enjoyed fully until he returns (see for example Matt 6:10). Therefore, the teaching that there should be no sickness or poverty among believers cannot be true for the present world of sin, but in the next. To place too much emphasis on realized eschatology and hence teach that believers should not experience illness is to deny the reality of physical mortality. Such eschatology, in my view, is unbalanced and a total deviation from Christian orthodoxy.

On Theological Formation

Prosperity theology has an ambivalent attitude towards knowledge; it promotes anti-intellectualism and at times portrays Christianity as illogical. Kasera quotes Oyedepo as saying "God's Word is not scientific; neither is it logical; God's Word is divine."[156] By this assertion, Oyedepo is saying that divine knowledge is illogical. If so, then we need not approach Scriptures with our thinking capabilities.[157] Yet, he calls on people to obey the Scriptures. Reinhard Bonnke is also noted for propagating the same attitudes of anti-intellectualism

---

154. Kwateng-Yeboah, "Re-appraisal of Prosperity Gospel," 88.
155. Idahosa, *I Choose to Change*, 7.
156. Kasera, "Biblical and Theological Examination," 64.
157. Kasera, 64.

and experientialism. Gifford notes how Bonnke has removed critical thinking from his theology, and thus uses experience as the ultimate judge of spiritual truth.[158]

The situation in Africa today is no different. It is a common belief among African prosperity preachers that serious academic study is not required for Christian ministry.[159] So instead of building a solid theological foundation through serious academic study, most prosperity preachers are of the view that once the (prophetic) gift is working, academic work is irrelevant, with some of them even going to the extent of claiming that the Holy Spirit will "drop" interpretations into their minds.[160] Their focus in ministry is on exorcisms, healing and prosperity. Such ministers who are not ready to learn eventually become biblicists, interpreting the Bible overly literally.

Conclusion

This chapter presented the shortcomings of using prosperity theology as a model for dealing with Africa's poverty. A general overview of this theology was given, followed by a brief discussion of the factors that make it appealing to the people of Africa. We have examined the main teachings of prosperity theology and found them to focus on material prosperity, faith healing, positive confession of faith, and seed sowing. Despite some positive contributions of prosperity theology to Christianity and the socioeconomic needs of people in the continent, in terms of promoting positive mind-set, cultural transformation, and personal, societal and national development, the model is largely inadequate as an approach for reducing poverty in Africa. I have demonstrated various flaws in the biblical hermeneutics approach of this model. It encourages unbiblical attitudes such as commercialization of the gospel, materialism, covetousness (which is idolatry), unethical and manipulative fund-raising techniques, and greed. It opposes the African communal view of life and the interdependence in especially poor communities. It also fails to provide any sustainable answer to the real causes of poverty because it has an obscured view of poverty. Clearly, the prosperity theology approach is not contextually, theologically, and biblically appropriate for Africa.

---

158. Gifford cited in Kasera, 64–65.
159. Amevenku and Boaheng, "Use of Imprecatory Prayers," 92.
160. Amevenku and Boaheng, 92.

6

A Contextual Approach for Poverty Reduction in Africa

In the previous chapter, I assessed the prosperity theology approach of poverty alleviation and found that while it has some positive aspects, its biblical, theological, and cultural bases are weak. In view of this, in this chapter I will set out to formulate a contextual theology of poverty alleviation that seeks to address the weaknesses we have found in the various approaches discussed earlier. The major stakeholders in the formulation and implementation of a more contextual theology for the continent include both poor and rich Africans in urban and rural areas, the African church, and governments. I begin with a brief description of what contextual theology is and how it could be applied in Africa.

Contextual Theology in Africa

According to Bevans, contextual theology is "a way of doing theology in which one takes into account the spirit and message of the gospel; the tradition of the church; the culture in which one is theologizing; and social change within that culture, whether brought about by Western technological process or the grass-roots struggle for equality, justice and liberation."[1] For Nicholls it is "a dynamic process of the Church's reflection . . . on the interaction of the text as the Word of God and the context as a specific human situation."[2] In short, contextual theology is what the word of God says in a particular situation.

---

1. Bevans, *Models of Contextual Theology*, 1.
2. Nihinlola, *Theology Under the Mango Tree*, 38.

From these definitions, we identify three partners of contextual theology, namely, Scripture, tradition, and the sociopolitical and economic situation of the culture the theology is addressing. First, contextual theology is based on Scripture. Scripture is the final authority for any authentic theology including contextual theology. The second element of contextual theology is tradition, by which is meant the teachings and practices of the church since its establishment. For contextual theology to arrive at acceptable results, biblical scholars must dialogue with past and present customs and beliefs of the church within a society. Third, contextual theology is culturally conditioned, meaning it takes into consideration both the worldview and the existential (social, political, economic) issues of the people for whom it is formulated. Therefore, the teachings from Scripture, the teachings (traditions) of the church, Africa's socioeconomic situation and African folk wisdom will guide the formulation of a contextual theology for poverty in the continent.

The history of scholarly attempts at formulating a Christian theology for the African continent can be traced to the 1950s and 1960s.[3] Bevans outlines (among other issues) two external factors that triggered the move to develop an African Christian theology: the "general dissatisfaction with classical approaches to theology" which fail to take African needs into consideration and "the oppressive nature of older approaches."[4] Browers identifies the pioneers of African theology as including Harry Sawyer of Seirra Leone, Vincent Mulago of Congo, and Bolaji Idowu of Nigeria, among others.[5] He notes the crucial role of the 1966 conference of African theologians in Nigeria which resulted in the publication of *Biblical Revelation and African Beliefs* in 1969.[6] In addition scholars such as K. A. Dickson, J. S. Pobee, Kwame Bediako, Emmanuel Martey, J. K. Asamoah-Gyadu, Paul K. Boafo, and Emmaunel K. Asante have also contributed to the development of African Christian theology.

Nihinlola defines African Christian theology as "the Christian Theology that is formulated in the African worldview."[7] By worldview I mean the way a person or a group of people understand physical and non-physical reality. African Christian theology must therefore be "Christian, biblical and African."[8] Emmanuel Martey identified four theological trends in Africa based on issues

---

3. Browers, *African Theology*, 28–29.
4. Bevans, *Models of Contextual Theology*, 5–6.
5. Browers, *African Theology*, 30.
6. Browers, 30.
7. Nihinlola, *Theology Under the Mango Tree*, 18.
8. Nihinlola, 18.

related to culture, poverty, gender, and race.⁹ He classified them into two major streams of African theologies, namely inculturation (or contextualization) and liberation (political and socioeconomic) theologies.

The contextualization of theology is not an option but a mandate to the church. Without contextual theology the word of God will always be alien to all communities that have a different culture from the formulating community. Oduyoye rightly observes that contextual theology "requires deep analysis of the context of the people's experience; hence contemporary theology has to be overtly contextual and take into account the whole scope of life's offerings and challenges."¹⁰ The task, however, is not always easy, as it can lead to compromise and syncretism.¹¹

In terms of poverty studies, Asamoah-Gyadu, Boafo, and Asante are some of the leading African scholars who have attempted to contextualize biblical teachings for the African situation.¹² What I present below is a further development of the efforts by these and other African scholars in the following thematic areas: work ethics, material ethics, human development, female empowerment, cultural transformation, social and structural transformation, spiritual transformation, solidarity with the poor, fruitfulness of spirituality and work, contentment, modesty and simplicity, job creation, fighting of extravagance in the church, and financial ethics. The contextual theology presented below not only addresses the theological and biblical needs of Africans but also their sociocultural needs.

Proposed Approach to Poverty Reduction in Africa
Work Ethics

The approach to poverty reduction proposed in this book begins with a look at work ethic because the attitude of many Africans towards work does little to promote poverty reduction. Since what we do is a significant part of our daily lives, work ethic plays an important role in formulating a model for poverty alleviation. J. N. Kudadjie and Robert K. Aboagye-Mensah argue that work must relate to three areas of human life, namely, the human-divine relationship, the human-human relationship and the human-environment relationship.¹³

---

9. Martey, *African Theology*, 69.
10. As cited by Asante, *Theology in Society*, 119.
11. Nihinlola, *Theology Under the Mango Tree*, 19.
12. Asamoah-Gyadu, "Poverty, Wealth," 55–69; Boafo, *John Wesley's Theology*.
13. Kudadjie and Aboagye-Mensah, *Christian Social Ethics*, 105.

The biblical understanding of work is outlined below. First, the Christian concept of work is informed by God's nature and his activities. The two creation accounts (Gen 1 and 2) illustrate that God himself is a worker. Zwingli states that "[t]here is nothing in the universe so like God as the worker."[14] The opening verse of the entire Bible is that "In the beginning God created the heavens and the earth" (Gen 1:1 NIV). The creation stories further reveal that God did not only create with word of mouth (as in Gen 1:3, 6, 9, 14, 20, 24) but also with his hands (Gen 1:26–27; 2:7). Throughout history God has been involved saving, preserving and judging humanity. In the incarnation, God (in Christ) affirmed the dignity of human labor by taking part in manual work as a carpenter (Mark 6:3). Jesus makes it clear to us that the Father has always been working and he (Jesus) is working as well (John 5:17). Manual work is therefore not to be looked down upon.

Human beings were made to be distinct from other creations in two respects—only humans were made in the image of God (Gen 1:26–27) and only humans "were given the privilege and responsibility to work" (Gen 2:15).[15] As we can see, God ordained human work before the fall. Since that time, human beings have made attempts to work and take dominion of the universe through crop farming and rearing of animals (see for example Gen 4).

Even though human work is a pre-fall institution, the Fall of humanity had consequences on the nature of work.[16] As a result of the Fall, God cursed the ground. The effect was that the earth became reluctant to produce food; it began to produce thorns and weeds (Gen 3:17–18). It was through toil, sweat, and tears that humankind would eat of it (Gen 3:19). From this time "work will have to be accomplished in the midst of many tensions, conflicts and crises."[17] The consequence of the Fall on human work is illustrated in the story of Cain and Abel (Gen 4). This is seen not only in the hatred that Cain had for Abel, but also in Cain's murder of Abel. Though the primary issue has to do with their offerings, the products for their offerings came from their occupations, which involved toil. In contemporary times, "labour disputes, strikes, cheating at work places," bribery and corruption, and loitering could be seen as the consequences of the fall on human work.[18] One may conclude

---

14. As cited by Asante, *Stewardship*, 32.
15. Kudajie and Aboagye-Mensah, *Christian Social Ethics*, 106.
16. Kudajie and Aboagye-Mensah, 107.
17. Kudajie and Aboagye-Mensah, 107.
18. Kudajie and Aboagye-Mensah, 107.

that God's purpose for human work was hindered, though not destroyed, by the fall; therefore, human labor has both joyful and unpleasant dimensions.[19]

Second, work is a divine command.[20] Human work was not the initiative of humankind but a command from God (Gen 2:15). Therefore, God wants everyone (including the poor) to work hard in order to improve their standards of living. Through human work, God makes provision for human needs (Ps 128:2). Nihinlola supports this view when he declares that "God has designed the human life in such a way that work is a means to create wealth, possess material blessings and prosperity."[21] This view informs the Akan saying "There is no other results of laziness than poverty." I believe that Africa cannot develop if we work less than what God expects us to do. Through work we affirm our true state as humans, creatures who bear the image of God.

Diligence is therefore the means by which humans participate in God's efforts to heal and redeem all creation. The poor should entrust their lives into God's care and take advantage of any opportunities offered by the church, the society, and the government to enhance their living conditions. No one should sit aloof and expect God to supply their need through miracles. People must, however, not be discouraged when their efforts become fruitless because life is a struggle. African traditional wisdom encourages people to work hard to earn their living. It also encourages those who face challenges in life to not give up, but work hard again towards their success. For example, the Akan saying "Life is a struggle" or "Strive hard, you will succeed" serves as a source of comfort and courage to those who fail in one enterprise. This is a form of social creativity that must be encouraged among African societies in order to instill in the populace the attitude of perseverance. This dimension of the contextual approach to poverty reduction addresses the shortfall of prosperity theology approach which does little to encourage hard work.

Third, Christians have limitations when it comes to work. God is infinite; he works forever; humans are finite and they work only as long as they live (Ps 146:3–6). Human work is not an end in itself but "a means of sustaining the individual and family; and a means of serving the community"; its end is to glorify God.[22] Any economic enterprise that does not glorify God, help one's neighbor, and improve the society is not worth undertaking.[23] In the African

---

19. Kudajie and Aboagye-Mensah, 107.
20. Kudajie and Aboagye-Mensah, 107.
21. Nihinlola, *Theology Under the Mango Tree*, 141.
22. Kudajie and Aboagye-Mensah, *Christian Social Ethics*, 109.
23. Boafo, *John Wesley's Theology*, 220.

context, the production and sale of alcohol falls under this category due to its devastating economic and psychological effects on the individual and the society. In addition, bankers, ministers of the gospel, doctors, pharmacists, lawyers and leaders who make money through exploitation, stealing, fraud and gambling act against the principle of love for one's neighbor. In my opinion, this category would also include those who cheat in examinations, those who lie at their visa application interviews about their bank statements and/or their purpose of traveling, individuals or officials of high rank (for example, senior pastors) who pay their own salaries and allowances and refuse to pay those who serve under them (for example, assistant pastors) and those who use foul means (such as receiving bribes) to generate money in their organizations. This dimension of the proposed approach to poverty reduction can deal with the current widespread practice in Africa whereby people use any means to get money regardless of the ethical implications.[24]

There is the need for people to rest from diligent industry and still trust God to provide for them. Work should not be at the center of the life of the Christian. The Sabbath economy expounded in the exegesis of Deuteronomy 15:1–11 (and Exod 16) underlines the fact that God is capable of providing for human needs even when human beings cease from active work. God made the Israelites cease from their physical activities during the weekly Sabbaths and Sabbatical Years (Exod 20:8; Deut 5:12–13); yet no one went hungry. Therefore, though hard work is encouraged, God expects us to take our rest and regain energy for future work. God's own Sabbath rest (Gen 2:2) serves as an example for humanity. God expects humankind to have periods of rest for revitalization, just as he wants the land to be left fallow after several years of cultivation (Exod 23:21).

God does not expect people to undertake any economic enterprise that "harms the body, mind or spirit, or saps health or perverts one's character or weakens one's faith and joy in God."[25] This principle applies to work that deprives people of their food or sleep in the proportion naturally required by the body. It has something to tell people who have migrated to other places for greener pastures and undertake certain works that are detrimental to their health, and yet consider them appropriate to gain wealth for their families back home. The reason for prohibiting the Christian from earning money by means that risk one's life is that life is more valuable than food, and the body more than clothing. From our exegesis of Matthew 6:19–34 we note that food,

---

24. Kudajie and Aboagye-Mensah, *Christian Social Ethics*.
25. Boafo, *John Wesley's Theology*, 220; Moltmann et al., *Economy of Salvation*, 96.

clothing, and shelter have instrumental value. They are not the reason why humans live and so one does not have to worry about them to the point of being disloyal to God (Matt 6:25).

Fourth, since human work is part of a believer's calling from God, it must not only meet the needs of the worker but also those of the community.[26] In this sense, human work becomes the means by which believers participate in sustaining God's creation. From this fact comes the deduction that believers should not engage in any vocation with the primary aim of pursuing wealth or gaining favor from others. Rather, they must consider their work as part of their service to God and humanity. This means that people who migrate from Africa to seek greener pasture in the West while their home countries lack the services they provide may need to return to their home countries to help improve the lives of others. This is to say that if the motivation for traveling to work outside one's country is solely financial gain, then such a decision should be reconsidered in the light of Scripture. Kudajie and Aboagye-Mensah rightly argue that "[t]he worth of human work is judged, not by how much it makes a few people in the community rich and powerful but, by how much it serves the cause of all humanity."[27]

The point is that one person's work should not be isolated from the life of the community; it must be regarded as an integral part of the entire society. If work is to serve the community, then one's work should not in any way be detrimental to the life of one's neighbor or the environment.[28] Again, if one's work is to serve the community, then they should render the service in the community that needs it most rather than the community which can pay the highest remuneration. Undertaking an enterprise that harms or has the potential of harming one's neighbor does not show the love Christians are required to show towards their neighbor (Matt 22:39). Human activities that pollute the environment or endanger the lives of workers contradict this principle. Illegal mining, illegal fishing, and similar ventures fall under this category.

The love requirement in human work is depicted in Deuteronomy 15:1–11. In verse 1, God required that creditors cancel the debt of their debtor every Sabbatical Year. Then in verses 7–9 he commanded the rich to give freely to the poor even when the Sabbatical Year was approaching. In both instances,

---

26. Kudajie and Aboagye-Mensah, *Christian Social Ethics*, 110; Boafo, *John Wesley's Theology*, 221.

27. Kudajie and Aboagye-Mensah, 110.

28. Boafo, *John Wesley's Theology*, 221.

God is teaching moneylenders that their work should not be for selfish gain but a service to the community. Such service requires love for humanity. Therefore, business transactions must not only be based on a profit-oriented principle but also on the principles of love and mercy towards others. This way, Christians can pursue heavenly goals rather than earthly goals in their worldly employments (cf. Matt 6:19).

Building upon the foregoing discussion, Kudajie and Aboagye-Mensah claim that the human-labor relationship is an ethical one.[29] Therefore, corporate enterprises must pay their taxes and appropriate salaries of workers promptly; ensure the safety and health of their workers by providing a healthy working environment; maintain good relations with their employees and refrain from threatening them.[30] Modern-day employers who refuse to pay salaries or statutory funds such as income tax and pension contributions fall short of this standard.

The above understanding of work has some ethical implications for correcting some negative work attitudes in Africa. The first negative work attitude is "laziness and lack of devotion to duty."[31] Both attitudes may arise when people regard the work they do as not befitting them or when they consider work as a necessary evil (that is, they work just because work is inescapable). The discussion above has shown that work is part of what it is to be human; it is therefore not to be regarded as a necessary evil. As God's image bearers, human beings are expected to be diligent and creative just as God is. It is therefore unchristian to be lazy. Another common negative work attitude is lateness. Lateness to work and other important activities such as school costs African countries huge sums of money. The concept of "African-time" is slowing down development in Africa. This attitude has made many Africans, including some of our government officials, insensitive to time to the point of never being punctual at work and elsewhere." This way of life must be stopped if we are to address successfully the challenge of poverty among our people. Time delays are too costly for Africa in the twenty-first century.

Corruption at our workplaces including favoritism and cronyism, and poor supervision and management at work also inform people's attitude to work and lead to low productivity. The African church needs to sensitize members about the damaging effects of these unethical practices. Governments also have a role to play in ensuring prosecution of those involved in corrupt activities.

---

29. Kudajie and Aboagye-Mensah, *Christian Social Ethics*, 114.
30. Kudajie and Aboagye-Mensah, 115.
31. Kudajie and Aboagye-Mensah, 112.

Finally, the "get-rich-quick attitude" that is now common across Africa is a challenge to the development of the nation and must be dealt with. This attitude is driving many African youth to engage in ritual money (money obtained through [human] sacrifices). The fight against this attitude must come from at least two institutions, the church and the society. The church must teach that money is not an end in life but simply a means. Attention should also be drawn to Jesus's teaching that life does not consist in the among of our possessions (Luke 12:15). Based on the outcome of the exegesis of Matthew 6:19–34, the church should encourage members to not worry about their lives but to work hard and trust God to provide their basic needs. The one-day-at-a-time mentality taught in Matthew 6:34 must be promoted. Africans must teach and encourage diligence and perseverance towards work using the many rich proverbs, sayings, and folk stories that pass along these didactic values. For example, the Akan saying "It is a man who drinks bitter medicine," can be used to teach that everyone faces difficulties and failure, which are part of life and must be faced with courage and determination until one overcomes. While promoting such teachings, the society should also not shower praises upon the wealthy and hail them without considering the source of their wealth. People who become rich overnight must explain the source of their wealth. This will help reduce the tendency of the young developing a "get-rich-quick" attitude to wealth, which can encourage idleness and eventually make people poor or ritualists.

The involvement of many Africans (especially the youth) in gambling activities is another result of this "get-rich-quick" attitude and needs mention at this point. Though the Bible does not discuss gambling explicitly, there are some biblical principles to apply. First, gambling contradicts biblical principles because while the Bible stresses God's sovereignty (Matt 10:29–30), gambling is based upon chance which becomes the determining factor of one's decisions in life. The principle of gambling goes against the biblical teaching that humans are to be responsible beings whose lives are not conducted by chance but by purposeful planning under God's providence. Gambling undermines the fundamental principle that humans need to labor for a living (Eph 4:28; 2 Thess 3:10). It also promotes greed and selfishness because in the practice, one aims at winning and taking the money of the losers. Ethically, it is wrong for a person's success to be based on other's failure. Finally, the Bible condemns materialism (Matt 6:24–25) while gambling promotes it.

Material Ethics

A people's attitude to wealth influences their perception of poverty and the measures they take to alleviate poverty in a community. The desire for wealth and its accumulation among many people in Africa hinders efforts to reduce poverty, because it keeps many rich Africans from caring about the well-being of the poor and taking action to alleviate their destitution. It is therefore important that our contextual theology outlines the biblically and culturally appropriate ethic of material things.

First, there is the need to recognize and accept the fact that material things and any other resources are God's, not humans'.[32] This foundation of our material ethics is found both in the African cultural teachings and Scripture. Africans recognize God as the Creator and owner of all that is, the source of rain and sunlight. Just as our being (soul and body) does not belong to us but to God, so does everything we have; it is God's, not ours. The Bible makes it clear that God is the Creator and owner of all that is in the universe (cf. Gen 1:1; Ps 24:1–2; Hag 2:8). Both Deuteronomy 15:1–11 and Matthew 6:19–34 underscore the fact that there is no individual on earth who has the right to claim complete ownership of the resources available to them because whatever one possesses was created by God. Humans can use technology to change wood into paper and then transform paper into money; yet neither the wood nor the wisdom used in the process comes from them. This principle can be applied to all that humans make and "own" (e.g. vehicles, houses, electronic devices, airplanes, and so on).

The first principle leads to the second, which is the principle of accountability for material possessions. Humans are accountable to God for all the resources he has entrusted to them. At the day of judgment, each person will account for the resources entrusted to them (see Matt 25:14–30). The Akan saying "Money has wings" underscores the belief that apart from the final judgment, God can, in this life, judge those who are not using resources according to his will by taking what they have and giving to others. According to the Akan, this saying explains why wicked trustees sometimes lose their wealth in dramatic ways.

The third principle is that material things are meant for the common good of God's people just as spiritual things are (1 Cor 12:7). God taught Israel to apply this principle when he demanded that the rich open their hands to the poor. Money lenders could not use an approaching sabbatical debt release as an excuse for not lending to the poor (Deut 15:7–9). African social and cultural

---

32. Asante, *Stewardship*; Boafo, *John Wesley's Theology*.

values such as relationships, sacrifice for others, unity, peaceful coexistence, cooperation, hospitality, and inclusiveness support this biblical teaching.

Africans are interconnected by blood; hence the saying "I am related by blood, therefore, I exist or I exist because I belong to a family." In the same way Christians are linked by a common Creator, faith, Lord, Spirit, and baptism. The interconnection among Christians implies interdependence. Interdependence requires sharing of resources. People should willingly share their food, clothing, land, money, and other resources with their neighbors as traditional African values demand.[33] No traditional African will be unconcerned with the suffering of the needy in the community. Both the Sabbath economy of Deuteronomy 15:1–11 and Exodus 16 and the one-day-at-a-time mentality of Matthew 6:34 encourage sharing of resources. Paul also encourages Christians to share resources with others (1 Tim 6:17–19). In God's economy, wealth is a means to an end and not an end in itself. Sharing of resources is therefore both African and biblical and must be a key ethical principle for the Christian community in the continent. Material things should be used to supply the material needs of other people.

At the same time, since wealth belongs to the entire society rather than the one to whom it has been entrusted, it is not acceptable to possess too much while others have too little. Therefore, accumulating wealth for one's own benefits is a sin; it hinders God's plan to reduce the plight of the poor. In order to build up the ecclesiastical community and preserve its unity, there is the need to cater for one another. Therefore, Christians "have a fundamental calling to create a community of radical sharing and mutual interdependence."[34] To achieve this, the African communal view of wealth must be upheld, developed and incorporated in whatever model of poverty one choses for the African context. The African church must reject any individualistic view of wealth not only because it is unbiblical but also because it is not acceptable within the African cultural setting.

A Christian perspective of giving and sharing of material resources needs to be outlined at this point. These views were developed from Wesley's economic principles.[35] First, Wesley regards giving as service to God and humanity. Therefore, the primary motivation of giving should not be the material blessing that may accompany this act. Rather, those who give must regard it as part of the service they are rendering to God and their fellow

---

33. Nihinlola, *Theology Under the Mango Tree*, 85.
34. Goliama, "Gospel of Prosperity," 293.
35. Asante, *Stewardship*.

humankind. Sharing one's resources with others is a demonstration of love for God and humanity (as noted earlier). It is the act of sharing as the fulfilment of the great commandment of love for God and neighbor.

Second, Wesley says giving has a christological dimension. He regards giving as a way of emulating Christ, who gave us everything including his life. The act of giving is therefore part of Christian discipleship. The disciple grows in giving as they grow in discipleship. In line with this thought, Wesley views tithing as a Christian practice but argues that the believer must strive to give more than ten percent because all belongs to God.[36] This means that a believer's giving must relate directly with his or her level of spiritual growth.

Third, giving, in Wesley's view, includes more than money. It may be in the form of labor such as farming, teaching, nursing, carpentry and so on. One's vocation, seen as God's call, must be done as a form of giving to individuals and to the society as a whole. Seeing employment as a calling helps us to think of employment not only in monetary terms, but in terms of a higher purpose of fulfilling our calling.

Furthermore, frugal living in response to the needs of others is a form of giving. The believer may decide to cut down expenses on their basic life needs (for a period) in order to have abundance to share with the poor. Such a life constitutes giving. The one who desists from corruption and the one who takes good care of the environment is also giving because such acts go a long way towards helping the government save money (which would have been spent on maintaining the environment) for other projects.

In addition, Wesley's concept of giving has a soteriological dimension. He says that one should not just help the poor through giving but also lead them to salvation in Christ. For this reason, he argued that social concern must involve personal contact and visitation. Therefore, Wesley's social concern for the poor was not only meant to relieve the poor from their plight but also to win them for Christ. He also argues that social concern for the poor should go beyond charity to building a Christian community in which justice and compassion will develop among interconnected groups of people. The promotion of these principles would significantly reduce poverty in Africa.

Human (Capacity) Development

Human development is core to all forms of economic development. By human development I mean the steps towards improving the quality (or capabilities)

---

36. Wesley, *Wesley's Notes*, 36.

of the people in our societies. Hope defines capacity development as "the enhancement of the competency of individuals, public sector institutions, private sector entities, civil society organizations, and local communities to engage in activities in a sustainable manner for positive development impacts."[37] Capacity development (also referred to as capacity building or capacity enhancement) goes beyond mere improvement in individual abilities and skills to include the provision of incentives.

Its basic aim is to bring about "change and transformation at the individual, institutional, and societal levels."[38] The individual level of capacity building has to do with giving the individual members of the society opportunities to have adequate training that helps them to accumulate knowledge and skills, which they can then expand into new directions to create additional opportunities. The institutional level of capacity development has to do with enhancing the efficiency of existing state institutions, rather than establishing new institutions. Many African countries have relatively more ministers of state than developed countries because governments keep on creating new departments and appointing ministers to manage them, rather than improving the capacity of the existing ministries and maintaining or reducing their number to cut down the cost of running the government. Capacity building at the societal or organizational level has to do with the creation of "opportunities in both the private and public sectors to allow people to use and expand their capacities to the fullest for the benefit of the society in general."[39] For the capacity building to be effective, its process must be owned by the individual African countries rather than by external donors who support the program.[40] Again capacity development program should be tailored to meet the needs of individual countries in their peculiar situations.

I find the following principles from Hope useful for planning and implementing capacity development programs. Capacity development programs must: (1) be "locally owned and controlled by those committed to the objectives of capacity development initiatives as well as by those who will be responsible and accountable for it"; (2) be "addressed as a dynamic, continuous, and long-term process" rather than "fragmented short-term interventions"; (3) build on "existing local capacity across the public, private, and civil society sectors" rather than "foreign expertise." This does not, however,

---

37. Hope, *Poverty, Livelihoods, and Governance*, 157.
38. Hope, 157.
39. Huque and Zafarullah, *International Development Governance*, 591.
40. Hope, 157.

imply no foreign expertise is requires; rather, the core must be locally-based efforts; (4) involve "a broad-based and participatory approach to increase awareness, understanding, and acceptance across the public, private and civil society sectors"; (5) be "comprehensive in approach to the extent possible, so that individuals, institutions, and communities are able to simultaneously benefit"; and (6) be "included in each sector plan, in the context of sector wide approaches, as a critical entry point and as part of development objectives."[41]

A country's economic development in the twenty-first century depends not so much on its natural resources but rather on human resources which can provide the skills needed to manage and harness a country's natural resources efficiently. Many African countries have many natural resources but lack the technical expertise required for harnessing these resources. Africa needs to promote balanced universal education to improve the technical skills of its people and their living conditions. In addition to technical, scientific and vocational development, the African context requires leadership and citizenry development as part of strategies towards poverty reduction. Africa is currently experiencing mediocre leadership or governance and irresponsible citizenship and this situation makes it imperative for the continent to have a theology of human development that attends to this need. Africa lacks "good political, economic, and corporate governance systems" which are "necessary foundations to create, stabilize, nurture and utilize capacity for development."[42] Leadership is "an influential relationship that is God-given to develop others."[43] Leaders are made, not born; the opportunity to lead comes from God and so leadership may be considered as a gift from God. The major task has to do with identifying people's potential and helping them develop their God-given abilities. To bring these about may require frequent leadership training and seminars for the youth and opportunities for them to take up leadership in society. Africa's leaders must also make a conscious effort towards grooming the youth so that they can take up leadership roles.

Leadership development should also stress the servanthood role of the leader. The understanding that leaders are to be served must be opposed by the biblical teaching that leaders ought to serve (Mark 10:42–43). Africa needs selfless and committed leaders, who have the interest of their community at heart rather than their own interest. The need for a proper understanding of power is key to this step. The Greek word *exousia* suggests "absolute

---

41. Hope, 158.
42. Hope, 155.
43. Nihinlola, *Theology Under the Mango Tree*, 138.

unrestricted authority" (e.g. Luke 12:5) when used of God; when used of humans it refers to "delegated authority" (Rom 13:1–2).[44] When God entrusts people with power he expects them to use it in ensuring the well-being of their subjects. To achieve this, there is the need "to promote justice, ensure peace and tranquility, a fairer distribution of income and a wiser use of resources, particularly the human and natural resources."[45] The obvious conclusion is that humans are accountable to God for their stewardship of the power entrusted to them. Through leadership development, Africa will be free from the hypocrisy, mediocrity and incompetence that currently marks the political and ecclesial leadership in the continent.

In addition, there is the need to develop the citizenry to be responsible citizens, not spectators. For a society to develop, its members need opportunities to give constructive criticism about what is happening around them. Ninhilola identifies complacency and illiteracy as two major factors that need to be dealt with to enable Africans to become more responsible members of their communities. Complacency among Africans is attested to by the "lack of passion for excellence."[46] There is the need for individuals, communities, and countries to strive towards excellence in all aspects of human life.

To achieve this, Africans must be educated. The reason is that illiteracy hinders many aspects of life, including political, religious, social and economic participation. I have mentioned earlier in this book that many Africans are poor due to lack of education. According to Nihinlola, "because of illiteracy, the electorates do not know the power of their vote, their rights to elect and change their leaders in a democracy."[47] People may sell their votes during elections because of illiteracy. People receive machetes, salt, meat, money and so on, to vote for wrong but popular candidates. Illiteracy may also be the reason for which citizens tolerate maladministration, tyranny and oppression or "compromise their welfare and allow politicians to deceive them."[48] In my view, Africa needs to structure and conduct its education in a way that makes Africans better prepared and more efficient for national development.

---

44. Asante, *Stewardship*, 68.
45. Asante, 69.
46. Nihinlola, *Theology Under the Mango Tree*, 140.
47. Nihinlola, 140.
48. Nihinlola, 140–141.

Female Empowerment

In Africa and many other parts of the world, women and children are the most destitute when it comes to issues related to poverty. This makes it crucial for the Africans to make conscious effort at educating and empowering women to raise their social and economic status. More females in Africa must be encouraged to enroll for formal education. There is a popular saying among Ghanaians that "If you educate a man, you simply educate an individual, but if you educate a woman you educate a nation." Women are key in the upbringing of children and the education they acquire contributes to the quality of the children they raise. Enrolling more women in school will go a long way towards reducing, for example, the number of female head porters on our streets. In the job market, females should be given the same opportunities as males. Females with good leadership qualities must be given the chance to lead. If leadership is a gift that God gives people regardless of their gender, race, age and the like, then people should not be denied opportunities to lead simply because of their gender.

In addition, cultural practices that hinder the socioeconomic progress of women must be discarded. For example, widowhood rites, which prohibit women from working after they lose their husbands and deny females the right to own property and other economic resources, must be reviewed. Traditions that ban females from contributing to socioeconomic development must also be addressed to empower women in Africa. More females must be encouraged to take active part in the democratic process of the country by vying for elective posts and positions in government and civil society.

Cultural Transformation

In my view, the culture of a society informs its socioeconomic progress. This means that our contextual theology of poverty alleviation needs to touch on African cultural practices. Coote and Stott rightly assert that "the process of communicating the gospel cannot be isolated from the human culture from which it comes, or from that in which it is to be proclaimed."[49] Therefore, to be effective, the gospel can and should permeate the ethos of a group, its essential attitudes, its institutions and all its structures without necessarily becoming an obstacle to the promotion of African heritage. The cultures of Africa, like any others, have both positive and negative aspects. The extremes of rejecting every human culture and adopting every human culture must be

---

49. Coote and Stott, *Down to Earth*, 311.

avoided. What the church needs to do is to seek to transform culture to make the society a better place to live.

Cultural practices that contradict the Christian faith must be rejected; the rest can be adopted (or modified) to enhance the gospel. Therefore, the gospel-culture encounter must result in a radical change in African cultural practices such as gender injustice, child marriages, widowhood rites with its associated exclusion from work, female genital mutilation, sexual exploitation of the vulnerable, expensive funerals, child trafficking and child labor, and shelving crimes such as rape.

Expensive funerals need special consideration because of their huge impact on the economic life of Africans. I indicated earlier in the book that expensive funerals can make people and their families poor. I give the following recommendations for addressing the practice of expensive funerals.[50]

First, our people need to be educated on the implications of spending too much money on funerals. In this regard, traditional and religious leaders to sensitize their followers on more cost-effective and simple way of organizing funerals.

Second, people should not copy blindly the funeral practices of those who are more affluent. Poor families should not borrow to organize expensive funerals because they want to have a ceremony similar to that of another family. As much as possible, funerals should be organized within the means of the bereaved family. No family, whether economically sound or not, should use all its available resources to organize funeral ceremonies. To this end, expensive caskets and decorations, death announcements, which are duplicated on radio and television stations, and newspapers; billboards of the deceased; prescription of different mourning cloths for a funeral; giving out of souvenirs with the picture of the deceased; and the use of many musical groups at funerals should be discouraged by the church. I suggest that the cost of food, drinks, and entertainment be minimized since a funeral is not for enjoyment but mourning. After all, no amount of display of wealth at a funeral can bring the dead back to life or change their eternal destiny.

The third proposal has to do with the duration of a corpse's stay in the morgue. Preserving a body scientifically for a long time, for whatever reason, tends to increase the cost of funerals. Dealing with the dead promptly, usually within twenty-four hours of one's demise, is highly recommended. However,

---

50. What follows has been gleaned from Amevenku and Boaheng, *African Biblical Christianity and Contemporary Ethics*, 110–111.

as a general rule, in my view, a dead person should not be kept at the morgue for more than two weeks.

Fourth, the use of alcohol at funerals must cease since most people get drunk and cause confusion at the end. I agree with Palmer-Buckle's view that "the surest way to remember the dead is not the type of coffins used to bury them nor [is it] the type of cloth or T-shirt worn during their funerals, but doing something positive for the dead which would benefit the living."[51] Therefore, reducing the cost of funerals can make available resources that can be channeled into assisting in areas such as healthcare and education.

Social and Structural Transformation

Poverty alleviation cannot be achieved without radical transformation in our societies. Dulles observed that "a failure to accept the social implications of the Gospel would be a lack of responsiveness to the Gospel itself."[52] The church is therefore expected to speak to contextual social problems such as injustice, bribery, corruption, and smuggling and hoarding of goods, among other ills that prevail in our societies and impoverish people. Some practical steps towards social transformation include calling on Christians to be responsible, compassionate, law-abiding citizens; to speak for the voiceless and oppressed; to maintain or restore righteousness and justice; and to advocate for the fair sharing of national resources. Christians are charged by God to oppose policies that cause poverty or widen the economic gap between the rich and the poor. They are to make useful suggestions to the governing authorities on how poverty can be addressed in a way that honors what God has said in Scripture. The society ought to monitor government to ensure that the right structures are in place for economic empowerment of the citizenry. Africans should participate in the governance of their countries and offer constructive critiques to political leaders with the aim of improving governance and fostering development to make life meaningful for all people, especially the poor.

Asante believes that part of the solution to Africa's poverty is to address the problem of structural injustice.[53] He identifies two ways in which structural injustice may occur: injustice in an organizational activity, for example, exploitation and oppression of the poor, and injustice in an organizational

---

51. Newton, "Long Goodbye," http://edition.cnn.com/2014/03/11/world/africa/on-the-road-ghana-funerals/.

52. As cited in Asante, *Theology in Society*, 118.

53. Asante, *Stewardship*, 186.

design.⁵⁴ For example, many African countries are highly indebted to developed countries. Year after year, poor countries pay debts to the rich developed countries without hope of ever paying off all that they owe. One thing that comes out clearly from this situation is the unfair distribution of the world's resources. Asante observes that the world's production is geared towards the needs of the rich minority.⁵⁵ He observes that in order to satisfy the drinking need of the rich, vast amount of land, which could have been used to cultivate nutritious local crops, are usually used to produce cash crops such as cocoa, coffee and tea.⁵⁶ Also, a lot of grain needs to be produced in order to feed cattle to produce beef for the rich. These commodities (cocoa, coffee, tea, beef, and others), according to Asante, are not really needed by the poor who form the majority of the world's population.⁵⁷ The poverty situation in Africa cannot be tackled without addressing these global economic inequalities.

At the heart of the message of Deuteronomy 15:1–11 is economic justice and compassion. God's requirement that the Israelites cancel the debt of their fellow Israelites every seventh year was one of the mechanisms God established to ensure that neither poverty nor wealth developed to an extreme. This requirement is based on God's divine ownership of resources (Ps 24:1–2). Matthew 6:19–34 places a limit on the extent to which ownership and control of basic resources of production could be concentrated in the hands of a few people (see especially vv. 19, 24). These passages underline the need to care for the poor. Asante concludes then that "justice and mercy are the guiding principles of social behavior for the Bible."⁵⁸

In light of Africa's poverty problem, the foregoing discussion points to the need for a new economic paradigm that promotes economic justice in the continent. Also, there is the need for world leaders to find a way of sharing the world's resources equitably. Asante concludes that "[w]hat we need more than anything else in our present situation is the rejection of the Master Economy and its system of values and the adoption of a Servant Economy with its new system of human centered and nature-oriented values."⁵⁹ To this I add that it would not be out of place for wealthy countries to cancel the debts owed by poor countries just as God required the Israelites to do. This will offer poor

---

54. Asante, 186.
55. Asante, 186.
56. Asante, 186.
57. Asante, 188.
58. Asante, 190.
59. Asante, 193.

countries an opportunity to reorganize their economy to improve the welfare of their people.

Spiritual and Moral Transformation

The fight against poverty in Africa must involve not only economic solutions but also spiritual and moral remedies. Africans are deeply spiritual and so the importance of the spiritual dimension in any kind of theology of poverty for Africa cannot be overemphasized. In view of the fact that poverty may have spiritual antecedents, the church should encourage its members to develop counselling, and healing and deliverance ministries. Abuses in such ministry must however be checked. The church must use its God-given power to deal with forces that retard the socioeconomic growth of believers. In my opinion, this task must not be left to certain denominations (such as Pentecostal and charismatic churches) but should be encouraged and practiced by all Christian denominations. While there is nothing wrong with Christians praying for God's blessings, favor and prosperity, overemphasis of spiritual solutions to poverty at the neglect of other practical steps of addressing the problem must be checked.

For example, Christian spirituality should not undermine the need for hard work. Genuine spirituality, as Nihinlola points out, "is a wholistic concept, a balance of good relationship with God and meaningful co-existence with fellow humans."[60] Unfortunately, there are Christian leaders in Africa who teach their members to assemble every day to pray for miracles and blessings. People believe these leaders, act according to their instruction and pay dearly with the burden of poverty. What Africa needs at the moment is a balance between worship (prayer) and work. The contextual model of poverty alleviation calls for a balance between time spent at worship centers and time spent on work. As Nihinlola adds, "church vigil becomes false spirituality when it is not combined with or if it hinders practical work."[61] A churchgoing contractor who executes a government contract poorly is not spiritual. A church leader who evades taxes or import expired goods is not spiritual; neither is a church member who cheats in an examination. A churchgoing civil servant with a lackadaisical attitude towards work lacks spirituality. By developing true Christian spirituality, African countries can be freed from bribery, corruption, and mismanagement of state funds, which hinder the continent's socioeconomic progress.

---

60. Nihinlola, *Theology Under the Mango Tree*, 143.
61. Nihinlola, 143.

Another aspect of African Christian spirituality is its effect on family life. How does Christian spirituality affect family life in Africa? In recent times, Africans have become so "spiritual" that they tend to spend all their time in the church at the expense of work and family life. Many churches in Africa today have programs and activities organized that require members' participation throughout the week from Monday to Sunday. The common lifestyle of most parents in much of urban Africa today can be described as follows: Early in the morning, parents leave for work when their children are still asleep or they leave home with their children who are going to school. From school, the children come home and find no parent and so are received by and have to enjoy the company of house helps. The parents come home in the evening only to leave the children in a rush to attend a church activity or a church meeting. They come back and find their children asleep and go through the same set of activities the following day. On weekends and during vacations, the schools also engage pupils in extra classes or extracurricular activities. Consequently, parents and their children hardly stay together to build the family. Unfortunately, on school holidays, which are meant to be used for family gatherings and socializing, churches fix programs which deprive families the opportunity to come together and think about family issues. The result of this loss of "family time" is a moral decline which may lead to children failing in school or dropping out of school entirely; situations which have the potential of making them jobless and hence poor.

In my candid opinion, true spirituality should enhance family building rather than destroying family bonds. Pastors should encourage members to spend time with their families, giving them time to think about their family's welfare and to build their Christian life as a family. The church should be a place where one goes to receive teaching that applies to real-life situations at home, but most service to God takes place outside the church buildings. Christianity is practiced in the home (society) not in the chapel. By this I mean it is during our stay in the community that our Christian values are mostly tested, not when we are worshiping in the chapel where almost everyone behaves like an angel.

Solidarity with the Poor

In chapter 2 I noted that poverty is a form of social exclusion. Socially excluded poor people encounter a lot of psychological problems. Also we noted earlier that the teachings of prosperity theology have created a negative psychological effect on the poor. Some poor Christians feels disappointed by God because they have been giving and yet have not received the expected material blessing.

Others feel neglected or cursed by God because of their economic situation. There is the need to deal both with the psychological effects on the poor created by prosperity teachers and the social exclusion of the poor by the African society. Following the example set by Jesus in his ministry, the African church must also identify with the poor and the social outcasts. One way of achieving this is for Christian ministers to live among the poor in their communities. This will offer them an opportunity to observe, listen, and share the problems that the poor face. As Bongo puts it, "[b]y being with them in their distress, taking their side, supporting them pastorally and showing them God's love, one starts gaining their trust and acquiring existential knowledge of that situation."[62] This move is a development of Wesley's principle of visiting the poor before donating to them rather than just sending one's donation to them through another person. The church should consider putting up mission houses within as many poor communities as possible. Chapels must also be built within poor communities.

The church as a body must also make the poor and marginalized in the society, such as women and orphans, the targets of its social services (which includes offering counselling and career guidance). It must intensify its visitations to the poor and use these visits as a platform to share the gospel. Boafo rightly says that "[m]ission alongside the poor in [Africa] must consider setting up Inner City Mission centers to provide for the spiritual and physical needs of the poor in the cities."[63] Such mission must include providing the basic needs of the vulnerable including orphans, street children, widows, and others. This will reduce the number of people hawking in our streets or begging for alms. In addition, poverty alleviation programs in Africa must protect the poor from destitution, exploitation, sharp fluctuations in income and social insecurity. The poor must be involved in rural works, and be provided with food subsidies to help them fight against destitution. Again, they must be encouraged to start some economic activities on their own through provision of productive assets and appropriate skills, subsidies and loan facilities, and other support services for sustained employment and development.[64]

---

62. Wilson and Letsosa, "Biblical Principles," 6.
63. Boafo, *John Wesley's Theology*, 234.
64. Enquobahrie, *Understanding Poverty*, 12.

Contentment, Modesty and Simplicity

Both the biblical teaching expounded in this book and the traditional African society support a simple and modest way of life. Both Matthew 6:19–34 and 1 Timothy 6:6–10 bring out the need for contentment, modesty, and simplicity in life. These virtues will help the Christian to avoid worry and anxiety that tend to distract them from the Lord. Contentment, modesty, and simplicity can only be applied if believers learn to distinguish between the necessities of life and wants. The choice between available commodities (for example, cellphone, food, furniture, or dressing mirror) is therefore crucial to the Christian. Asante believes that right choices between commodities can be made if believers are able to distinguish between commodities of intrinsic value and those with instrumental value. He writes, ". . . even though the human has instrumental need for food, clothing and shelter, which are basic values to be taken care of, given that the human also has a spiritual component, there are ends beyond these instrument needs, which the Christian must pursue to fulfil his nature."[65] Having made this distinction, one can choose appropriately based on their scale of preference.

The biblical data examined in this book shows that human life has intrinsic value while items such as food, clothing, shelter, and others have instrumental value (Matt 6:25). It is for this reason that Jesus maintains that life does not consist in the abundance of wealth (Luke 12:15). Asante maintains that human beings "eat to live" but "do not live to eat."[66] This means that food is a means to an end and not an end in itself. Hence, it is unethical to consider food or wealth as the reason for which Christians live. Therefore, no matter one's economic situation there is the need to pursue higher goals which have eternal values. If so, then there is no justification for engaging in ungodly vocations such as robbery or prostitution as a means of one's survival. Asante explains further that "the right use of things [resources] is defined and informed by the law of love, other-centeredness, the needs of neighbor."[67] Therefore, the law of love must be the guiding principle for any choice made in one's life. Love for neighbor requires modesty and simplicity in order to get surplus to share with others. At the same time, modest living will save one from the dangers associated with accumulated wealth.

---

65. Asante, *Theology in Society*, 117.
66. Asante, 116.
67. Asante, 117.

Job Creation

One of the major factors that contribute to poverty in Africa is unemployment. Our discussion on work ethics has pointed out that every able person needs to engage in some kind of productive work. For people to work, there must be opportunities for work available. The state has the biggest role to play in creating jobs for the populace. With governments leading the campaign against unemployment, entities such as individuals, non-governmental organizations, the church and others should also help in providing jobs for the unemployed. African governments should set up policies that support the expansion of national economies and industry. There is the need to set out industrial policies that can help Africa countries process some of their raw materials into finished goods before export. This will not only create employment but also increase government revenue as well.

The road networks in African countries need particular attention and should be improved to facilitate easy transport of food stuffs from farming communities to the cities. This in turn will encourage many people to engage in farming because they would be certain that their yield will not rot on the farm due to bad roads. As another strategy of making farming attractive, governments should work towards making markets available and accessible to farmers. In other words, there should be government agencies that will buy or determine the price of farm produce. This will help fight exploitation of farmers by buyers. With vast land available in Africa, many unemployed people can engage themselves in farming if it becomes lucrative enough to attract them.

Africa's high unemployment can also be dealt with through the expansion of vocational and technical education. This kind of education has the potential of giving learners the practical skills required for employment including self-employment. People with such expertise can be assisted to start their own enterprises. The church should also educate its members on job opportunities available and how people can also start their own businesses. The church should also consider providing financial assistance or other forms of help to the needy.

Financial Ethics

This aspect seeks to address the issues of gambling and hoarding of resources, and financial investments undertaken by Christians in Africa. Unethical uses of money include hoarding and all kinds of gambling such as betting, pools and raffles, sweepstakes and similar uses.[68] Hoarding money or other treasures,

---

68. Asante, 64.

such as food or fuel, is a sign of selfishness. It opposes the idea of Christian stewardship which teaches sharing of resources. Gambling is wrong because it "makes luck or chance the determining factor of human's decisions."[69] Humans are to be responsible beings whose life is conducted not by chance but by purposeful planning ahead under God's providence. Gambling is contrary to the fundamental principle that humans should work for a living. "Gambling replaces the link between work and income with chance and income," says Asante.[70] Using God's resources to sponsor ungodly activities such as beauty pageants, liquor production and promotion are also some of the unethical uses of wealth in Africa that must be discouraged among Christians.

Between 2013 and 2016, some financial institutions and supposed fun clubs[71] (including Dele Kundeni Martin [DKM] financial services, God Is Love, Jastar Motors, Perfect Edge, Little Drops and others) sprang up in Ghana (especially in the Bono, Bono East and Ahafo regions) and promised to offer their customers very high interest rate (some of them as high as 200%).[72] At the end, these institutions collapsed and customers' deposits were lost.[73] At the same time, many other financial institutions in Africa charged very high interest on loans given to their customers.[74] This situation has a lot of lessons for Africa in general. The biblical principles taught by Deuteronomy 15:1, 7–9 include the fact that Christians are not expected to charge huge interest on loans. I reason this way because God expected the Israelites to cancel debts every seven years. It is deducible from this principle that God does not want debt to be the burden of the poor throughout their lifetime. By reducing interest on loans to the barest minimum, God's desire for the Christian community will be accomplished.

In my opinion, Christians should always consider the sustainability and credibility of the enterprises they engage in, and they should consider their involvement with Christian financial ethics in mind. We have noted earlier that "God's command in Genesis 2:15 that humankind should work and till the land and his subsequent statement that humankind will have his or her daily bread from the sweat of his or her brow, is an indication that God does

---

69. Asante, 64.

70. Asante, 65.

71. These organizations were really financial institutions which operated like fun clubs (or keep fit clubs). They were not actual betting companies.

72. Boaheng, "Christian Discipleship," 24.

73. Boaheng, 24.

74. Boaheng, 24–25.

not sanction enterprises that aim at making everybody rich, even the lazy."[75] Therefore, Christians (in their attempts to seek financial gains) should apply biblical principles regarding the source and the sustainability of the source. The get-rich-attitude of the young must be discouraged. People must work hard through the guidance of God in order to succeed. Investments whose chances of sustainability are unknown must be avoided.

Reducing Extravagance and Materialism in the Church

The extravagant and materialistic nature of the contemporary African church needs attention. The twenty-first century African church is very materialistic. Materialism among pastors is evident in the multi-million-dollar empires many of these churches and Christian ministries have become, the mansions that some pastors live in, the fleet of ostentatious and luxurious cars they own, and the expensive electronic gadgets they use. For example, the net worth of some famous pastors has been estimated as follows: Bishop David Oyedepo, $150 million; Pastor E. A. Adeboye (Nigeria), $130 million; Pastor Chris Oyakhilome, $50 million; and Uebert Angel $50 million.[76] It is against this backdrop that J. K. Asamoah-Gyadu says that "anybody who has cared to pay attention to the life of the church today is likely to see a church that is committed not to the core business of mission or the things of the Spirit as defined by the Cross, but carnality that manifests in foolish jesting, ecclesiastical pomposity, and the exploitation of the Gospel for economic gain."[77] The need for wealthy ministers to help the poor in the society is obvious. Since no one will take any wealth to the grave, it is important that ministers of the gospel share their wealth with the poor and help them in other ways to improve their living standards. Caring for the needy can only be realized if we control our materialistic tendencies. Jesus's example of compassion for the poor is a model for the Christian community, including pastors.

Another key issue that raises a lot of theological and ethical questions is the high cost of chapels we find in Africa today. Are buildings a legitimate ministry expense? If so, what kinds of buildings and how many buildings are legitimate? Can this extensive accumulation of material wealth be justified in the light of the world's needs? Alcorn argues that "Spending money on buildings for ministries is inherently neither right nor wrong" because in

---

75. Boaheng, 24.
76. https://indapaper.com/richest-pastors-in-africa/3/, accessed 21 May 2020.
77. Asamoah-Gyadu, *Jesus Our Immanuel*, 140.

certain cases, we glorify God "through the financing, construction, and use of a building."[78] However, we dishonor God when church building results in "massive indebtedness, disunity, extravagance, pride, and misuse."[79] Alcorn balances this argument by saying that criticizing the church for spending money on buildings and not giving it to the poor or not using it for missions is not always justifiable, because "by providing for a growing congregation's needs, a building can serve purposes of evangelism and edification, broadening and deepening the home base so that much more money, prayer, and personal involvement are ultimately given to missions and to the poor than otherwise would have been."[80]

I see nothing wrong with the wise use of church funds in putting up practical and attractive—but not extravagant—buildings as an investment in eternity. On the other hand, there are some buildings which could have served the churches purpose but are pulled down for the sake of putting up a more expensive one so that a church can make a name for itself. Alcorn is right in saying the church must ensure that "the construction of a building doesn't detract us from giving to meet needs and evangelize our community and the world."[81] Therefore, there is everything wrong "when a church spends more money paying interest on its construction loans than on world missions. If missions spending declines during a building program, this reflects poorly on a church's priorities."[82] Churches that major in chapel buildings tend to externalize the body of Christ, and thereby forget that human beings—not the physical building—are God's dwelling place (1 Cor 3:16). The contextual model of poverty alleviation in Africa therefore demands that the church focuses on building people, not building buildings. It is only when the African church applies the principles of contentment, modesty, and simplicity that it will have enough funds to help alleviate poverty in society. As it is now, the church in Africa is always in dire need of funds for one project or the other. This situation makes it turn a blind eye to its social responsibility of helping the poor through sharing of resources. The sooner the church does something about this situation the better.

---

78. Alcorn, *Money, Possessions, and Eternity*, 430.
79. Alcorn, 430.
80. Alcorn, 430.
81. Alcorn, 431.
82. Alcorn, 431.

Conclusion

The model of poverty alleviation formulated in this chapter is multifaceted, touching on the individual, the state, and the church. This means that the fight against poverty cannot be achieved by any one institution alone. The need for collective efforts by different stakeholders in the fight against poverty is very crucial. The implementation of a contextual model for poverty reduction in Africa is expected to yield improved health, increased literacy, increased income, spiritual growth, and improved investments for the people of Africa. In addition, it will help reduce the seductive attraction and harmful effects of wealth on Christians, help promote modest living, and reduce greed and anxiety in life. It will also help Christians to focus first on the kingdom of God and his righteousness, and in so doing accumulate eternal treasures.

Afterword

The book set out to develop an approach to poverty that is both theologically sound and culturally appropriate for the context of Africa. I have shown the extent, causes, and effects of poverty in Africa. I have also shown that contextual poverty alleviation model is an alternative to the prosperity theology model. Thus, I have contended that a contextual theology of poverty offers a better paradigm for the understanding and alleviation of poverty among African Christians. In other words, poverty among Christians in Africa will decrease if contextual theological principles for poverty reduction are formulated, taught and applied. The contextual model of poverty for Africa has a number of practical implications for the poor, the church, and the society. To these I now turn.

First, the book has shown that it is biblically unsound and culturally inappropriate for the poor to do nothing about their state, thinking that poverty is a requirement for entering the kingdom of God. God really does not command voluntary poverty and it is not a requirement for entrance into the kingdom of God. This means that each person must work hard under the guidance of God to improve their status in life. While the poor may not necessarily trust that their hard work will lead to success in life, they can nevertheless trust God to bless their labor and help them overcome their challenges.

Second, wealth should not be considered a sign of righteousness. God is the source of all good things. Wealth comes with a responsibility to ensure that the needy are cared for. Those who have wealth have the responsibility of ensuring that they do not idolize it. The dangers associated with wealth possession, including pride, luxury, religious laxity, selfishness, and oppression, must be guarded against.

Third, the church must intensify teachings on wealth and poverty to help members understand God's will on this subject. A small survey conducted in some key Pentecostal and charismatic churches in Africa indicates that members lack effective and sound teaching on wealth and poverty. What is often taught is prosperity theology which, as we have seen, is biblically and culturally inappropriate. Rather than promoting materialism, the church ought to be teaching stewardship of resources, contentment, modesty and simplicity not only by words but also by example. This means that extravagance in ministry must be checked.

Fourth, the church in Africa should contribute to the nurturing of leaders who will exhibit Christ-like leadership principles in all spheres of life. Teaching based on the examples of leaders in the Bible such as Moses, Joshua, Solomon, David, and most importantly, Jesus Christ, may be helpful in this regard. Their experiences can help model good leadership skills as a way of addressing the bad leadership that is found in many African nations. Leaders who are worthy of emulation are selfless, humble, hard-working, truthful, and Spirit-led. The church must also encourage African believers and their leaders to not privatize God or take biblical principles out of national discourse and decisions. Africans, regardless of their age or status in society, should be encouraged to see themselves as leaders in their own small or big ways. For example, parents are leaders in the home, teachers are leaders in school, and so on. Everyone should lead with dedication and be guided by the truth in whatever duty and work they do, so that together, we can build a better continent.

Fifth, the church should work towards societal transformation by teaching about the devastating effects of sin not only on the sinner but also on the society. The disciple-making task of the church must be reworked so that we focus on making more disciples of Christ rather than just churchgoers and church members. Christian discipleship must promote contentment, generosity, good stewardship, simplicity and modesty, and other similar virtues.

Sixth, the church must work with traditional leaders to promote positive African traditions and mores and do away with negative and outdated cultural practices that hinder the socioeconomic development of Africans. We have identified expensive funeral rites, widowhood rites, and patriarchal structures that sideline women as some of the negative practices contributing to poverty. The church must be well informed about these practices and their effects and then, together with the traditional authorities, negotiate with communities and help them to give a contextual expression to the practice in question from a Christian perspective. Involving Christian opinion leaders in such negotiations can help the church more effectively reach communities.

Seventh, the government must work towards bridging the economic inequality gap between the rich and the poor. For fair sharing of the national resources priority should be given to the mostly rural communities that lack basic social amenities such as potable drinking water, motorable roads, electricity, and other services. This will make rural communities attractive not only to the inhabitants but also to investors to commit their resources towards developing these regions, which can create employment opportunities for the youth in rural communities. Rural development contributes to lessening rural urban migration and bridging the income gap between rural and urban dwellers.

Last, the success of the contextual model for poverty alleviation will require collaboration between African governments and national, international, and multilateral partners to form and implement plans that will enhance national economies. Education, good governance, crime prevention, tackling the canker of corruption and the development of local agricultural industries, and manufacturing are examples of programs that such collaboration could support. Providing good roads, water, sanitation, energy supply and renewal, mining and local industry, the provision of health infrastructure, and the prevention of post-harvest losses will also contribute greatly towards enhancing national economies and improving living standards in Africa.

Bibliography

Adeboye, E. A. *Behold He Cometh*. Lagos: Christ the Redeemer's Ministries, 2003.

Aderonmu, Jonathan A. "Local Government and Poverty Eradication in Rural Nigeria." *Canadian Social Science* 6, no. 5 (2010): 200–208.

Adjei, Nyarko G. "Poverty in Ghana: Theological Reflection on the Response of Some Churches in Kumasi Metropolitan Area." Unpublished MPhil thesis, Kwame Nkrumah University of Science and Technology [KNUST], 2012.

Adogla-Bessa, Delali . "Man, 70, Dies after 7 Hospitals 'Rejected Him' over Lack of Beds." Posted 11 June 2018. Accessed 21 May 2020. https://citinewsroom.com/2018/06/man-70-dies-after-7-hospitals-rejected-him-over-lack-of-beds/.

Alcorn, Randy. *Money, Possessions, and Eternity*. Carol Stream, IL: Tyndale, 2011.

Amevenku, Frederick M. "Faith Healing in Ghanaian Christianity: An Examination of Attitudes and Practices Based on an Exegesis of James 5:13–18." *Trinity Journal of Church and Theology* 18, no. 4 (2015): 87–101.

———. "The Reinterpretation of the Law in Matthew's Sermon on the Mount: Exploring Its Contextual Interpretation among the Ewes of Ghana." Unpublished PhD dissertation, University of Stellenbosch, 2019.

Amevenku, Frederick M., and Isaac Boaheng. *African Biblical Christianity and Contemporary Ethics*. Accra: Noyam Publishers, 2020. Ebook, https://noyam.org/e-books/.

———. "Theological Interpretations of the Sermon on the Mount: Making an Old Sermon Relevant for Our Time." *Trinity Journal of Church and Theology* 18, no. 5 (2016): 69–90.

———. *Tithing in the Christian Church*. Tema: Kabkork Publication, 2018.

———. "Use of Imprecatory Prayers in Contemporary African Christianity: A Critique." *E-Journal of Religious and Theological Studies* 1, no. 2 (2015): 86–104.

Amoah, E. "African Traditional Religion and the Concept of Poverty." In *Religion and Poverty: Pan-African Perspectives*, edited by P. J. Paris, 111–127. Durham and London: Duke University Press, 2009.

Ampong, Ebenezer A., and Benyah, Francis. "Imposition of Hands: A Theological Assessment of Contemporary Ghanaian Christian Exorcistic Practice." *Trinity Journal of Church and Theology* 19, no. 1 (2017): 84–108.

Anderson, Allan H. *An Introduction to Pentecostalism: Global Charismatic Christianity*. Cambridge: Cambridge University Press, 2014.

Anim, Emmanuel K. "The Prosperity Gospel in Ghana and the Primal Imagination." *Pentvars Business Journal* 4, no. 2 (2010): 66–76.

Anyanwu, John C. "Working Paper 180 - Marital Status, Household Size and Poverty in Nigeria: Evidence from the 2009–2010 Survey Data." Working Paper Series 978,

African Development Bank (2013). https://ideas.repec.org/p/adb/adbwps/978.html.

Archer, Gleason L., Jr. *New International Encyclopedia of Bible Difficulties*. Grand Rapids, MI: Zondervan, 1982.

Ardington, Cally, Till Bärnighausen, Anne Case, and Alicia Menendez. "The Economic Consequences of Death in South Africa." SALDRU Working Paper no. 91. Southern Africa Labour and Development Research Unit, University of Cape Town, 2012.

Arichea, Daniel C., and Howard A. Hatton. *A Handbook on Paul's First Letter to Timothy*. New York: UBS Handbook Series, 1995. Electronic edition.

Arthur, G. K. *Cloth as Metaphor: (Re)reading the Adinkra Cloth Symbols of the Akan of Ghana*. Beltsville: Cefiks Publications, 2001.

Asamoah-Gyadu, Johnson K. *African Charismatics. Current Developments within Independent Indigenous Pentecostalism in Ghana*. Leiden: Brill, 2005.

———. *Contemporary Pentecostal Christianity: Interpretations from an African Context*. Oxford: Regnum Africa, 2013.

———. "Did Jesus Wear Designer Robes?" *Christianity Today*, 27 October 2009. https://www.christianitytoday.com/ct/2009/november/main.html.

———. *Jesus Our Immanuel*. Accra: African Christian Press, 2013.

———. "Poverty, Wealth and Social Justice in Africa." *Religions* (2012): 55–69. https://www.qscience.com/docserver/fulltext/rels/2012/2/rels.2012.justice.13.pdf?expires=1590053129&id=id&accname=guest&checksum=4B29D54E351670D4A31390A9D319D676.

———. *Sighs and Signs of the Spirit*. Oxford: Regnum Africa, 2015.

Asante, Emmanuel K. *Culture, Politics and Development: Ethical and Theological Reflections on the Ghanaian Experience*. Accra: Combert Impressions, 2007.

———. *Issues in African Traditional Religion, Ethnicity and Development: Impact on African Christianity*. Accra: SonLife Press, 2017.

———. *Stewardship: Essays on Ethics of Stewardship*. Kumasi: Wilas Press, 1999.

———. *Theology in Society in Context: A Theologist's Reflection on Selected Issues*. Accra: SonLife Press, 2014.

Atiemo, Abamfo O. "Crowds that Bring no Rains: Religious Revivals and Corruption in Ghana." *Trinity Journal of Church and Theology* 18, no. 5 (2016): 6–23.

Awumbila, M. *Gender and Poverty Reduction Strategies in Ghana: Poverty, Health and Gender; Proceedings of the NUFU Workshop*. Accra: Media Design, 2004.

Ayegboyin, Deji. *The Synoptics: Introductory Notes on the Gospels According to Matthew, Mark and Luke*. Ibadan: Global Estida Publishers, 2015.

Baker, M. "Isaiah." In *Eerdmans Commentary on the Bible*, edited by J. D. G. Dunn and J. W. Rogerson, 489–542. Grand Rapids, MI: Eerdmans, 2003.

Barrett, David B. *Schism and Renewal in Africa*. Lusaka: Oxford University Press, 1968.

Bax, Pauline. "In Ghana, Funerals Have Become Big Business: Insurers and Entrepreneurs Profit by Helping Stage Lavish Funerals." *Bloomberg*. Posted

23 August 2013. https://www.bloomberg.com/news/articles/2013-08-22/in-ghana-funerals-have-become-big-business.

Beegle, Kathleen et al. *Poverty in a Rising Africa*. Washington, DC: International Bank for Reconstruction and Development / The World Bank, 2016.

Bevans, Steven B. *Models of Contextual Theology*. Maryknoll, NY: Orbis Books, 1992.

Bitrus, Daniel. "Amos." In *Africa Bible Commentary*, edited by Tokunboh Adeyemo, 1059–1066. Nairobi: WordAlive Publishers, 2006.

Blomberg, Craig L. "On Wealth and Worry: Matthew 6:19–34 – Meaning and Significance." *Criswell Theological Review* 6, no. 1 (1992): 73–89.

Boaheng, Isaac. "Exploring the Relationship between Divine Sovereignty and Human Responsibility in Relation to God's Plan for Salvation." Unpublished master of divinity thesis, Trinity Theological Seminary, 2016.

———. "Christian Discipleship in the Contemporary Church: Lessons from the Matthean Beatitudes." Unpublished essay, Methodist Church Ghana, 2017.

———. "Early Christian Missions in West Africa: Implications for Rethinking the Great Commission." In *Rethinking the Great Commission: Emerging African Perspectives*, edited by Emmanuel Asante and D. N. A. Kpobi, 207–230. Accra: Type Company, 2018.

Boafo, Paul K. *John Wesley's Theology and Public Life: His Socio-Political Thought in the Ghanaian Context*. Accra: Asempa Publishers, 2014.

Bonhoeffer, Dietrich. *The Cost of Discipleship*. London: SCM Press, 2015.

Bosch, David J. *Transforming Mission: Paradigm Shifts in Theology of Mission*. Maryknoll, NY: Orbis, 1991.

Bowler, K. *Blessed: A History of the American Prosperity Gospel*. Oxford: Oxford University Press, 2013.

Bratcher, R. G., and H. A. Hatton. *A Handbook on Deuteronomy*. New York: UBS Handbook Series, 2000. Electronic edition.

Browers, W. P. "African Theology." In *Evangelical Dictionary of Theology*, edited by Walter A. Elwell, 28–34. Grand Rapids, MI: Baker Academic, 2001.

Calef, S. "'Prophet Margins' in the Economy of Salvation: Having, Being, and Doing in the Gospel of Luke." *Journal of Religion & Society*. Supplementary Series 10 (2014): 106–131.

Cannon, K. G. "An Ethical Mapping of Trans-Atlantic Slave-Trade." In *Religion and Poverty: Pan-African Perspectives*, edited by P. J. Paris, 19–38. Durham and London: Duke University Press, 2009.

Carson, D. A. "Matthew." In *The Expositor's Bible Commentary Vol. 8*, edited by F. E. Gaebelein. Grand Rapids, MI: Zondervan, 1984.

Chianeque, Luciano C., and Samuel Ngewa. "Deuteronomy." In *Africa Bible Commentary*, edited by Tokunboh Adeyemo, 209–254. Nairobi: WordAlive Publishers, 2006.

Chimfwembe, Richard M. "*Pastoral Care in a Context of Poverty: A Search for a Zambian Contextual Church Response*." PhD Dissertation, University of Pretoria, 2013.

Chukwuma, Onyekachi Gift. "Reducing Poverty in Nigeria in the Light of Deuteronomy 15:7–18." Unpublished master's thesis, University of Nigeria, 2014.

Citro, F., and R. T. Michael, eds. *Measuring Poverty: A New Approach*. Washington, DC: National Academy Press, 1995.

Coote, Robert T., and John R. W. Stott. *Down to Earth: Studies in Christianity and Culture: The Papers of the Lausanne Consultation on Gospel and Culture*. Grand Rapids, MI: Eerdmans, 1980.

Cotterell, P. *Prosperity Theology*. RTSF Booklets 23. Leicester: Religious and Theological Studies Fellowship, 1993.

Coulombe, Harold, and Quentin Wodon. "Poverty, Livelihoods, and Access to Basic Services in Ghana." In *Ghana CEM: Meeting the Challenge of Accelerated and Shared Growth*, 2007. https://pdfs.semanticscholar.org/5381/dd2567a04b8c406e699d4c286ea9eb5b15ff.pdf?_ga=2.48894502.1259371377.1591181975-1959360548.1591181975.

Cunguara, B. "Assessing Strategies to Reduce Poverty in Rural Mozambique." Unpublished doctoral thesis, Institute of Agricultural and Forestry Economics, Vienna, 2011.

Dahir, Abdi Latif. "These Charts Show Migrants Aren't South Africa's Biggest Problem." *Quartz Africa*. Posted September 13, 2019. https://qz.com/africa/1708814/what-is-behind-south-africas-xenophobic-attacks-on-foreigners.

De Witte, M. "Spirit Media: Charismatics, Traditionalists, and Mediation Practices in Ghana." PhD thesis, University of Amsterdam, 2008.

Deere, Jack S. "Deuteronomy." In *The Bible Knowledge Commentary*, edited by John F. Walvoord and Roy B. Zuck, 259–324. Colorado: David C. Cook, 1983.

Domeris, William R. *Touching the Heart of God: The Social Construction of Poverty among Biblical Peasants*. T & T Clark Library of Biblical Studies. New York: T&T Clark, 2007.

Donkor, T. K. "The Role of MMDAS in Poverty Alleviation: A Case Study of Amansie Central District Assembly." Unpublished master's thesis, KNUST, 2011.

Duncan-Williams, Nicholas. *You Are Destined to Succeed*. Accra: Action Faith, 1990.

Earle, Ralph. "1 Timothy." In *The Expositor's Bible Commentary, Vol. 11*, edited by Frank E. Gaebelein, 339–390. Grand Rapids, MI: Zondervan, 1984.

Edoun, Emmanuel Innocents, and Dikgang Motsepe. "Critical Assessment of Highly Indebted Poor Countries (HIPIC) Initiative in Africa and the Implication of the New Partnership for Africa's Development (NEPAD) (2001–2016): A Theoretical Perspective." In *Investment Management and Financial Innovations* 13, no. 3 (Oct. 2016): 380–386. http://dx.doi.org/10.21511/imfi.13(3-2).2016.10.

Edu-Bekoe, Yaw Atta, and Enoch Wan. *Scattered Africans Keep Coming: A Case Study of Diaspora Missiology on Ghanaian Diaspora and Congregations in the USA*. Portland, OR: Institute of Diaspora Studies, 2013.

Enquobahrie, Asmamaw. "Understanding Poverty: The Ethiopian Context." A Paper presented at the Gambia AAPAM Roundtable Conference, Banjul, The Gambia, April 19–23, 2004.
https://pdfs.semanticscholar.org/f52a/37ced8e2dd5f4176e679d2f33d86bd2c52ec.pdf
Eze, G. T. *Understanding Poverty*. Onitsha: Good Time Press, 2011.
Filson, F. V. *The Interpreters Bible, Vol. 10*, edited by G. A. Buttrick et al. Nashville: Abingdon, 2004.
Geisler, Norman L. *Systematic Theology*. Minneapolis: Bethany House, 2011.
Genyi, George Akwaya. "Widowhood and Nigerian Womanhood: Another Context of Gendered Poverty in Nigeria." *Research on Humanities and Social Sciences* 3, no. 7 (2013): 68–73.
Ghana Statistical Service. *Ghana Living Standards Survey Round 6*. Accra: Ghana Statistical Service, 2014.
———. *Ghana Poverty Mapping Report*. Accra: Ghana Statistical Service, 2015.
———. *Population and Housing Census 2010*. Accra: Sankofa Press Limited, 2012.
Gifford, Paul. *African Christianity: Its Public Role*. London: Hurst & Company, 1998.
———. *Ghana's New Christianity: Pentecostalism in a Globalized African Economy*. London: Hurst & Company, 2004.
———. "The Prosperity Gospel in Africa: Expecting Miracles." *Christian Century* 10 (July 2007): 20–24.
Goliama, Castor M. "The Gospel of Prosperity in African Pentecostalism: A Theological and Pastoral Challenge to the Catholic Church – With Reference to the Archdiocese of Songea, Tanzania." Unpublished doctoral thesis, University of Vienna, 2013.
Gomez, Brandi. "The Main Causes of Poverty in Ethiopia." *The Borgen Project*. Posted July 29, 2017. https://borgenproject.org/main-causes-of-poverty-in-ethiopia/.
Goodrick, Edward W., and John R. Kohlenberger III. *The NIV Exhaustive Concordance*. Grand Rapids, MI: Zondervan, 1990.
Grogan, G. W. "Isaiah." In *The Expositor's Bible Commentary Vol. 6*, edited by F. E. Gaebelein. Grand Rapids, MI: Zondervan, 1984.
Hagin, Kenneth E. *The Believer's Authority: Legacy Edition*. Broken Arrow, OK: Faith Library Publications, 2009.
———. *Seven Things You Should Know about Divine Healing*. Tulsa, OK: Faith Library, 1979.
Hastings, James. *A Dictionary of the Bible*. Peabody, MA: Hendrickson, 1988.
Heward-Mills, Dag. *Why Non-Tithing Christians Become Poor and How Tithing Christians Become Rich*. Wellington: Lux Verbi.BM (Pty) Ltd., 2009.
Hick, R. "Poverty as Capability Deprivation: Conceptualizing and Measuring Poverty in Contemporary Europe." *European Journal of Sociology* 55, no. 3 (2014): 295–323.
Hope, Kempe Ronald, Sr. *Poverty, Livelihoods, and Governance in Africa: Fulfilling the Development Promise*. New York, NY: Palgrave Macmillan, 2008.

Howell, Timothy D. "Examining the Jewish Origins Employed in the Matthean Beatitudes Through Literary Analysis and Speech Act Theory." PhD dissertation submitted to South African Theological Seminary, 2011.

Huque, Ahmed Shafiqul, and Habib Zafarullah, eds. *International Development Governance*. New York: Taylor & Francis, 2006.

Idahosa, Benson. *I Choose to Change: The Scriptural Way to Success and Prosperity*. Crowborough: Highland Books, 1987.

Johnson, Sherman E. *The Interpreters Bible Vol. 7*, edited by G. A. Buttrick et al. Nashville: Abingdon, 2004.

Johnson, T. F. "1, 2 & 3 John." In *Understanding the Bible Commentary Series*. Grand Rapids, MI: Baker, 2011. https://books.google.com.gh/books?id=ZEMa7AMLO 0cC&pg=PT37&dq.

Kasera, Basilius M. "The Biblical and Theological Examination of Prosperity Theology and Its Impact Among the Poor in Namibia." Unpublished master's thesis, SATS, 2012. https://www.sats.edu.za/wp-content/uploads/2019/10/THE-BIBLICAL-AND-THEOLOGICAL-EXAMINATION-OF-PROSPERITY-THEOLOGY.pdf.

Keener, Craig S. *A Commentary on the Gospel of Matthew*. Grand Rapids, MI: Eerdmans, 1999.

———. *The IVP Bible Background Commentary*. 2nd edition. Downers Grove, IL: InterVarsity Press, 2014.

Khan, Jabir Hasan, and Shamshad Tarique Hassan. "Incidence of Poverty and Level of Socio-Economic Deprivation in India." In *The Journal of Developing Area* 48, no. 2 (2014): 21–38.

Khan, Rumman, Oliver Morrissey, and Paul Mosley. "Colonial Legacy and Poverty Reduction in Sub-Saharan Africa." In *CREDIT Research Paper No. 16/01*. https://www.nottingham.ac.uk/credit/news/papers/1601.aspx.

Kimilike, Lechion Peter. "An African Perspective on Poverty Proverbs in the Book of Proverbs: An Analysis for Transformational Possibilities." Unpublished PhD thesis, University of South Africa, 2006. http://uir.unisa.ac.za/bitstream/handle/10500/2372/?sequence=1.

Kissi, Seth. "Reading Hebrews in the Light of Social Creativity in Akan Society of Ghana." In *Ghana Journal of Religion and Theology* (New Series) 7, no. 1 (2017): 32–49.

Kudadjie, J. N., and Robert K. Aboagye-Mensah. *Christian Social Ethics*. Accra: Asempa Publishers, 1992.

Kwateng-Yeboah, James. "A Re-appraisal of the Prosperity Gospel in African Neo-Pentecostalism: The Potency of 'Multiple Modernities' Paradigm." Unpublished master's thesis, Queen's University, 2017.

Kyeremanteng, Nkansah K. *The Akan of Ghana: Their Customs, History and Institutions*. Kumasi: Sebewie De Ventures, 2010.

Kyle, R. G. *Evangelicalism: An Americanized Christianity*. New Brunswick, NJ: Transaction Publishers, 2006.

Larbi, Emmanuel K. *Pentecostalism: The Eddies of Ghanaian Christianity*. Accra: Blessed Publications, 2001.

Lasor, William S., David A. Hubbard and Frederick W. Bush. *Old Testament Survey: The Message, Form, and Background of the Old Testament*. Grand Rapids, MI: Eerdmans, 1996.

Lathem, R. Warren. *Our Father . . . I Believe: A Fresh Look at Prayer and Faith*. 2nd edition. Lathemtown: JRJ Publishing, 2010.

Lausanne Theology Working Group. "A Statement on Prosperity Teaching." Africa chapter, at its consultations in Akropong, Ghana, 8–9 October, 2008, and 1–4 September 2009. *Christianity Today*. http://www.christianitytoday.com/ct/2009/decemberweb-only/gc-prosperitystatement.html.

Lausund, Maria Elisabeth. "*Social Protection for Enhanced Food Security in South Sudan*." Unpublished master's thesis, University of Oslo, 2017.

Lavender, A. E. *Are You a Full Gospel Christian?: The True Meaning and Message of the Gospel of Jesus Christ*. N.p: Xulon Press, 2007.

Liddell, H. G., and R. Scott. *A Greek-English Lexicon*, revised by H. S. Jones and edited by G. W. H. Lampe. Oxford: Clarendon Press, 1961.

Lieu, J. M. *I, II & III John: A Commentary*. London: Westminster John Knox Press, 2008.

Litfin, A. Duane. "1 Timothy." In *The Bible Knowledge Commentary*, edited by John F. Walvoord and Roy B. Zuck, 727–748. Colorado: David C. Cook, 1983.

Longenecker, R. N. *New Testament Social Ethics for Today*. Grand Rapids, MI: Eerdmans, 1984.

Longman, T., and Raymond B. Dillard. *An Introduction to the Old Testament*. 2nd edition. Grand Rapids, MI: Zondervan, 2006.

Lundbom, J. R. *Deuteronomy: A Commentary*. Grand Rapids, MI: Eerdmans, 2013.

Mackay, John L. *Isaiah Chapters 1–39*. Darlington: Evangelical Press, 2008.

Maier, K. *This House Has Fallen: Midnight in Nigeria*. New York: Public Affairs, 2000.

Martey, Emmanuel. *African Theology*. Maryknoll: Orbis Books, 1995.

Mathole, Ezekiel M. K. "The Christian Witness in the Context of Poverty with Special Reference to the South African Charismatic Evangelicals." Unpublished PhD dissertation, University of Pretoria, 2005.

Mbiti, John S. *African Religions and Philosophy*. Oxford: Heinemann, 1990.

McConnell, Dan R. *A Different Gospel*. Peabody, MA: Henderson, 1995.

———. "The Encounter of Christian Faith and African Religion." *Christian Century* 97, no. 27 (1980): 817–820.

———. *The Promise of Health and Wealth*. Sevenoaks: Hodder & Stoughton, 1990.

Merrill, E. H. "Deuteronomy." In *The New American Commentary 4*, electronic edition. Nashville: Broadman & Holman, 2018.

Joyce Meyer, "Living in Financial Freedom." Accessed 19 May 2020. https://joycemeyer.org/everydayanswers/ea-teachings/living-in-financial-freedom.

Mkandawire, T. "On Tax Efforts and Colonial Heritage in Africa." *Journal of Development Studies* 46 (2010): 1647–1669.

Moltmann, Jurgen, T. R. Eberhart, and M. W. Charlton, eds. *The Economy of Salvation: Essays in Honor of M. Douglas Meeks*. Eugene, OR: Cascade Books, 2015.

Moody, M., and B. Breeze. *The Philanthropy Reader*. London and New York: Routledge, 2016.

Morris, R. A., and D. T. Lioy. "A Historical and Theological Framework for Understanding Word of Faith Theology." *Conspectus* 13 (2012): 73–116.

Morton, Steven, David Pencheon, and Neil Squires. "Sustainable Development Goals (SDGs) and Their implementation: A National Global Framework for Health, Development and Equity Needs a Systems Approach at Every Level." *British Medical Bulletin* 124, no. 1 (2017): 81–90.

Moyo, J. "Preaching the Gospel of Bling in Zimbabwe." Nehenda Radio. https://nehandaradio.com/2012/04/05/preaching-the-gospel-of-bling-in-zimbabwe/.

Newman, B. M., and P. C. Stine. *A Handbook on the Gospel of Matthew*. New York: UBS Handbook Series, 1993. Electronic edition.

Newton, Paula. "The Long Goodbye: Why Funerals Are Big Deals in Ghana." In CNN's "On the Road Series," March 11, 2014. http://edition.cnn.com/2014/03/11/world/africa/on-the-road-ghana-funerals/.

Nihinlola, Emiola. *Theology Under the Mango Tree: A Handbook for African Christian Theology*. Lagos: Fine Print & Manufacturing, 2013.

Nlkamiti, Boniface. "Does Corruption Affect Poverty? The Case Study of Kenya." Master of arts thesis, University of Nairobi, 2004.

O'Donoghue, Darrell. "A Biblical-Theological Analysis of Matthew 6:19–34 to Clarify the Relationship between the Christian Disciple and Money." Unpublished master of theology thesis: SATS, 2011. https://www.sats.edu.za/wp-content/uploads/2020/02/Biblical-theological-analysis-of-Matt.pdf.

O'Donovan, Wilbur. *Biblical Christianity in African Perspective*. 2nd edition. Carlisle: Paternoster, 1996.

Odotei, I. "Pre-colonial Economic Activities of Ga." *Research Review* (Ns) 11, nos. 1 & 2 (1995): 59–74.

Ogundele, Samuel Oluwole. "Understanding Nigeria within the Context of the Atlantic World." In *The African Diaspora Archaeological Network* 13, no. 3 (2010): 1–17. https://scholarworks.umass.edu/adan/vol13/iss3/2

Okosun, D. E. "Poverty, Illiteracy cum Prosperity Theology: A Quantitative Study." *International Journal of Social Sciences (IJSS)* 8, no. 1 (2018): 83–92.

Oluoch, S. *Concerning Prosperity Gospel: A Glimpse into One of the Popular Gospels of Today*. Bloomington, IN: Xlibris Corporation, 2012.

Omanson, R. G., and J. A. Ellington. *Handbook on Paul's Second Letter to the Corinthians*. New York: UBS Handbook Series, 1993. Electronic edition.

Ononogbu, D. C. "Unemployment among Youths: A Study on the Role of the Nigerian Church." *Religion and Democracy in the 21st Century*. Ilorin: Decency Printers and Stationeries, 2010.

Onyinyechukwu, I. P. "Old Testament Concept of Poverty and Its Application to the Contemporary Nigerian Church." Unpublished PhD thesis, University of Nigeria, 2010.

Osteen, Joel. *Your Best Life Now: 7 Steps to Living at Your Full Potential*. New York: Faith Words, 2007.

Otabil, Mensah. *Beyond the Rivers of Ethiopia: A Biblical Revelation on God's Purpose for the Black Race*. Accra: Altar International, 1992.

Otu, J. E. et al. "Analysis of Poverty Indices in Underdeveloped Countries: Nigeria Scenario." *Mediterranean Journal of Social Sciences* 2, no. 2: (2011): 175–183. https://www.richtmann.org/journal/index.php/mjss/article/view/10792/10405.

Owusu, K. G. "Military Coups in Ghana, 1969–1985: A By-product of Global Economic Injustices?" Unpublished MSc thesis, Linköpings Universitet-Sweden, 2008.

Osborne, Grant R. *The Hermeneutical Spiral: A Comprehensive Introduction to Biblical Interpretation*. Downers Grove: IVP Academic, 2006.

Oyedepo, David O. *Possessing Your Possession*. Lagos: Dominion Publishing, 2007.

———. *Understanding Financial Prosperity*. Ikeja: Dominion Publishing, 1997.

Pantazis C., D. Gordon, and R. Levitas. *Poverty and Social Exclusion in Britain*. Bristol: Policy Press, 2006.

Picard, A., and M. Habets, eds. *Theology and the Experience of Disability: Interdisciplinary Perspectives from Voices Down Under*. London and New York: Routledge, 2016.

Pobee, John S. *Towards an African Theology*. Nashville: Abingdon, 1979.

Poku-Boansi, M., and S. Afrane. "Magnitude and Impact of Youth Unemployment in Ghana." *West Africa Review* 18 (2011): 73–89.

Powell, Mark Alan. *Introduction to the New Testament: A Historical, Literary, and Theological Survey*. Grand Rapids, MI: Baker Academic, 2009.

Renn, Stephen D., ed. *Expository Dictionary of Bible Words*. Peabody, MA: Hendricks, 2005.

Sangmor, V. M. "The Impact of Colonialism on Cultural Identity: A Comparative Study of Ghana and South Africa." Unpublished master of arts thesis, University of Ghana, 2013.

Sarpong, Peter K. *People Differ: An Approach to Inculturation in Evangelism*. Accra: Sub-Saharan Publishers, 2002.

Scheffler, Eben. "Luke's View on Poverty in Its Ancient (Roman) Economic Context: A Challenge for Today." *Scriptura* 106 (2011):115–135.

Scott, R. B. Y. *The Interpreters Bible Vol. 5*, edited by G. A. Buttrick et al. Nashville: Abingdon, 2004.

Seale, C., and S. van der Geest. "Good and Bad Death: Introduction." *Social Science and Medicine* 59, no. 5 (2004): 883–886.

Settles, Joshua Dwayne. "The Impact of Colonialism on African Economic Development." Unpublished honours thesis, University of Tennessee, 1996. https://trace.tennessee.edu/utk_chanhonoproj/182.

Sen, A. K. "Capabilities, Lists, and Public Reason: Continuing the Conversation." *Feminist Economics* 10, no. 3 (2004): 77–80.

———. *Development as Freedom*. Oxford: Oxford University Press, 1999.

Smeeding, T. M. "Public Policy and Economic Inequality: The United States in Comparative Perspective." *Social Science Quarterly* 86 (2005): 955–983.

Soboyejo, J. O. "Prosperity Gospel and Its Religious Impact on Sustainable Economic Development of African Nations." *Open Access Library Journal* 3 (2016): 1–13.

Stott, John R. *A Deeper Look at the Sermon on the Mount: Living Out the Way of Jesus*. Nottingham: Inter-Varsity Press, 2013.

———. *Issues Facing Christians Today*. Grand Rapids, MI: Zondervan, 2006.

Strickland, Carol Moir. "Money Matters: Living Faithfully amid a Materialistic Culture." Unpublished doctor of ministry thesis, McCormick Theological Seminary, 1997. http://zacchaeus.org/pdfs/strickland_thesis.pdf.

Sweeney, M. A. *Isaiah 40–66*. Grand Rapids, MI: Eerdmans, 2016.

Taylor, J. V. *The Primal Vision: Christian Presence and African Religion*. London: SCM, 1963.

Temitope, Ogunlusi Clement. "Prosperity Gospel Preaching and Its Implications on National Developments." *International Journal of Humanities and Cultural Studies* 5, no. 1 (2018): 313–330.

Thomson, J. A. "Deuteronomy." In *Believer's Bible Commentary*, edited by Art Fastard, 201–232. Nashville: Thomas Nelson, 1995.

Towner, Philip H. "The Letters to Timothy and Titus." In *The New International Commentary on The New Testament*. Grand Rapids, MI: Eerdmans, 2006.

Transparency International. *Corruption Perceptions Index 2018*. Berlin: Transparency International, 2019.

Tryon, Denzil B. *"Accounting for Anxiety: An Analysis of an Early First-century Material Ethic from Matt 6:19–34."* Unpublished master of theology thesis, Stellenbosch University, 2006.

Umoh, Dominic. "Prosperity Gospel and the Spirit of Capitalism: The Nigerian Story." *African Journal of Scientific Research* 12, no. 1 (2013): 654–667.

United Nations Educational, Scientific and Cultural Organization (UNESCO) Institute for Statistics. "Literacy Rates Continue to Rise from One Generation to the Next (Fact Sheet No. 45)." Fact Sheet No. 45, September 2017. FS/2017/LIT/45.

van Wyk, Ilana. "A Look at the 'Prosperity Gospel' in South Africa." *CNBC Africa*. Posted February 25, 2019. https://www.cnbcafrica.com/news/special-report/2019/02/25/a-look-at-the-prosperity-gospel-in-south-africa/.

Vincent, Marvin R. *Vincent's Word Studies in the New Testament*. Peabody, MA: Hendrickson, 2009.

Vogt, P. T. "Social Justice and the Vision of Deuteronomy." *Journal of the Evangelical Theological Society* 51, no. 1 (2008): 35–44.

Wagle, Udaya. "Multidimensional Poverty Measurement." *Springer Science+Business Media* (2008): 15–53. https://link.springer.com/chapter/10.1007%2F978-0-387-75875-6_2.

Walton J. H, V. H. Matthews, and M. W. Chavalas. *IVP Background Commentary: Old Testament*. Downers Grove: IVP Academic, 2000.

Wesley, John. *Wesley's Notes on the Bible (The Old Testament): Genesis – Ruth*. Edited by Anthony Uyl. Ontario: Woodstock, 2017.

White, Paula. *Living the Abundant Life: Why Not Me? Why Not Now?* Tampa, FL: Paula White Ministries, 2003.

Wiersbe, Warren W. *The Wiersbe Bible Commentary*. Colorado Springs: David C. Cook, 2007.

Williams, David T. *Christian Approaches to Poverty*. San Jose: Authors Choice Press, 2001.

Wilson, A., and R. Letsosa. "Biblical Principles towards a Pastoral Strategy for Poverty Alleviation amongst the Youth in Uganda." *HTS Teologiese Studies/Theological Studies* 70, no. 2 (2014): https://hts.org.za/index.php/hts/article/view/1328/4520.

Wilson, William. *Wilson's Old Testament Word Studies*. Peabody, MA: Hendrickson, n.d.

World Bank, *Somali Poverty Profile 2016: Findings from Wave 1 of the Somali High Frequency Survey*. Washington, DC: World Bank, 2017.

Wright, Christopher J. H. *Old Testament Ethics for the People of God*. Nottingham: Inter-Varsity Press, 2004.

Yeboa-Mensa, S. "Reducing Poverty in Sub-Saharan Africa: Two Development Theories and the Role of the Church." Unpublished master's thesis, University of Helsinki, 2012.

Youngblood, R. F. ed. *New Illustrated Bible Dictionary*. Nashville: Thomas Nelson, 1995.

Zodhiates, Spiros, and Warren Baker, eds. *The NIV Key Word Study Bible*. Chattanooga, TN: AMG Publishers, 1996.

Subject Index

A
accumulation of wealth 73, 98, 100, 126–127
Adinkra 6, 174
ānāwîm 47, 49–50
ancestors 9–10, 28
ānî 47–48, 50
anxiety 2, 73, 77–79, 87–88, 94, 98–99, 130–131, 163, 168, 182

B
blessing 16, 58, 60, 76, 109–112, 121, 127, 129, 151, 161
bribe 35, 65

C
capabilities 20–21, 139, 152, 182
capability deprivation 21, 177
Christians 35, 72, 74, 86–87, 92, 94–95, 99–100, 103, 112–113, 116–117, 122, 131, 133, 145, 147–148, 151, 158, 160–161, 163–166, 168–169, 177, 182
colonialism 11–14, 181
contentment 2, 76, 90–93, 95, 127, 130, 143, 163, 167, 169–170
contextualization 143
contextual theology 141–143, 150, 156, 169, 175
corruption 34–35, 62–63, 82, 94, 110, 119–120, 135–137, 144, 148, 152, 158, 160, 171, 174, 180, 182
cultural practices 15, 36, 121, 123–124, 156–157, 170

D
dal 47, 49–50
debt 14, 16, 26, 33, 50, 54–55, 57–58, 75, 95, 97, 109, 120, 128, 147, 150, 159, 165
deliverance 61, 116–117, 121, 124, 160
destiny 6, 10, 157
divinities 5, 7–8

E
'ebyôn 47, 49–50
education 2, 13, 15, 22, 28–29, 31, 37–38, 41–42, 44–45, 106, 118–119, 154–156, 158, 164, 171, 185
emigration 41–42
exclusion 20–23, 27, 102, 157, 161–162, 181
exploitation 24, 63, 65, 67, 95–96, 98, 102–103, 119, 126, 146, 157–158, 162, 164, 166

F
faith healing 110–111, 140, 173
financial ethics 143, 164–165

G
gambling 40, 146, 149, 164–165
generosity 27–28, 55, 59–60, 69, 78, 80, 83, 99, 110, 139, 170
government 1, 11, 30, 33–35, 43, 62, 119, 145, 148, 152–153, 156, 158, 160, 164, 170, 173
Greco-Roman world 75, 79, 84
greed 81, 89–90, 130–131, 140, 149, 168

H
healing and deliverance 116–117, 121, 124, 160
human development 29, 143, 152, 154

I
illiteracy 37–38, 44, 111, 119, 155, 180
inequality 29–31, 35, 38, 75, 170, 182
injustice 24, 48–50, 56, 62, 64, 95, 100–103, 119–120, 135, 137, 157–158
intermediaries 7
Israel 52–53, 55–58, 60–63, 65, 83, 95, 97, 128, 150

J

Jubilee Year 55, 97
justice 2, 15, 35, 54, 56, 58, 63–65, 68, 88, 95, 100, 102–103, 135, 141, 152, 155, 158–159, 174, 182

L

laziness 39–40, 86, 96, 110, 134, 145, 148
love of money 54, 80, 93–94, 127

M

mammon 74, 84–85, 88, 99–100
materialism 2, 75, 80, 92, 97–98, 126, 134, 140, 149, 166, 169
miskēn 47, 50
modesty 2, 143, 163, 167, 169–170
money 23, 25, 28, 32, 35, 37, 45–46, 50–51, 54–55, 66–67, 74, 77–80, 93–95, 98, 100, 112, 115, 120, 125–128, 131, 135–139, 146, 148–152, 155, 157, 164, 166–167, 173, 180, 182

N

natural disasters 40, 43
Noah 121

O

orphans 28, 51, 53, 58, 62, 64, 66, 76, 95, 162

P

positive confession of faith 105–106, 113–114, 140
possessions 74, 80–81, 84, 89, 91, 93–95, 97–100, 125, 129, 131, 134, 137, 149–150, 167, 173
poverty alleviation 105, 120, 128, 141, 143, 156, 158, 160, 162, 167–169, 171, 176, 183
power 7–8, 23, 33, 62–64, 67, 86, 88, 96, 98–101, 110, 114–115, 117, 119, 128, 131, 154–155, 160
pride 62, 98, 126, 167, 169
prosperity preachers 107, 109–135, 138–140
prosperity theology 1–2, 105–109, 112, 114–118, 120, 122, 124–129, 131–132, 134–141, 145, 161, 169, 176, 178, 180
ptōchos 47, 51

R

rush 47, 50, 161

S

Sabbath economy 56, 97, 125, 146, 151
Sabbath Year 54–55
Sabbatical Year 53–55, 57, 59, 97, 147
salvation 92–93, 110, 116, 121, 130, 146, 152, 175, 180
seed-sowing 106, 111
Sermon on the Mount 73–74, 80, 88, 173, 182
simplicity 2, 82, 95, 143, 163, 167, 170
slave 13–14, 83–85, 99
social exclusion 20–23, 27, 102, 161–162, 181
spiritual world 7

T

tithe 53, 66, 102, 112, 130
treasures 74, 77–80, 91, 113, 128, 164, 168

U

Ujamaa 15
unemployment 1, 31, 39, 45, 114, 118, 164, 180–181

W

widows 28, 36–37, 51, 53, 58, 62, 64–66, 76, 95, 102, 162
worldview 5, 7–9, 14, 17, 19, 23, 27, 114, 131, 138, 142
worry 2, 74, 77, 84–87, 89, 98–99, 130–131, 147, 149, 163, 175

www.ingramcontent.com/pod-product-compliance
Lightning Source LLC
Chambersburg PA
CBHW070535170426
43200CB00011B/2435